William Shakespeare

HENRY IV, PART I

Edited with a Commentary by Peter Davison
Introduced by Charles Edelman

PENGUIN BOOKS

PENGUIN BOOKS

Published by the Penguin Group
Penguin Books Ltd, 80 Strand, London WC2R ORL, England
Penguin Group (USA) Inc., 375 Hudson Street, New York, New York 10014, USA
Penguin Group (Canada), 10 Alcorn Avenue, Toronto, Ontario, Canada M4V 3B2
(a division of Pearson Penguin Canada Inc.)
Penguin Ireland, 25 St Stephen's Green, Dublin 2, Ireland (a division of Penguin Books Ltd)
Penguin Group (Australia), 250 Camberwell Road, Camberwell, Victoria 3124, Australia
(a division of Pearson Australia Group Pty Ltd)
Penguin Books India Pvt Ltd, 11 Community Centre, Panchsheel Park, New Delhi – 110 017, India
Penguin Group (NZ), cnr Airborne and Rosedale Roads, Albany, Auckland 1310, New Zealand
(a division of Pearson New Zealand Ltd)
Penguin Books (South Africa) (Pty) Ltd, 24 Sturdee Avenue, Rosebank 2196, South Africa

Penguin Books Ltd, Registered Offices: 80 Strand, London WC2R ORL, England

www.penguin.com

This edition first published in Penguin Books 1968
Reissued in the Penguin Shakespeare series 2005

9

This edition copyright © Penguin Books, 1968
Account of the Text and Commentary copyright © Peter Davison, 1968, 1996
General Introduction and Chronology copyright © Stanley Wells, 2005
Introduction, The Play in Performance and Further Reading copyright © Charles Edelman, 2005

ISBN-13: 978-0-14-101366-4

www.greenpenguin.co.uk

Contents

General Introduction

Every play by Shakespeare is unique. This is part of his greatness. A restless and indefatigable experimenter, he moved with a rare amalgamation of artistic integrity and dedicated professionalism from one kind of drama to another. Never shackled by convention, he offered his actors the alternation between serious and comic modes from play to play, and often also within the plays themselves, that the repertory system within which he worked demanded, and which provided an invaluable stimulus to his imagination. Introductions to individual works in this series attempt to define their individuality. But there are common factors that underpin Shakespeare's career.

Nothing in his heredity offers clues to the origins of his genius. His upbringing in Stratford-upon-Avon, where he was born in 1564, was unexceptional. His mother, born Mary Arden, came from a prosperous farming family. Her father chose her as his executor over her eight sisters and his four stepchildren when she was only in her late teens, which suggests that she was of more than average practical ability. Her husband John, a glover, apparently unable to write, was nevertheless a capable businessman and loyal townsfellow, who seems to have fallen on relatively hard times in later life. He would have been brought up as a Catholic, and may have retained

Catholic sympathies, but his son subscribed publicly to Anglicanism throughout his life.

The most important formative influence on Shakespeare was his school. As the son of an alderman who became bailiff (or mayor) in 1568, he had the right to attend the town's grammar school. Here he would have received an education grounded in classical rhetoric and oratory, studying authors such as Ovid, Cicero and Quintilian, and would have been required to read, speak, write and even think in Latin from his early years. This classical education permeates Shakespeare's work from the beginning to the end of his career. It is apparent in the self-conscious classicism of plays of the early 1590s such as the tragedy of *Titus Andronicus*, *The Comedy of Errors*, and the narrative poems *Venus and Adonis* (1592–3) and *The Rape of Lucrece* (1593–4), and is still evident in his latest plays, informing the dream visions of *Pericles* and *Cymbeline* and the masque in *The Tempest*, written between 1607 and 1611. It inflects his literary style throughout his career. In his earliest writings the verse, based on the ten-syllabled, five-beat iambic pentameter, is highly patterned. Rhetorical devices deriving from classical literature, such as alliteration and antithesis, extended similes and elaborate wordplay, abound. Often, as in *Love's Labour's Lost* and *A Midsummer Night's Dream*, he uses rhyming patterns associated with lyric poetry, each line self-contained in sense, the prose as well as the verse employing elaborate figures of speech. Writing at a time of linguistic ferment, Shakespeare frequently imports Latinisms into English, coining words such as abstemious, addiction, incarnadine and adjunct. He was also heavily influenced by the eloquent translations of the Bible in both the Bishops' and the Geneva versions. As his experience grows, his verse and prose become more supple, the patterning less apparent, more ready to accommodate the rhythms of ordinary speech, more colloquial in diction, as in the speeches of the Nurse in *Romeo and Juliet*, the characterful prose of Falstaff and Hamlet's soliloquies. The effect is of increasing psychological realism, reaching its greatest heights in *Hamlet*, *Othello*, *King Lear*, *Macbeth* and *Antony and Cleopatra*. Gradually he discovered ways of adapting the regular beat of the pentameter to make it an infinitely flexible instrument for matching thought with feeling. Towards the end of his career, in plays such as *The Winter's Tale*, *Cymbeline* and *The Tempest*, he adopts a more highly mannered style, in keeping with the more overtly symbolical and emblematical mode in which he is writing.

So far as we know, Shakespeare lived in Stratford till after his marriage to Anne Hathaway, eight years his senior, in 1582. They had three children: a daughter, Susanna, born in 1583 within six months of their marriage, and twins, Hamnet and Judith, born in 1585. The next seven years of Shakespeare's life are virtually a blank. Theories that he may have been, for instance, a schoolmaster, or a lawyer, or a soldier, or a sailor, lack evidence to support them. The first reference to him in print, in Robert Greene's pamphlet *Greene's Groatsworth of Wit* of 1592, parodies a line from *Henry VI, Part III*, implying that Shakespeare was already an established playwright. It seems likely that at some unknown point after the birth of his twins he joined a theatre company and gained experience as both actor and writer in the provinces and London. The London theatres closed because of plague in 1593 and 1594; and during these years, perhaps recognizing the need for an alternative career, he wrote and published the narrative poems *Venus and Adonis* and *The Rape of Lucrece*. These are the only works we can be certain that Shakespeare himself was responsible for putting into print. Each bears the author's dedication to Henry Wriothesley, Earl of Southampton (1573–1624), the second in warmer terms than the first. Southampton, younger than Shakespeare by ten years, is the only person to whom he personally dedicated works. The Earl may have been a close friend, perhaps even the beautiful and adored young man whom Shakespeare celebrates in his *Sonnets*.

The resumption of playing after the plague years saw the founding of the Lord Chamberlain's Men, a company to which Shakespeare was to belong for the rest of his career, as actor, shareholder and playwright. No other dramatist of the period had so stable a relationship with a single company. Shakespeare knew the actors for whom he was writing and the conditions in which they performed. The permanent company was made up of around twelve to fourteen players, but one actor often played more than one role in a play and additional actors were hired as needed. Led by the tragedian Richard Burbage (1568–1619) and, initially, the comic actor Will Kemp (d. 1603), they rapidly achieved a high reputation, and when King James I succeeded Queen Elizabeth I in 1603 they were renamed as the King's Men. All the women's parts were played by boys; there is no evidence that any female role was ever played by a male actor over the age of about eighteen. Shakespeare had enough confidence in his boys to write for them long and demanding roles such as Rosalind (who, like other heroines of the romantic comedies, is disguised as a boy for much of the action) in *As You Like It*, Lady Macbeth and Cleopatra. But there are far more fathers than mothers, sons than daughters, in his plays, few if any of which require more than the company's normal complement of three or four boys.

The company played primarily in London's public playhouses – there were almost none that we know of in the rest of the country – initially in the Theatre, built in Shoreditch in 1576, and from 1599 in the Globe, on Bankside. These were wooden, more or less circular structures, open to the air, with a thrust stage surmounted by a canopy and jutting into the area where spectators who paid one penny stood, and surrounded by galleries where it was possible to be seated on payment of an additional penny. Though properties such as cauldrons, stocks, artificial trees or beds could indicate locality, there was no representational scenery. Sound effects such as flourishes of trumpets, music both martial and amorous, and accompaniments to songs were provided by the company's musicians. Actors entered through doors in the back wall of the stage. Above it was a balconied area that could represent the walls of a town (as in *King John*), or a castle (as in *Richard II*), and indeed a balcony (as in *Romeo and Juliet*). In 1609 the company also acquired the use of the Blackfriars, a smaller, indoor theatre to which admission was more expensive, and which permitted the use of more spectacular stage effects such as the descent of Jupiter on an eagle in *Cymbeline* and of goddesses in *The Tempest*. And they would frequently perform before the court in royal residences and, on their regular tours into the provinces, in non-theatrical spaces such as inns, guildhalls and the great halls of country houses.

Early in his career Shakespeare may have worked in collaboration, perhaps with Thomas Nashe (1567–*c*. 1601) in *Henry VI, Part I* and with George Peele (1556–96) in *Titus Andronicus*. And towards the end he collaborated with George Wilkins (*fl.* 1604–8) in *Pericles*, and with his younger colleagues Thomas Middleton (1580–1627), in *Timon of Athens*, and John Fletcher (1579–1625), in *Henry*

VIII, *The Two Noble Kinsmen* and the lost play *Cardenio*. Shakespeare's output dwindled in his last years, and he died in 1616 in Stratford, where he owned a fine house, New Place, and much land. His only son had died at the age of eleven, in 1596, and his last descendant died in 1670. New Place was destroyed in the eighteenth century but the other Stratford houses associated with his life are maintained and displayed to the public by the Shakespeare Birthplace Trust.

One of the most remarkable features of Shakespeare's plays is their intellectual and emotional scope. They span a great range from the lightest of comedies, such as *The Two Gentlemen of Verona* and *The Comedy of Errors*, to the profoundest of tragedies, such as *King Lear* and *Macbeth*. He maintained an output of around two plays a year, ringing the changes between comic and serious. All his comedies have serious elements: Shylock, in *The Merchant of Venice*, almost reaches tragic dimensions, and *Measure for Measure* is profoundly serious in its examination of moral problems. Equally, none of his tragedies is without humour: Hamlet is as witty as any of his comic heroes, *Macbeth* has its Porter, and *King Lear* its Fool. His greatest comic character, Falstaff, inhabits the history plays and *Henry V* ends with a marriage, while *Henry VI, Part III*, *Richard II* and *Richard III* culminate in the tragic deaths of their protagonists.

Although in performance Shakespeare's characters can give the impression of a superabundant reality, he is not a naturalistic dramatist. None of his plays is explicitly set in his own time. The action of few of them (except for the English histories) is set even partly in England (exceptions are *The Merry Wives of Windsor* and the Induction to *The Taming of the Shrew*). Italy is his favoured location. Most of his principal story-lines derive from printed writings; but the structuring and translation of these narratives into dramatic terms is Shakespeare's own, and he invents much additional material. Most of the plays contain elements of myth and legend, and many derive from ancient or more recent history or from romantic tales of ancient times and faraway places. All reflect his reading, often in close detail. Holinshed's *Chronicles* (1577, revised 1587), a great compendium of English, Scottish and Irish history, provided material for his English history plays. The *Lives of the Noble Grecians and Romans* by the Greek writer Plutarch, finely translated into English from the French by Sir Thomas North in 1579, provided much of the narrative material, and also a mass of verbal detail, for his plays about Roman history. Some plays are closely based on shorter individual works: *As You Like It*, for instance, on the novel *Rosalynde* (1590) by his near-contemporary Thomas Lodge (1558–1625), *The Winter's Tale* on *Pandosto* (1588) by his old rival Robert Greene (1558–92) and *Othello* on a story by the Italian Giraldi Cinthio (1504–73). And the language of his plays is permeated by the Bible, the Book of Common Prayer and the proverbial sayings of his day.

Shakespeare was popular with his contemporaries, but his commitment to the theatre and to the plays in performance is demonstrated by the fact that only about half of his plays appeared in print in his lifetime, in slim paperback volumes known as quartos, so called because they were made from printers' sheets folded twice to form four leaves (eight pages). None of them shows any sign that he was involved in their publication. For him, performance was the primary means of publication. The most frequently reprinted of his works were the non-dramatic poems – the erotic *Venus and Adonis* and the more moralistic *The Rape of Lucrece*. The *Sonnets*, which appeared in 1609, under his name but possibly without his consent, were less successful, perhaps because the vogue for sonnet sequences, which peaked in the 1590s, had passed by then. They were not reprinted until 1640, and then only in garbled form along with poems by other writers. Happily, in 1623, seven years after he died, his colleagues John Heminges (1556–1630) and Henry Condell (d. 1627) published his collected plays, including eighteen that had not previously appeared in print, in the first Folio, whose name derives from the fact that the printers' sheets were folded only once to produce two leaves (four pages). Some of the quarto editions are badly printed, and the fact that some plays exist in two, or even three, early versions creates problems for editors. These are discussed in the Account of the Text in each volume of this series.

Shakespeare's plays continued in the repertoire until the Puritans closed the theatres in 1642. When performances resumed after the Restoration of the monarchy in 1660 many of the plays were not to the taste of the times, especially because their mingling of genres and failure to meet the requirements of poetic justice offended against the dictates of neoclassicism. Some, such as *The Tempest* (changed by John Dryden and William Davenant in 1667 to suit contemporary taste), *King Lear* (to which Nahum Tate gave a happy ending in 1681) and *Richard III* (heavily adapted by Colley Cibber in 1700 as a vehicle for his own talents), were extensively rewritten; others fell into neglect. Slowly they regained their place in the repertoire, and they continued to be reprinted, but it was not until the great actor David Garrick (1717–79) organized a spectacular jubilee in Stratford in 1769 that Shakespeare began to be regarded as a transcendental genius. Garrick's idolatry prefigured the enthusiasm of critics such as Samuel Taylor Coleridge (1772–1834) and William Hazlitt (1778–1830). Gradually Shakespeare's reputation spread abroad, to Germany, America, France and to other European countries.

During the nineteenth century, though the plays were generally still performed in heavily adapted or abbreviated versions, a large body of scholarship and criticism began to amass. Partly as a result of a general swing in education away from the teaching of Greek and Roman texts and towards literature written in English, Shakespeare became the object of intensive study in schools and universities. In the theatre, important turning points were the work in England of two theatre directors, William Poel (1852–1934) and his disciple Harley Granville-Barker (1877–1946), who showed that the application of knowledge, some of it newly acquired, of early staging conditions to performance of the plays could render the original texts viable in terms of the modern theatre. During the twentieth century appreciation of Shakespeare's work, encouraged by the availability of audio, film and video versions of the plays, spread around the world to such an extent that he can now be claimed as a global author.

The influence of Shakespeare's works permeates the English language. Phrases from his plays and poems – 'a tower of strength', 'green-eyed jealousy', 'a foregone conclusion' – are on the lips of people who may never have read him. They have inspired composers of songs, orchestral music and operas; painters and sculptors; poets, novelists and film-makers. Allusions to him appear in pop songs, in advertisements and in television shows. Some of his characters – Romeo and Juliet, Falstaff, Shylock and Hamlet – have acquired mythic status. He is valued

for his humanity, his psychological insight, his wit and
humour, his lyricism, his mastery of language, his ability
to excite, surprise, move and, in the widest sense of the
word, entertain audiences. He is the greatest of poets,
but he is essentially a dramatic poet. Though his plays
have much to offer to readers, they exist fully only in
performance. In these volumes we offer individual introductions, notes on language and on specific points of the
text, suggestions for further reading and information
about how each work has been edited. In addition we
include accounts of the ways in which successive gener-
ations of interpreters and audiences have responded to
challenges and rewards offered by the plays. The Penguin
Shakespeare series aspires to remove obstacles to understanding and to make pleasurable the reading of the work
of the man who has done more than most to make us
understand what it is to be human.

                                              Stanley Wells

The Chronology of
Shakespeare's Works

A few of Shakespeare's writings can be fairly precisely dated. An allusion to the Earl of Essex in the chorus to Act V of *Henry V*, for instance, could only have been written in 1599. But for many of the plays we have only vague information, such as the date of publication, which may have occurred long after composition, the date of a performance, which may not have been the first, or a list in Francis Meres's book *Palladis Tamia*, published in 1598, which tells us only that the plays listed there must have been written by that year. The chronology of the early plays is particularly difficult to establish. Not everyone would agree that the first part of *Henry VI* was written after the third, for instance, or *Romeo and Juliet* before *A Midsummer Night's Dream*. The following table is based on the 'Canon and Chronology' section in *William Shakespeare: A Textual Companion*, by Stanley Wells and Gary Taylor, with John Jowett and William Montgomery (1987), where more detailed information and discussion may be found.

Introduction

One of the Elizabethan age's most delightful books is
John Florio's *Second Fruits* (1591), from which one could
learn to speak Italian through a series of typical conver-
sations, Italian and English on facing pages. In this
example some young Londoners discuss how to spend
their day:

And then after dinner we will go see a play.
The plays that they play in England, are not right comedies.
Yet they do nothing else but play every day.
Yea but they are neither right comedies, nor right tragedies.
How would you name them then?
Representations of histories, without any decorum.

Unenthusiastic about seeing such a play, they decide on a
game of tennis instead. Had Florio written his book about
six years later, the play 'without any decorum' they missed
could well have been the latest effort of London's most
popular playwright, William Shakespeare, about King
Henry IV, his famous son and the son's very fat friend, Sir
John Falstaff.

As with most of Shakespeare's plays, we have no sure
knowledge of when *Henry IV, Part I* was first performed,
but the year 1597 has gained general, if not unanimous,

acceptance. Nor do we know exactly what the play was originally called; the first Quarto edition of 1598 had the title *The History of Henry the Fourth; with the battle at Shrewsbury, between the King and Lord Henry Percy, surnamed Henry Hotspur of the North, With the humorous conceits of Sir John Falstaff*.

To label a play a 'History' was unusual – between 1578, when George Whetstone's comedy *The Right Excellent History of Promos and Cassandra* was published, and 1597, only three other Elizabethan plays, all of them printed in 1594, had been so identified on their title pages. Two were by Robert Greene, *The Honourable History of Friar Bacon and Friar Bungay* and *The History of Orlando Furioso*; the third was *A Pleasant Conceited History, called The Taming of a Shrew*, which may have been another version of Shakespeare's famous play or an earlier work that Shakespeare adapted. The varied subject matter and styles of these plays are a reminder that in Shakespeare's day 'history' did not automatically carry a connotation of a record of past events, or of a branch of knowledge such as Roman or English history. Those meanings certainly existed, but the primary definition of 'history' was simply 'story', a shorter form of the same word, with the same derivation.

To regard *Henry IV, Part I* as a story rather than a history may bring us closer to the sort of work it actually is, for Shakespeare makes no pretence of being a historian or historiographer – his occupation is poet. Edmund Spenser, in dedicating *The Faerie Queene* to Sir Walter Raleigh, writes,

an historiographer discourseth of affairs orderly as they were done, accounting as well the times as the actions, but a poet thrusteth into the middest, even where it most concerneth him, and there recoursing to the things forepast, and divining of things to come, maketh a pleasing analysis of all.

In constructing his own 'pleasing analysis', Shakespeare freely mixes 'real' people – King Henry IV, the Earl of Northumberland – with 'fictional' ones – Falstaff, Poins, Mistress Quickly – but even the real people are fictional in that they speak words (usually in verse) that no one is to believe they actually said. 'Truth', in the sense of sticking to facts, does not matter: Hotspur is made a youth, the same age as the Prince of Wales, even though the real Hotspur was two years older than the Prince's father.

When Shakespeare's former partners, John Heminge and Henry Condell, collected his plays for publication in 1623, they grouped them into three categories and called the book *Mr William Shakespeare's Comedies, Histories, and Tragedies*. Each of the ten Histories has an English king in its title, but in poetic style, dramatic construction and the ways in which what might be called the 'historical record' is used, differences outnumber similarities: to place a play originally known as *The Tragedy of King Richard the Second* with the Histories, and then put the *True Chronicle History of the Life and Death of King Lear* (the title of the 1608 Quarto) among the Tragedies, is arbitrary to say the least.

Heminge and Condell took an even more radical step in giving our play a new title, *The First Part of Henry the Fourth*, one it never had during Shakespeare's lifetime. Although *The Second Part of Henry the Fourth* was performed in 1597 or 1598 and was published in 1600, *The History of Henry the Fourth* was reprinted *eight* times, more than any other Shakespeare play, between 1598 and 1639, without changing the title. One can understand how the play eventually became *Part I*, given the existence of a *Part II*, and in some ways the subject is unimportant, since every Shakespeare play is known today by a shorthand title, which can vary from edition to edition.

The words 'part one' do, however, affect how the play
is to be understood and appreciated by all readers, from
students preparing essays to actors rehearsing their roles:
there is an obvious difference between a text that is
complete in itself and one that is only the first half of
something.

Critics have long argued over whether or not
Shakespeare had a second part in mind while writing *The
History of Henry the Fourth*. It is hard to believe that plans
for at least one more play about Henry V were not present
early on: the Prince's eventual throwing off of his former
companions is foreshadowed clearly in his soliloquy of
Act I, scene 2 and in the mock-rejection of Falstaff in
the 'play extempore' of Act II, scene 4. This event,
however, need not occur at the end of a second play,
before going on to a third about the reign of Henry V,
with its moving scene (II.3) describing Falstaff's last
moments. If a two-part Prince/Falstaff play was fore-
seen from the beginning, then Shakespeare made a poor
job of it – no amount of explaining away will account
for the glaring inconsistencies in the narrative, with the
relationship of the King and the Prince in *Part II* showing
little awareness that the events of *Part I* ever happened.
It is not that Shakespeare was new at this game, since
two of his earliest efforts, *Henry VI, Parts II* and *III*
(not their original titles) do form a coherent historical
narrative.

There is no one right answer to the one- or two-play
question, which is taken up later in the essay on The Play
in Performance; in some respects it is more of a problem
for readers of *Part II*, since our play did have an inde-
pendent existence, however brief, as the only Shakespeare
work about Henry IV and his wayward son. It is that
play I would like to recover in this Introduction, in the

hope that it could provide a path to a deeper appreciation of what, by all accounts, was Shakespeare's greatest hit.

Let us imagine ourselves as London playgoers, some time in 1597. What might we be expecting as we approach the theatre? If we had attended Shakespeare's *Richard II* a few years ago, we would remember the newly crowned Henry IV promising 'a voyage to the Holy Land' (V.6.49) to wash the blood of Richard II from his hands, along with the brief appearance of Harry Hotspur of the north. We would also recall King Henry asking,

> Can no man tell of my unthrifty son?
> 'Tis full three months since I did see him last.
> If any plague hang over us, 'tis he.
> I would to God, my lords, he might be found.
> Inquire at London 'mongst the taverns there;
> For there, they say, he daily doth frequent
> With unrestrainèd loose companions . . . (V.3.1–7)

Perhaps we would also have seen *The Famous Victories of Henry V* (c. 1586) at the Bull Inn, where the wild Prince Harry cavorted with his cronies Ned, Tom and 'Jockey' Oldcastle, only to reject them upon becoming king and going off to fight the battle of Agincourt.

There is nothing particularly surprising in the first scene of today's play. The action begins in 1402, about twelve months after *Richard II* left off; hopes of a crusade to the 'sepulchre of Christ' (I.1.19) have been repeatedly put off by the King's ill health and by continued civil strife at home. We hear 'heavy news' that the Earl of Mortimer has been captured in Wales by 'the irregular and wild Glendower', but 'smooth and welcome news' arrives from Holmedon in the north: 'the Earl of Douglas

is discomfited', and much of his force taken prisoner
(I.1.37–67). A promise of some adventures with the
Prince of Wales is also given, as the King expresses his
envy that Northumberland 'Should be the father to so
blest a son' while 'riot and dishonour stain the brow' of
his 'young Harry' (79–85). Again, nothing surprising,
but the second scene opens with a fat man asking, 'Now
Hal, what time of day is it lad?' Obviously, 'Hal' is the
Prince of Wales, but who is his friend?

'Seneca cannot be too heavy, nor Plautus too light' (*Hamlet*)

Gordon Crosse was a London barrister who attended no
fewer than 576 performances of Shakespeare between
1890 and 1953, and recorded his impressions in a series of
diaries now kept at the Shakespeare Library, Birmingham.
After his first *Henry IV, Part I* in 1896, he wrote, 'the play
consists of two sides, the serious and the comic interest,
the one led by King Henry and Hotspur, the other by
Falstaff, while Prince Hal, who participates in both, binds
the two together'. It is both reassuring and instructive that
Crosse was neither an English professor nor a profes-
sional drama reviewer; he felt no need to back his opinion
by citing the critics. Had he wished to do so, there were
plenty from whom to choose: Dr Samuel Johnson writes
of the play's 'comic and tragic part', William Hazlitt
compares the 'heroic and serious' with the 'comic and
farcical'; to Victor Hugo, 'all these changes of scene, cease-
lessly alternating comedy with tragedy, are not mere
caprices of a strange imagination; they have their reason
in the plan of a great genius' (Bevington, *'Henry IV': Critical
Essays; Henry the Fourth, Part 1*, New Variorum edition).

To see a play as alternately serious and funny does not take us very far; it describes the (presumably intended) effect on the audience, not the actual content. However, there is another, more revealing pattern: 'the plan of a great genius' is not only to alternate comedy with tragedy but also to alternate the past with the present.

A common observation about the plays of Shakespeare and his contemporaries is that they lack any sense of historical chronology. To the Elizabethans, life centuries ago was more or less the same as life in their own era: Cleopatra plays billiards, a clock strikes three in *Julius Caesar* and cannons thunder in *King John*. *Henry IV, Part I* is seemingly no different – if the setting is the early 1400s, what is Falstaff doing with a pistol case at the battle of Shrewsbury (V.3.52), many years before the wheel-lock pistol was known in England? A closer look at this and other apparent anachronisms reveals an interesting pattern, however: nearly all occur within the so-called 'comic' world of Falstaff, Poins and, for the first half of the play, Prince Hal, where they are not anachronisms at all. Shakespeare has not placed these scenes in the time of Henry IV; they are in his own and the audience's time, late in the 1590s.

After over a century of realistic drama we tend to assume that a play can have only one historical setting, but *Henry IV, Part I* (and *Part II*) are written in a very different way. When the King, Glendower or Hotspur is onstage, the time was, for the original spectators, nearly two hundred years before, but *'enter Falstaff'* and they were in the present. That 'present' is often called the 'age of Shakespeare' – perhaps strange, since except for the brief Induction to *The Taming of the Shrew* our only opportunity to get a close look at Shakespeare's England in his plays is with Sir John Falstaff as our guide, in the two parts of *Henry IV* and *The Merry Wives of Windsor*. Here, Falstaff can be 'fat-witted with drinking of old sack', and, according to Poins, would sell his soul for 'a cup of Madeira' (I.2.2–3, 113–14), sweet wines from Spain, the Canary Islands and Portugal that were first imported into England during Tudor times; indeed, the *Oxford English Dictionary* cites *Henry IV, Part I* as the earliest recorded use of both 'madeira' and 'anchovies', another newly fashionable item in Falstaff's tavern bill (a bill with 1590s not 1400s prices). Westmorland's report of the 'artillery' employed at Holmedon and Hotspur's ire at the 'certain lord, neat and trimly dressed' who would have been a soldier 'but for these vile guns' (I.3.32, 62) are unhistorical, but not anachronistic; the artillery at that battle was indeed bow and arrow, since cannon, at that time, was rarely used as a field weapon. However, Henry IV made full use of 'vile guns' when besieging rebel strongholds two years later.

Students of German drama might find something familiar in all this: much of what later came to be called 'epic theatre', as developed primarily by the great dramatist Bertolt Brecht in the 1920s and 1930s, can be found in *Henry IV, Part I*. Of course, Shakespeare could not employ Brecht's slide projections, written captions and other appurtenances of the 'alienation effect', intended to discourage the spectator from empathizing with the characters, but then he had no need to, for there was no realistic theatre, with its painted scenery and linear plot, to overturn. Critics have often debated who the central character of *Henry IV, Part I* is, a difficult question given that Prince Hal, Hotspur and Falstaff have roughly the same number of lines. The best answer might be that this play does not, indeed cannot, have one central character, since there is no one plot which they inhabit. Like the great

plays of the epic theatre, it presents a series of episodes
that interrelate freely in both time and place, without
restriction, and instead of a subsequent scene being the
next thing that happens in the story, it is often a parodic,
alternative version of what has just occurred. The past
informs the present, and the present informs the past.

The events of the past in *Henry IV, Part I* take place
over a mere ten months, by far the shortest period of
time among the Folio's ten Histories, plays noted, as the
Chorus of *Henry V* says, for 'Turning th'accomplish-
ment of many years | Into an hour-glass' (I.Prol.30–31).
Relying mostly on Raphael Holinshed's *Chronicles of
England* (1587), Shakespeare shows the breaking up of
Henry IV's alliance with the powerful northern lords and
their subsequent rebellion, put down (temporarily) at
Shrewsbury. These conflicts are foretold in *Richard II*,
King Richard warning Northumberland,

> Thou shalt think,
> Though he divide the realm and give thee half,
> It is too little, helping him to all,

while the King

> . . . shall think that thou, which knowest the way
> To plant unrightful kings, wilt know again,
> Being ne'er so little urged another way,
> To pluck him headlong from the usurped throne.
>   (V.1.59–65)

King Henry's dilemma is one that greets every ruler
who seizes power by force. The Florentine statesman
Niccolò Machiavelli (1469–1527) advises in his treatise
on political power, *The Prince* (1513), 'you may find

that you have enemies in all those whom you have
injured in seizing the Princedom, yet cannot keep the
friendship of those who helped you to gain it, since you
can neither reward them as they expect, nor yet, being
under obligations to them, use violent remedies against
them'. As for those who place the new Prince on his
throne, they are never safe. Machiavelli writes, 'he who
is the cause of another's greatness is himself undone,
since he must work either by address or force, each of
which excites distrust in the person raised to power'.
Most importantly, Machiavelli sees this as part of an
inevitable historical process, a 'general axiom, which
never or rarely errs', an axiom Worcester knows, as he
refuses to tell Hotspur of Henry IV's 'liberal and kind
offer' (V.2.2) of pardon:

> It is not possible, it cannot be,
> The King should keep his word in loving us.
> He will suspect us still, and find a time
> To punish this offence in other faults. (4–7)

Appeals to the likely reactions of those in Shakespeare's original audience are all too easy, since they
always think whatever we want them to, but it must be
fair to say that almost everyone watching this play in
1597 would know that Queen Elizabeth's grandfather,
Henry VII, took the throne by force, and had to defend
it the same way.

Although the rebels seek to depose Henry IV, what is
at stake in *Henry IV, Part I* is not so much who the
rightful King of England is but how England itself is to
be defined. For all the eloquence of John of Gaunt's
famous evocation in *Richard II* of 'This precious stone
set in the silver sea, | Which serves it in the office of a

wall' (II.1.46–7), that silver sea does not surround England – as Owen Glendower says, it 'chides the banks of England, Scotland, Wales' (III.1.42). Even south of the Cheviot Hills that form England's border with Scotland, the authority of the crown was the subject of bitter contention, constantly challenged by the northern barons seeking to maintain their rule under the old feudal system. When Mortimer, Glendower, Worcester and Hotspur divide their map, Glendower is to keep Wales, while England is to be split in two, Mortimer's kingdom ending at the River Trent.

The driving force behind this effort to divide England is, as in the Quarto title, 'Lord Henry Percy, surnamed Henry Hotspur of the North'. Where Hotspur comes from is as important as who he is: Prince Hal speaks of the 'Hotspur of the north', Falstaff of 'that same mad fellow of the north, Percy' (II.4.101,328). Any comparison of Hal and Hotspur involves more than their ideas of honour, as is discussed below; it is a comparison, as the Elizabethan mapmaker and historian John Speed writes in his *Theatre of the Empire of Great Britain* (1612), between London, 'the seat of British kings, the chamber of the English, the model of the land and the mart of the world', and the north country, 'exposed to extremity of weathers, as great winds, hard frosts, and long lying of snows', with its 'warlike people . . . made fierce and hard by the several encounters of the Scots'.

Hotspur died at Shrewsbury only weeks after first engaging in open rebellion, but northern affairs remained a constant source of worry to the crown. Once Henry VIII broke with the Papacy and established a separate English church the conflict became religious as well as political – in those times the distinction hardly existed – much of the north remaining staunchly Catholic. In 1569

the five-year-old Shakespeare may have seen the soldiers
of Henry VIII's daughter, Queen Elizabeth, march
through Stratford on their way to put down the 'Rising
of the North', led by the seventh Earl of Northumberland,
Thomas Percy.

'All westward, Wales beyond the Severn shore'

Henry IV, Part I ends with the northern rebellion in
abeyance, as King and Prince head 'towards Wales, | To
fight with Glendower and the Earl of March' (V.5.39–40).
Owen Glendower is one of the many memorable
Shakespearian characters who seem to have much larger
parts than they actually do – he speaks fewer than eighty
lines, in only one scene, but when well acted, Glendower
never fails to make a lasting impression. Before he appears
descriptions range from Westmorland's 'irregular and
wild Glendower . . . that Welshman' (I.1.40–41), to the
King's 'that great magician, damned Glendower' (I.3.82),
to Hotspur's 'great Glendower' (I.3.100), to Falstaff's
colourful 'he of Wales that gave Amamon the bastinado,
and made Lucifer cuckold' (II.4.329–30). Anyone who
could be even some of these things would be something
of a marvel; upon meeting him, we find he is indeed, as
he himself claims, 'not in the roll of common men'
(III.1.40). His son-in-law Mortimer attests,

> In faith, he is a worthy gentleman,
> Exceedingly well read, and profited
> In strange concealments, valiant as a lion,
> And wondrous affable, and as bountiful
> As mines of India. (III.1.159–63)

These are the very qualities Hotspur enjoys debunking, without quite succeeding in doing so.

A major distinction between the northern and Welsh revolts of the early 1400s should be kept in mind – one indicated by the small 'n' and capital 'W' in this sentence. While the crown's conflict with the Percies was a political dispute among Englishmen, the Welsh were engaged in a nationalist insurrection, wanting to keep their separate language, culture and political-judicial system from being completely absorbed into a greater Britain. These cultural and linguistic differences are first presented through Glendower's retort to Hotspur's deriding of his accent,

> I can speak English, lord, as well as you,
> For I was trained up in the English court,
> Where being but young I framèd to the harp
> Many an English ditty lovely well,
> And gave the tongue a helpful ornament –
> A virtue that was never seen in you. (III.1.116–21)

and are then brought home with great force, in a manner that is silent on the page but often stunning in performance. Glendower's daughter, Lady Mortimer, who speaks and then sings in Welsh, is a far cry from the Welshwomen who committed 'Such beastly shameless transformation' (I.1.44) upon the bodies of Herefordshire soldiers. The impression one receives of this Welsh household is one of love, warmth and good feeling in a rich and sophisticated culture.

One factor lying behind Shakespeare's positive depiction of the Welsh is that Glendower is not the play's only Welshman. Prince Hal, as Hotspur twice says, is also 'Harry Monmouth', named for the town of his birth. As

Henry V, he proudly asserts his nationality to the Welsh
Captain Fluellen, promising to wear the traditional leek
in his cap on St David's day: 'I wear it for a memorable
honour; | For I am Welsh, you know, good countryman',
Fluellen replying, 'All the water in Wye cannot wash
your majesty's Welsh plood out of your pody, I can tell
you that' (*Henry V*, IV.7.102–5).

If Henry V actually did observe St David's day, he
was not the last king of England to do so: Henry VII,
grandson of the Welshman Owen Tudor, was born in
Pembrokeshire, and returned the English crown to Welsh
hands after landing at Milford Haven, defeating the last
Plantagenet king, Richard III, at the battle of Bosworth.
From that day to the end of his reign, the first Tudor
king advertised his Welsh heritage and its association
with the legendary King Arthur as a means of establishing his legitimacy.

Elizabeth did not promote her Welsh background to
the extent her grandfather did, perhaps because Wales's
many connections with Tudor rule were so well established by her time. The soldier and poet Thomas
Churchyard dedicated his book *The Worthiness of Wales*
(1587) to the Queen, describing it as 'a work to the honour
of Wales, where your highness' ancestors took name', and
informed 'every loving and friendly reader' that 'some of
our greatest Kings (that have conquered much) were born
and bred in that country . . . among the same Princes, I
pray you give me leave to place our good Queen Elizabeth'.
In *Henry IV*, *Part I* and *Henry V*, where questions of royal
legitimacy are always present, it would have been astonishing had Shakespeare chosen to present anything other
than a favourable picture of Wales and its people.

Prince Hal does not assert his Welsh nationality in
Henry IV, *Part I*, but then there is little opportunity or

need to do so. Questions of national identity do not
concern him for the first half of the play; they are truly
a world and two centuries away from Eastcheap and Sir
John Falstaff.

'There is a devil haunts thee in the likeness of an old fat man'

The character whom many, not without justification,
consider to be Shakespeare's greatest creation got his
name over an unusually lengthy process. Originally, he
was Sir John Oldcastle, one of three names Shakespeare
took for Hal's companions from *The Famous Victories of
Henry V*, the others being Ned and Gadshill. Since the
Famous Victories survives only in a very poor and probably corrupt text, any conclusion drawn from it must be
treated with caution. Even so, one can say with some
certainty that the most noteworthy thing about 'Jockey'
Oldcastle in that play is how unnoteworthy he is. The
Prince's closest companions are Ned and Tom, and they,
not Oldcastle, are rejected by Henry V and told to mend
their ways; Jockey is present, but ignored.

Why the author of the *Famous Victories* used this one
historical name among other fictional ones is a mystery.
Sir John Oldcastle, the fourth Lord Cobham (1378–1417),
served both Henry IV and Henry V as a military
commander. As a follower of John Wycliffe, he was
condemned as a heretic, but escaped from the Tower and
fled to Wales; four years later he was captured and brought
to the scaffold. Oldcastle is celebrated in John Foxe's *Acts
and Monuments* (1563) as a martyr to the Protestant cause.

Whether or not Shakespeare adopted Oldcastle for his
character knowing it would offend the present Lord

Cobham is a matter of historical debate. In any event, either the powerful descendant of Oldcastle's widow, Sir William Brooke, or his son Henry, or both, did indeed object, and some time between the first performance and 25 February 1598, when the play was registered for publication at the London Stationers' Company, Oldcastle became Falstaff, another name taken from history.

Sir John Fastolf, as it is usually spelled, a powerful knight and landowner, was born in the same year as Oldcastle, but lived until 1459. He served Henry V and Henry VI with great distinction in their French wars but, according to some chroniclers, while engaging Joan of Arc's forces at Patay he beat a hasty retreat, was charged with cowardice and expelled from the Order of the Garter. These incidents, dramatized by Shakespeare in *Henry VI, Part I*, are unlikely to have actually taken place, for soon after the battle of Patay Fastolf was occupying important positions of command.

Critics and editors have differed sharply on the significance of Oldcastle and, to a lesser extent, Fastolf – Stanley Wells and Gary Taylor have gone so far as to use Oldcastle (in *Part I* only) for their Oxford edition of the *Complete Works*. Whatever the merits of that editorial decision, history has made the debate (literally) academic: restaurants in Brussels, Maastricht, Cologne and Arnhem, a bar in Paris, hotels from Vienna to Johannesburg and an Austrian wine guide all bear the name 'Falstaff', as do many an English pub and a famous American brewery – ironic in that Sir John drinks sack, not beer.

When confronted by an institution, returning him to a character in a single play seems a foolhardy task, but let us try to put aside what Falstaff later became, and look at what the 'original' Falstaff, the Falstaff of *Henry*

IV, Part I, did to create such a demand for printed
copies of this play and the writing of more plays with
Sir John in them. Even before anything is said, Falstaff's
appearance tells spectators that he is to be something
new, since nothing in the surviving text of the *Famous
Victories* indicates that Sir John was fat in that play.
There is also something quite shocking in his first words,
'Now Hal, what time of day is it lad?' In the earlier
play the Prince is never addressed by a commoner as
'Hal' or any other nickname, but to Falstaff he is 'lad',
'sweet wag', 'mad wag' and, again and again, just 'Hal'.
The Prince seizes on Falstaff's enquiry about the time
as an opportunity to give us a better picture of his
friend's personality: he is not only fat, but 'fat-witted
with drinking of old sack'; he sleeps until afternoon,
and he spends as much time in brothels as he can. The
splendid tavern sequences are foreshadowed a few lines
later with mention of their mutual acquaintance, 'my
Hostess of the tavern' (I.2.40), and Falstaff's conceding
that the Prince always pays the bill.

   Here, comedy is in the 'quips and . . . quiddities'
(I.2.45), given in a style rarely seen before in Shakespeare.
The splendid repartee of plays such as *The Taming of
the Shrew* and *Love's Labour's Lost* is usually in verse and
between lovers; prose was used to brilliant effect in *A
Midsummer Night's Dream*, but Bottom's comedy does
not derive from his wit or intelligence. In their game of
'Can You Top This?' Hal is the first, and with the exception of three lines in *Henry VIII*, the only Shakespearian
English king ever to speak in prose: more than anything
he does, this establishes him as one who relates to
commoners as well or better than he does to the nobility.

   Through all the wordplay the conversation constantly
returns to the theme of 'What will happen when the

Prince of Wales becomes King Henry V?' For Hal, it will mean forsaking his companions and assuming the responsibilities of government; for Falstaff, it is a matter of survival, since in his second line he names the first of the two vocations he practises in the play: 'we that take purses go by the moon and the seven stars' (I.2.13–14). Falstaff delights himself, and us, with his extraordinary knowledge of scripture – no one in Shakespeare quotes the Bible more often, and no one in all of literature is more adept at claiming divine sanction for everything he does. There is no hypocrisy here, only a rather individual interpretation of how the Old and New Testaments serve as a guide to our daily lives: who can argue with Falstaff's reading of 1 Corinthians (7:20), 'Let every man abide in the same vocation wherein he was called', even if that vocation happens to be purse-taking (I.2.102–5).

Of any speech in the play, the interpretation of Hal's soliloquy at the end of Act I, scene 2 depends most upon the one-or-two-play question. 'I know you all, and will awhile uphold | The unyoked humour of your idleness' is commonly read as a prediction, and justification, of the rejection of Falstaff at the end of *Part II*; for Hal to state at the outset, 'My reformation, glittering o'er my fault, | Shall show more goodly' (I.2.193–4, 211–12), makes him seem cold, calculating and disloyal to his friends. If read only in the context of *Part I*, however, other meanings come to the surface.

So far, all the audience knows of the Prince of Wales's 'riot and dishonour' is a cultural tradition, the King's voicing his distress over his son's reputation, and Hal's agreeing to participate in Poins's plan for a practical joke on Falstaff. Furthermore, it is not yet clear how important a character Falstaff will be. Hal begins not with an apostrophe to Sir John but with the ambiguous 'I know

you all' – Falstaff, Poins, others who have yet to appear
– and this is the last we hear of his companions for
the rest of the soliloquy, a short one by Shakespearian
standards. The topic here is not Hal's friendships but
whatever seemingly irresponsible (and presumably enter-
taining) things he will do, offending 'to make offence
a skill', until his inevitable reformation, as required by
both tradition and written history. His premise, that good
behaviour 'Shall show more goodly, and attract more
eyes' when preceded by 'loose behaviour' (I.2.214, 212,
206), has some, but not much, logic to it, and A. C.
Bradley speaks for many in noting that Hal is behaving
much like his father, the 'vile politician' of Hotspur's estimation (*Henry the Fourth, Part 1*, New Variorum edition).

'Is there no virtue extant?'

As amusing as Falstaff's verbal dexterity in Act I, scene
2 may be, it is hardly the stuff of a character who is,
according to Harold Bloom, 'a miracle in the creation of
personality' (*Shakespeare: The Invention of the Human*),
but once at Gad's Hill in Act II we are able to see Sir
John in action and, more importantly, hear him speak
directly to us. The moment that Falstaff turned to the
original spectators and said, 'I am accursed to rob in that
thief's company' (II.2.10), they would have realized he
was to dominate the play. His willingness, indeed eagerness, to share his thoughts, another of his Brechtian qualities, marks him as the only character with whom we have
a personal relationship. Of course, the actor playing Hal
can, if he chooses, speak his Act I soliloquy while looking
spectators in the eye, but a calm and calculated plan for
the future does not engender much warmth.

Falstaff's inevitable accusation that the Prince and Poins are 'arrant cowards' advertises the glorious tavern scene to follow, the longest in the play. It does not start well; many audiences find Hal's teasing of Francis the Drawer (II.4.36–96) more cruel than funny, but the second episode, with the unmasking of Falstaff as liar, braggart and coward, is a triumph. That triumph is Falstaff's, for what answer can there be to the effrontery of 'By the Lord, I knew ye as well as he that made ye' (261–2)? A tradition going back to the nineteenth century has Sir John giving this line rather sheepishly, while peeping over his shield, but the most appropriate delivery must be as direct and straightforward statement of fact. Of course, Falstaff is not telling the truth in any literal sense, but there is a deeper truth at work here: Poins has asked, 'What trick hast thou now?' (260). The game is everything, and if Falstaff gives even the slightest hint of admitting his cowardice, that game is over, and our interest in Falstaff is over along with it.

Fortunately, Sir John has won, but the victory is short lived: a messenger from the court is at the door. Sir John Bracy's 'villainous news' (II.4.326) marks the first mention of Hotspur, Glendower and Douglas in Falstaff's Eastcheap; that Hal will be 'horribly chid' (366) when he confronts his father awakens Falstaff's fears, not spoken of since Act I, scene 2, about his fate once Hal becomes King.

Amazingly, the 'play extempore' was usually omitted in the eighteenth and nineteenth centuries, a practice deplored by that most astute of Shakespearians Abraham Lincoln, who knew it to be 'one of the best scenes in the play'. Of all the episodes in *Henry IV, Part I*, none is more revealing about the relationship of Falstaff and the Prince. The first part, with Sir John impersonating Henry IV, has some wonderful parody of rival playwright John Lyly (II.4.384–410), but behind the parody we see a man who desperately seeks reassurance about his own future. This is the only time that Falstaff gives Hal fatherly advice, using the mask of Hal's real father to say, 'there is virtue in that Falstaff. Him keep with, the rest banish' (419–20).

When they switch roles Hal, as the King, directly challenges 'himself' about 'that grey iniquity' whose company he keeps. Although the scene is in prose, when spoken, the exchange

FALSTAFF (*as* HAL)
    My lord, the man I know.
PRINCE HAL (*as* KING)
    I know thou dost. (II.4.451–2)

comes across as a single, shared blank verse line of ten one-syllable words. Its terseness, with the repeated 'I know', signals that what follows, while said behind the mask of an impromptu play, is no joke.

Hal's response to Falstaff's famous 'Banish plump Jack, and banish all the world' (II.4.465) marks a turning point Actors have spoken 'I do, I will' in many different ways: Hal can address all four words to Falstaff, address the spectators, soliloquize or divide the line, moving from one mode to another after 'I do'. Any variation in the length of the pause before 'I will' is also going to carry a different meaning with it. However the line is given, the shift in tense from present to future seems to imply that Hal speaks 'I do' as the mock Henry IV, 'I will' as himself, the future Henry V. He used the very same words, 'I will', at the end of his soliloquy – the reformation he then promised occurs at this moment, almost precisely at the play's halfway point.

After reassurances to the 'oily rascal' of a Sheriff and the discovery of the sleeping Falstaff's tavern account, the Prince of Wales is all business – 'I'll to the court in the morning. We must all to the wars' – while giving reassurance that whatever Falstaff's ultimate fate, he will not be banished from this play: 'I'll procure this fat rogue a charge of foot' (II.4.511, 528–30). Hal never really returns to a life of companionship with Falstaff, either here or in *Henry IV, Part II*, where Falstaff's part is a small one, and where he and the Prince spend all of three or four minutes together onstage.

For all his notoriety, the wastrel Hal of popular tradition is mostly conspicuous by his absence in Shakespeare, less than remarkable, given that the tradition is without any historical basis except for a few scattered hints in Holinshed and in John Stow's *Chronicles of England* (1580) – perhaps the remarkable thing is that Shakespeare sustains it for half a play. How much of an actual thief Hal is remains unclear; his question 'where shall we take a purse tomorrow?' is contradicted several lines later by an initial refusal to join Poins and Falstaff on their next exploit. He changes his mind only when Poins reveals the real objective, to play a practical joke on Sir John.

Spectators in the playhouse do not *see* Hal do anything wrong, other than keep company with Poins and Falstaff. He does not rob anyone, except Falstaff, and has the money taken from the travellers at Gad's Hill 'paid back again with advantage' (II.4.532). This is some distance from the Prince of the *Famous Victories*, who enters having taken £500 from the King's Receivers, proceeds to spend it and gleefully promises, 'if the old king my father were dead, we would be all kings'.

What makes *Henry IV, Part I* unique among treatments of the Henry V legend, including Shakespeare's own *Henry IV, Part II* and *Henry V*, is that the Prince's reformation occurs while he is still Prince; in the other versions it comes suddenly, when he becomes King. The *Famous Victories* has Henry V turning Ned, Tom and Oldcastle aside at his coronation; in *Henry IV, Part II* the new king tells the amazed court,

> The tide of blood in me
> Hath proudly flowed in vanity till now.
> Now doth it turn, and ebb back to the sea,
> Where it shall mingle with the state of floods,
> And flow henceforth in formal majesty. (V.2.129–33)

In *Henry V* the Archbishop of Canterbury recalls:

> The breath no sooner left his father's body
> But that his wildness, mortified in him,
> Seemed to die too. (I.1.25–7)

Nothing in Hal's Act I soliloquy would lead one to expect something different. He does not say what positive action he will undertake to make up for his past faults, so the playgoers of 1597 would have every reason to presume that later that afternoon a wild prince would suddenly become a great king. Shakespeare turns the tables on tradition by having Hal seek to pursue the qualities of a king while still the Prince of Wales. Hal does not choose the means of doing this — that decision is made for him when he confronts his father.

'I am your son'

A most interesting oddity can be found in the critical

response to *Henry IV, Part I*, particularly in the nineteenth century: whether commentators see the Prince as
a heroic figure who is temporarily misled by the wiles of
Falstaff or as a priggish hypocrite, loyal to Falstaff only
as long as he has use for him, they usually refer to someone
named 'Prince Henry', even though there is no such
character in the play. He is always 'Hal' to Falstaff, except
during the play at the Boar's Head; both the mock king
and then the real one address their son as 'Harry', not a
diminutive but the original English form of 'Henry'. In
halving Hotspur's age to create a wished-for son to the
King, Shakespeare neatly exploits the fact that they bear
the same name.

As Henry IV scolds his Harry for the 'barren pleas-
ures' he enjoys and 'rude society' he keeps (III.2.14)
there is no recognition on his part how barren the relationship to his son appears to be; one can easily understand why Harry would prefer to be where he is known
as Hal. This is a king speaking to a prince, not a father
to his son: matters of state are being neglected, and the
Prince is in danger of losing his crown, just as 'the skipping King', Richard II, lost his to Henry Bolingbroke:

> For all the world
> As thou art to this hour was Richard then
> When I from France set foot at Ravenspurgh. (III.2.93–5)

Hal listens contritely, in near silence, until the King likens
himself to Hotspur, 'even as I was then is Percy now'
(96), and launches into a passionate tribute to the honours
Hotspur has won. Reverse the word order, and the
meaning, if not the metre, is the same: 'as Percy is now,
I was then' – like father, like son. This finally draws a
reply, and an impassioned one, from the Prince:

> I will redeem all this on Percy's head,
> And in the closing of some glorious day
> Be bold to tell you that I am your son. (132–4)

Like 'My lord, the man I know . . .', the last of these
three lines is ten one-syllable words. As any actor trained
to work with blank verse knows, such lines take longer
to say than those with polysyllables, inviting added
emphasis; Shakespeare's versification directs the actor to
show that nothing in Hal's long speech approaches the
vehemence and eloquent simplicity of 'I am your son'.
The imagery of the rest of the speech is of changing
places: Hal will demonstrate that he, not Hotspur, is the
'child of honour and renown' (139).

'What is in that word honour?'

The idea that Prince Hal represents a 'mean' between the
extremes of Hotspur, who cares only about honour, and
Falstaff, who dismisses it, has become something of a
critical orthodoxy. It has the advantage of giving the play
a moral, neatly placing ideas and themes into boxes; the
disadvantage is that they might be the wrong boxes,
obscuring rather than clarifying the text.

To say that characters represent different attitudes
to something, we must first agree on what that thing is,
and as with other 'big' Shakespearian words, from
'commodity' in *King John* to 'patience' in *King Lear*,
'honour' had a range of definitions in Elizabethan times.
At first glance it would seem nonsensical to say that
Hotspur represents an extreme: is one supposed to be
honourable, but not *too* honourable? Obviously not, if

we apply the most common modern definition of honour as 'integrity', 'honesty', or, as Samuel Johnson writes in his great *Dictionary* of 1755, 'nobleness of mind, scorn of meanness, magnanimity'. Surely, one cannot have too much of these qualities; they are fundamental to the concept of 'virtue', as famously expounded by Aristotle in his *Nicomachean Ethics*.

However, this is the *fifth* of Dr Johnson's definitions. The first four are 'dignity', 'reputation or fame', 'the title of a man of rank' and 'subject of praise'. Here, honour relies not upon personal integrity but upon being recognized by others, especially those in authority, for one's achievements. It is synonymous with 'glory', as when Hal promises

> That this same child of honour and renown,
> This gallant Hotspur, this all-praisèd knight,
> . . . shall render every glory up . . . (III.2.139–40, 150)

If one asked any Elizabethan to name the person who most deserved the title 'child of honour and renown', undoubtedly the answer would be Sir Philip Sidney. He was, as Ophelia says of Hamlet,

> The courtier's, soldier's, scholar's, eye, tongue, sword,
> Th' expectancy and rose of the fair state,
> The glass of fashion and the mould of form . . .
>   (*Hamlet*, III.1.152–4)

Son of the powerful courtier Sir Henry Sidney and nephew of the even more powerful Robert Dudley, Earl of Leicester, the young Philip Sidney was renowned throughout Europe as a statesman and poet. His *Apology for Poetry* (1579–80) must be accounted the first great

work of literary criticism to be written in English, his
Astrophel and Stella (1582) the first great English sonnet
sequence. As the most favoured of Elizabeth's young
courtiers, Sidney's only opportunity to emulate the gallant
knights of his prose romance, *Arcadia* (1590), was in
tournaments such as the Accession Day Tilts – more
lavish costume displays than tests of chivalric prowess.
Hence, like many an Elizabethan gentleman, he sought
the active life of honour by volunteering to fight in the
Low Countries. In July of 1586, during an assault against
the town of Zutphen, a bullet shattered his thigh bone
and he died from infection twenty-five days later. A
legend surrounding his death has him refusing a cup of
water in his last moments, saying to a dying soldier alongside him, 'Thy need is greater than mine.' All Europe
grieved for him; his state funeral was the most magnifi-
cent ever given a commoner.

   Hotspur embodies one aspect of Sidney's fame when
he declares his readiness to seek 'bright honour'
anywhere, 'from the pale-faced moon' to 'the bottom of
the deep, | Where fathom-line could never touch the
ground' (I.3.200 202). The honour that he seeks will add
to the glory he already owns, through his military exploits
against 'renownèd Douglas' (III.2.107). For Sidney's
other accomplishments, Hotspur has little time: he dislikes
'mincing poetry' (III.1.128), and the only music he cares
for is the sound of 'lofty instruments of war' (V.2.97);
his 'spirit within', according to his wife, Kate, 'hath been
so at war' that it occupies every sleeping as well as waking
hour (II.3.39–66).

   If honour is to be synonymous with glory, Harry Percy
has a monopoly on it for the first half of the play. The
only time Prince Hal utters the word, while in the world
of Eastcheap and Gad's Hill, is to say to Poins, 'I tell

thee, Ned, thou hast lost much honour that thou wert not with me in this action' (II.4.19–20), this action being a drinking contest. In his vow to prove he is the King's true son, he says 'honour' twice within four lines (III.2.139–42).

'The land is burning'

While Hal has been with the King things have changed for Falstaff. In Act III, scene 3, his last visit (for this play) to the Boar's Head, he is without employment, his career as thief apparently over, and there is no Poins or Hal with whom to exchange quips, only Bardolph. For the first time we see a melancholy Sir John, who observes, 'Company, villainous company, hath been the spoil of me' (III.3.9–10). He even entertains thoughts of repentance; in something of a parody of what Prince Hal had promised, he plans to do it 'suddenly, while I am in some liking' (5).

Fortunately, all such thoughts are put aside with the arrival of the 'marching' Hal with a new opportunity – to command an infantry company in the coming war. Although this scene contains some humorous repartee over who, if anyone, picked Falstaff's pocket, a change in the relationship is apparent. Having informed Falstaff, 'I have procured thee, Jack, a charge of foot', Hal ignores a further attempt at wordplay: 'I would it had been of horse. Where shall I find one that can steal well?' (III.3.184–6), and instead delivers a series of crisp orders to Bardolph, Peto and to Falstaff (speaking to him for the first time in verse), closing with 'The land is burning, Percy stands on high, | And either we or they must lower lie' (200–201). Also for the first time, Falstaff ends a scene alone onstage: 'Rare words! Brave world! Hostess, my breakfast, come! | O, I could wish this tavern were my drum!' (202–3); we sense that henceforth the two friends will be more apart than together, a situation placing Sir John in unaccustomed danger.

The play has left London, never to return. Assembled at Shrewsbury, the Percys and Douglas await the King's forces, who are approaching 'with strong and mighty preparation' (IV.1.93). Sir Richard Vernon's description of Prince Hal at the head of the army has aroused some critical controversy, due to the obscurity of its avian imagery (98–9), but the message is clear: Hal is no longer the 'sword-and-buckler Prince of Wales' of Hotspur's estimation (I.3.227). Now mounted on a 'fiery Pegasus', the Prince of the Eastcheap taverns has become 'young Harry . . . gallantly armed', his company 'Glittering in golden coats . . . As full of spirit as the month of May' (IV.1.94–110).

Such would not describe Falstaff's company, whom we meet in Shakespeare's home county of Warwickshire, as they make their way to Shrewsbury in a decidedly leisurely fashion. As both the Quarto and Folio texts have only '*Enter Falstaff and Bardolph*', it seems likely that the limited size of Shakespeare's acting company forbade the appearance of Falstaff's soldiers onstage, but then their actual appearance could never match the imaginary one Falstaff provides: 'scarecrows' so 'ragged' as to make a madman encountered along the road say he had 'unloaded all the gibbets and pressed the dead bodies' (IV.2.1–46).

In this his longest aside, an account of how he has 'misused the King's press damnably', Falstaff introduces himself in his new role, one he will occupy for the rest of the play. Falstaff as thief was relatively innocent fun,

Falstaff as captain is not: in giving Sir John his 'charge of foot' (III.3.184), Shakespeare creates a living picture of Queen Elizabeth's army, and with it some of the bitterest and most devastating social satire ever seen on the English stage.

Citing the two parts of *Henry IV* in his *History of the British Army* (1910–30), the noted military historian J. W. Fortescue says of Shakespeare, 'he is truly the painter of the English army in his own day'. What a picture it is! Falstaff has already collected 'three hundred and odd pounds' in bribes from all able-bodied men with money to buy their way out of serving, filling their places with 'a hundred and fifty tattered prodigals lately come from swine-keeping' (IV.2.14,30–34). As many historical documents show, this is no exaggeration. For example, Sir Anthony Wingfield speaks of the soldiers he commanded on the troubled expedition of 1589 to Portugal as 'our newest men, our youngest men, and our idlest men, and for the most part our slovenly pressed men, whom the justices . . . have sent out as the scum and dregs of their country' (*A True Copy*), just as Falstaff boasts of 'discarded unjust serving-men, younger sons to younger brothers, revolted tapsters, and ostlers trade-fallen, the cankers of a calm world and a long peace' (IV.2.26–9). Most of these men were recruited by conniving with Justices of the Peace (such as the brilliantly drawn Justice Shallow of *Part II*) to empty out the jails: 'Nay, and the villains march wide betwixt the legs as if they had gyves on, for indeed I had the most of them out of prison' (38–40).

Those sitting or standing at the playhouse in 1597, especially if they had seen military service, could not possibly have thought of Falstaff as a fictive fifteenth-century captain marching towards Shrewsbury – there before them was the rapacious and corrupt officer they knew from personal experience. The odds on their surviving that experience were not great, since so many of their own captains followed Falstaff's advice: 'Tut, tut, good enough to toss, food for powder, food for powder, they'll fill a pit as well as better' (IV.2.63–4). Not only does Falstaff allow anyone to bribe his way out of service, he deliberately sends those he is left with to their deaths so that he can pocket their pay: 'I have led my ragamuffins where they are peppered. There's not three of my hundred-and-fifty left alive' (V.3.35–7).

On 14 May 1590, seven years or so before Falstaff spoke these words on the stage, Queen Elizabeth signed an order for the immediate suppression of a book just published, Sir John Smythe's *Certain Discourses Military*, in which Smythe, who was something of a crank but had held some very important military and civilian posts, openly charged that English captains in the Low Countries were purposely having their men killed in order to keep their wages: 'they have presently devised some very dangerous enterprise to employ their bands and companies in, to make proof how many in such exploits should lose their lives, that they might enrich themselves by their dead pays'. The captains, meanwhile, 'remained in great towns feasting, banqueting, and carousing with their dames'. As for those soldiers who did manage to get back alive, Falstaff has the answer: 'they are for the town's end, to beg during life' (V.3.37–8).

'I have a truant been to chivalry'

As the Prince and Falstaff head towards Shrewsbury the play's interrogation of honour both expands and

intensifies. If Hotspur is to be regarded as too zealous in
his pursuit of honour, then it is hard to see how Hal is
any less so, for in order to 'save the blood on either side'
at Shrewsbury he challenges Hotspur to single combat
(V.1.83–100). Historically, no such challenge was offered
– it would have been a boy of sixteen against a seasoned
warrior of thirty-nine – but as is so often the case,
Shakespeare seeks a truth through fiction. The Prince,
no longer a 'truant' to chivalry, formally invokes the code
his father served when, as shown at the beginning of
Richard II, he sought to prove his loyalty to the crown
by 'all the rites of knighthood' (I.1.75). In challenging
the Duke of Norfolk to trial by combat, the then Henry
Bolingbroke set in motion the chain of events that ulti-
mately brought him to the throne.

For a war to be decided by a single combat seems the
stuff of Arthurian romance, and to some extent this is
true: throughout the Hundred Years War no battle was
ever called off for this reason. Nevertheless, such challenges were frequently offered, twice by Henry V himself;
they were part of the formal process by which rules of
engagement were established and maintained, rules
designed to equate the battle of two armies to a battle
between their Princes, leaving judgement over the right-
ness of their cause to God. The word 'battle' itself could
refer to either a clash of armies or one between two indi-
viduals, as when Bolingbroke promises he 'will in battle
prove' the Duke of Norfolk's perfidy (*Richard II*, I.1.92).

To proclaim oneself the King's champion and fight on
his behalf, as Hal does here, is the most public of all ways
to attain honour. No one knew this better than Robert
Devereux, the second Earl of Essex, who must be
accounted Sir Philip Sidney's successor as 'the theme
of honour's tongue' (indeed, he married Frances

Walsingham, Sidney's widow). At the age of twenty-two, Essex distinguished himself fighting alongside Sidney at Zutphen; in 1589 he joined the English expedition to Portugal against the Queen's wishes, and at the gates of Lisbon offered single combat to any in the Spanish garrison who was of his quality. Two years later he challenged the enemy commander at Rouen, arousing admiration from the French and fury from Queen Elizabeth, as this was a mere two months after Essex's younger brother Walter rode before the town in an act of bravado, and was shot dead.

Of course, known history dictates that the battle of Shrewsbury must be fought, but the King's 'considerations infinite' (V.1.102) forbidding the combat are easily misunderstood. Henry has already sent Blunt to the rebel camp with an offer of 'pardon absolute' (IV.3.50) should they lay down their arms; the offer is now repeated with a personal appeal to Worcester (V.1.103–14). If Henry is sincere in seeking to avoid war, then he cannot allow a trial by battle, for under the law of arms there is no difference between the two – armed rebellion will have taken place, so, whatever the outcome, 'Rebuke and dread correction' must follow.

Observing all this is Sir John Falstaff, who enters the discourse on honour with a brilliant parody of it: 'Can honour set to a leg?' (V.1.131). To many in the original audience, this question would have evoked the memory of Sir Philip Sidney; Sir John Smythe, from whom we have already heard (*Certain Discourses*), considered the death of 'that noble and worthy gentleman' unnecessary, for 'in the opinion of diverse gentlemen that saw him hurt with a musket shot, if he had that day worn his cuisses, the bullet had not broken his thigh bone'. As Falstaff continues his 'catechism' – the word itself a reminder that serious moral and ethical questions lie behind the comedy – there is no denying the sense of his attitude: 'What is that honour? Air. A trim reckoning! Who hath it? He that died a'Wednesday' (140, 134–6).

By Act V Falstaff is the play's sole remaining representative of the 'modern' age, and for him honour does indeed belong to those that 'died a'Wednesday'. From the thirteenth to the fifteenth century members of the nobility who sought honour by serving their prince in war could achieve it through singular achievements of horsemanship or swordsmanship. Individual combats, when they occurred, were relatively unlikely to have fatal consequences, since one gained far more honour by taking an opponent of quality prisoner than by killing him; it was in everyone's interest to observe the laws of capture, treatment of prisoners and ransom, for they served to maintain a vital part of the European economy. Legally, all such prisoners and the ransom they brought (often they were sent home to raise the money) belonged to the King, hence the quarrel over the disposal of Hotspur's prisoners at the start of *Henry IV, Part I*, and the formalities over the disposal of Douglas at the end.

In the Tudor era, with gunpowder weapons having replaced swords and lances, the system had broken down. Prisoners had been replaced as the 'honourable spoil' of war (I.1.74) by whatever could be taken from a captured town, a town that defended itself with cannon and musket. Sir Philip Sidney and young Walter Devereux provide sad examples of what can happen to soldiers, as Jaques describes them in *As You Like It*, when 'Seeking the bubble reputation | Even in the cannon's mouth' (II.7.153–4). Their pursuit of honour had simply become outmoded; in a letter written at about the same time Shakespeare was writing *Henry IV, Part I*, Sir Francis Bacon advised

Essex against depending upon military greatness to gain
the Queen's favour, for 'she loveth peace . . . and that
kind of dependence maketh a suspected greatness'
(Harrison, *Elizabethan Journals*).

The principles behind Bacon's private advice to Essex
had recently been given new and eloquent voice in the
Essays (1588) of Michel de Montaigne. In 'On Glory',
Montaigne draws on Aristotle's *Ethics*, with its idea of
the virtuous man, and Cicero's *De Officiis* (*On Moral
Obligations*) to ask, 'those who teach nobility to seek in
valour nothing but honour . . . as though it were not
honest except it were ennobled, what gain they by it?'
To Montaigne, honour as glory is meaningless, since
being noticed for one's martial deeds is a matter of
chance; true honour is found 'within ourselves, where no
eyes shine but ours'. Albeit for all the wrong reasons,
Falstaff's catechism enlivens and deepens the play's
debate on honour by implicitly recalling another of his
rhetorical questions, one that he asked upon his return
to Eastcheap from the Gad's Hill exploit: 'Is there no
virtue extant?' (II.4.115).

The final three scenes are really one continuous
sequence, where honour is sought, evaded, won and lost
near the town of Shrewsbury. Shakespearian battles are
often satirized as being a great deal of running in and
out, declamatory speeches and actors who are obviously
trying desperately not to hurt themselves or each other.
In today's theatre this is frequently all too true; in 1597,
when every actor would have known how to fence, the
effect would have been something quite different, and
any humour would be provided not by the swordsmanship, but by Falstaff's running commentary upon it.

Like Glendower, Sir Walter Blunt has an importance
far outweighing the number of his lines. In his limited

time onstage Blunt justifies what Falstaff says ironically of him: 'there's honour for you' (V.3.32–3). He is, in fact, the only courtier in the play, and provides an ideal model for one, earning Hotspur's respect by following his conscience in standing up to the King and defending him (I.3.69–75). As Henry IV's ambassador to the rebel camp, he is punctilious in delivering the King's offer, listens patiently to fifty-four lines of Hotspur's angry response, and then, his job done, he dispenses with formality for a brief moment and speaks personally: 'I would you would accept of grace and love' (IV.3.112). Blunt forgoes any opportunity of personal glory on the battlefield by fighting, as Shakespeare read in Holinshed, 'apparelled in the king's suit and clothing' – a standard tactic of medieval and Renaissance warfare, also employed by Richmond, the future Henry VII, in *Richard III*. If the play has an example of Montaigne's alternative to what some consider the 'extremes' of Hotspur and Falstaff, then Sir Walter Blunt, rather than Prince Hal, seems the best candidate.

When Falstaff enters and discovers Blunt's body he becomes the true prototype of the Brechtian hero, simultaneously a character in the action and someone who stands aside and comments upon it. That he sees himself 'fighting' alongside such as Sir Philip Sidney at Zutphen rather than Henry IV at Shrewsbury is shown by his telling us of having led his 'ragamuffins where they are peppered', the 'shot' he fears being bullets, not arrows: 'I am as hot as molten lead, and as heavy too. God keep lead out of me'. Shrewsbury was fought on a Saturday, not a Wednesday, but otherwise Falstaff has been proved correct: 'Sir Walter Blunt – there's honour for you! Here's no vanity!' (V.3.30–38).

In terms of the realistic theatre, Hal's apparent failure

to notice Blunt's body and his losing his sword, only to have it magically returned when he re-enters to fight Douglas moments later, are absurd; this episode is a perfect example of the play's multi-level, epic style. He has momentarily left the field near Shrewsbury and joined Falstaff on the latter's other plane of dramatic narrative, largely as a device to allow Sir John his quips about carrying a bottle of sack instead of a pistol. The Prince's angry departure, 'is it a time to jest and dally now?' (V.3.55), arouses a newly fatalistic attitude in Falstaff. Armed only with sword and sack, he may have to face Hotspur himself: 'I like not such grinning honour as Sir Walter hath. Give me life, which if I can save, so. If not, honour comes unlooked for, and there's an end' (58–61).

Falstaff's brief aside and the subsequent 'alarums and excursions' give the actor playing Hal a few moments in the tiring-house to collect a sword and apply some stage blood for what is obviously meant to be more than a 'shallow scratch' (V.4.10) – Hal's wound and Blunt's death at the hands of Douglas are the only parts of the battle taken from Holinshed. In having the Prince fight off Douglas and rescue the King, Shakespeare invites a comparison with that 'other' Prince, the one of the *Famous Victories*, who eagerly awaits his father's demise so that he can be king (50–51). King Henry then pronounces the process that Hal predicted in his soliloquy, and promised to him in Act III, scene 2, as complete: 'Thou hast redeemed thy lost opinion' (V.4.47).

Things have not gone precisely according to plan. The 'gallant Hotspur', not 'the noble Scot, Lord Douglas', was to be the 'factor' by which Hal would redeem his lost honour, so when the Prince is at last able to call Hotspur to a 'strict account', it is, for him, after the fact. Such is decidedly not the case for Harry Percy:

although Hal no longer needs to fight him, Hotspur needs
to fight Hal. History dictates that he will die on the battlefield; the way he does so is to bring some sense of
dramatic closure to his (fictively) short life.

Hotspur has sought this event as earnestly as has Hal —

> O, would the quarrel lay upon our heads,
> And that no man might draw short breath today
> But I and Harry Monmouth! (V.2.47–9)

— part of his eagerness may lie in the apparent fact that
they have never met. Although it is Hotspur who answers
Henry IV's question about his unthrifty son's whereabouts
in *Richard II*, 'My lord, some two days since I saw the
Prince, | And told him of those triumphs held at Oxford'
(V.3.13–14), in this play Shakespeare seems to be at pains
to emphasize that they are strangers to one another:

HOTSPUR
  If I mistake not, thou art Harry Monmouth.
PRINCE HAL
  Thou speakest as if I would deny my name.
HOTSPUR
  My name is Harry Percy. (V.4.58–60)

Hotspur's great error was to underestimate Hal right up
to the time they meet. He dismisses Vernon's description
of the courtesy with which Hal offered single combat
with the retort,

> Cousin, I think thou art enamourèd
> On his follies! Never did I hear
> Of any prince so wild a liberty (V.2.69–71),

and even at the very moment they go sword against sword he refuses to allow Hal the status of a worthy opponent: 'and would to God | Thy name in arms were now as great as mine' (V.4.68–9).

Some editors have wondered if Hotspur's 'O Harry, thou hast robbed me of my youth!' (V.4.76) is not a compositor's error, suggesting 'worth' or 'growth'; on the surface one would say that Hotspur's old age, not his youth, has been taken from him. The subsequent lines show that 'youth' is perfectly apt, for Hotspur's youth – emphasized throughout the play – has been defined by the 'proud titles' he had won, and must now surrender to Hal.

Of course, another of the play's heroes is 'killed' at this moment. While Falstaff cheers Hal on like a spectator at a prize fight, he suddenly finds himself face to face with the person he once called 'that sprightly Scot of Scots, Douglas' (II.4.335–6). Although the point seems to have eluded most Falstaffs, it cannot be stated too strongly that his falling down *as if he were dead* (V.4.75) must not in any way be obvious. The first audience did not study this play at school, nor can it have known for sure that Sir John would return in other plays. For Falstaff to die at the same time as Hotspur would be a sad but in many ways fitting means of bringing the play to a close; if the audience, along with the Prince, believes that Falstaff is actually dead, then Hal's speech over the bodies is informed with increased power and meaning.

Hal's generous tribute to Hotspur comprises thoughts often found in Renaissance texts, but that does not lessen its sincerity; it also provides our first real glimpse, and a tantalizingly brief one, into Hal's private beliefs. The Act I soliloquy was the working out of a plan, without any hint of reflection; since then he has always been with others. Now, alone onstage (or so he thinks) for the first

time since Act I, scene 2, Hal is given what amounts to a
second soliloquy, and that he reflects at all on the significance of Hotspur's life and death, however commonplace
those reflections may be, shows a seriousness of thought
heretofore unseen.

The eulogy over Falstaff has often been played for
laughs, Hal knowing that Falstaff is alive and purposely
using the word 'embowelled' to scare him. This creates
an inconsistency with Prince John's 'Did you not tell me
this fat man was dead?' (V.4.130), and also ignores the fact
that the last six lines are in rhyme, while the lines to Hotspur
are all blank verse. This is one speech, not two, in which
the affection shown for 'Poor Jack' is counterpoised to the
honour given Hotspur. If Hal were engaged in a parody
here, it seems unlikely that he would close with 'Till then
in blood by noble Percy lie' (109). Ever the survivor,
Falstaff '*riseth up*', delivers the famous and often misquoted
dictum 'The better part of valour is discretion' (118–19),
and then hits on an extraordinary plan to claim the credit
for killing Hotspur, who is perhaps again compared to Sir
Philip Sidney: 'Therefore, sirrah, with a new wound in
your thigh, come you along with me' (125–7).

In one of the play's many ironies, Hal's bold 'think not,
Percy, | To share with me in glory any more' (V.4.62–3)
loses much of its meaning, for no one is there to witness the
event. No one, that is, except Sir John Falstaff, who inad-
vertently ends up leading Hal to deeds of greater honour,
though of a different sort. When Falstaff, in his ultimate act
of brazenness, claims to have killed Hotspur himself, adding
that an appropriate award would be his becoming 'either earl
or duke' (140–41), Hal's response, 'For my part, if a lie may
do thee grace, | I'll gild it with the happiest terms I have'
(156–7), is the most generous thing he does in the play.

First Hal was dismissive of Hotspur's honour, then he

sought it avidly, won it, and now he gives it away, not because he denies its value but because he no longer has need for it. If, as many critics have argued, *Henry IV, Part I* deals with the education of the Prince, then this noble deed shows an understanding that however important one type of honour is, it remains only a part of what Hal must become to be a good king. Without saying so openly, in doing Falstaff this 'grace', Hal implies that Dr Johnson's fourth dictionary definition, 'nobleness of mind, scorn of meanness, magnanimity', is part of his answer to 'What is in that word honour?'.

Such magnanimity continues in the final scene, where the Prince speaks only of 'The noble Percy slain' without saying how, and asks that the 'noble Scot, Lord Douglas' (V.5.19,17) be released without ransom:

> His valours shown upon our crests today
> Have taught us how to cherish such high deeds,
> Even in the bosom of our adversaries. (29–31)

Falstaff hears none of this. At the close of the previous scene he remained alone onstage, looking forward to the reward for his great 'victory' over Hotspur: 'He that rewards me, God reward him! If I do grow great, I'll grow less, for I'll purge, and leave sack, and live cleanly as a nobleman should do' (V.4.161–4).

'An ancient and very fat sage called Sir John Falstaff' (George Bernard Shaw, *Back to Methuselah*)

As the world now knows, Falstaff's exit with Hotspur slung on his back was not to be his final one: from

Henry IV, *Part II* to Giuseppe Verdi's *Falstaff* (1893) and beyond, the great survivor continues to do just that. For Prince Hal, though his 'Poor Jack, farewell!' (V.4.102) is not quite as final as he expected, the association with Falstaff is indeed over. As noted, *Part II* has only a very brief and rather tame episode in which Hal and Poins, disguised as tapsters, overhear Falstaff abuse them to Doll Tearsheet, before King Henry V turns to Sir John at his coronation and says, 'I know thee not, old man' (V.5.50).

Falstaff's age is mentioned nearly as often as his girth, and the difference in years between him and Hal is as important as Hotspur and Hal being the same age. It immediately places Falstaff within a tradition going at least as far back as to Achilles and the Centaur, the sage who instructs the young man in the ways of the world – sometimes with good intent, sometimes otherwise – and to the Vice of the English morality play, relentless in his desire to lead the hero away from the path of piety and virtue.

Once we venture into the area of what Falstaff *is*, rather than what he *does*, we confront the controversial subject of character criticism, often derided as antithetical to the very idea of drama, since it relies on an extra-theatrical life for the characters – they become 'real people' in situations we create ourselves, those the playwright did not bother to include. There is nothing inherently wrong with this; treating characters as real people has always been the primary means, though not the only means, by which drama communicates, but there is only one valid way of verifying one's impression of what characters are, which is to go back to what they do.

If Falstaff is a 'villainous, abominable misleader of youth', as Hal says during the play extempore (II.4.449), then whatever Falstaff has done to deserve the accusation is not shown, although it may be inferred from a friendship that keeps the Prince away from his responsibilities. Neither is Hal's moral development ever called into question, not even by the King in Act III, scene 2; the sole subject of that episode is Hal's duties as a prince and future king. In all their time together, Falstaff never advises Hal as to what course to take, nor does he ever encourage him to ill deeds or a vain life – indeed, it is Hal who asks, 'Where shall we take a purse tomorrow, Jack?' (I.2.98–9). We never see Falstaff seeking Hal out: except for Act II, scene 4, when they meet by arrangement, Falstaff enters first, or they enter together. All in all, there is more than a modicum of truth in Falstaff's saying,

> Thou hast done much harm upon me, Hal, God forgive thee for it. Before I knew thee Hal, I knew nothing, and now am I, if a man should speak truly, little better than one of the wicked. (I.2.91–4)

To be sure, Falstaff exploits the friendship. He gets Hal to pay his bills, he hides behind Hal's authority to avoid arrest and he abuses the military commission Hal procures for him. What Falstaff wants, as he so eloquently pleads while pretending to be Hal in the tavern play, is to keep enjoying his 'Harry's company' (II.4.464), along with the material comforts that Harry's company brings. One thing is certain: Falstaff cannot be out to lead the Prince astray as he delivers his great philosophical discourses on honour, for the Prince is nowhere in sight. Falstaff is out to lead *us* astray.

As we, in our imaginations, leave the playhouse in 1597, we leave having been told by Sir John Oldcastle, as he was then known, that 'honour is a mere scutcheon' (V.1.139–40) and 'the better part of valour is discretion'. Whether or not we decide to become (or remain) cowards as a result is irrelevant – what counts is that we have loved and applauded the man who gave the advice. This is a paradox that has been with us since drama was invented – indeed, it is one of the reasons Plato wanted comedy, along with tragedy, banned from his ideal Republic. The greatest comic characters, from Falstaff to Tartuffe to Homer Simpson, are not loved in spite of their being cowards, hypocrites or gluttons; they are loved *because* they are cowards, hypocrites or gluttons, and proudly so.

Shakespeare's *Henry IV, Part I* confronts its audience with important questions, including those about honour, nationhood, family relationships, politics and government. Another question may be asked about Lord Cobham: would he have bothered to object to the use of his predecessor's name had the play been a flop, and had all of London not demanded to see and read more of Sir John, including, or so we are told, the Queen herself? The story that Shakespeare wrote *The Merry Wives of Windsor* in response to a royal request is probably apocryphal, but it is most certainly plausible. Why the Queen of England, personally responsible for the physical, moral and spiritual welfare of her subjects, would ask to see more of a thief who escapes her sheriffs and a captain who purposely sends her soldiers to their deaths might be the most interesting question of all. Here, perhaps, is where the extraordinary power of *Henry IV, Part I* lies, in what Bertolt Brecht, whose name has appeared often in this discussion, believed the theatre must be: a place where questions are asked, not answered.

Charles Edelman

The Play in Performance

Apart from its obvious excellence, several factors combine to make *Henry IV, Part I* the perfect work for the contemporary theatre. More than any other Shakespeare play, it requires an ensemble rather than an individual star, a mode of production that today's performers are trained for, and are comfortable working in. Every choice an actor makes affects how the other roles are to be played: whether Henry IV is Eric Porter's 'guilty, saddened father' (Ronald Bryden, *New Statesman*, 24 April 1964), or Julian Glover's 'stern, cold, and authoritarian' King (Stanley Wells, *The Times Literary Supplement*, 10 May 1991), the actor who plays Prince Hal must adjust accordingly. Similarly, a contrite Prince in Act III, scene 2 will affect the King's characterization differently from an openly bored or insolent one, as Michael Pennington learned during rehearsals in 1986, when John Castle as Henry IV slapped him hard across the face (Bogdanov and Pennington, *English Shakespeare Company*). How Hotspur is played depends on how Lady Percy is played, and so it goes, for every moment in the play.

Also, the movement begun in the early twentieth century to release Shakespeare from the confines of the proscenium arch (the picture frame separating the stage from the auditorium) has in most places been successful;

both the fluidity of the staging and the inter-relationship of the characters, especially Falstaff's relationship with the audience, are inevitably deepened and intensified in the intimacy of theatres wherein the audience nearly, or even completely, surrounds the players. It is hard to imagine that Michael Attenborough's splendid Royal Shakespeare Company production of 2002 would have been as good had it been performed in Stratford's main house, a very large theatre built in 1932 but in nineteenth-century style, instead of in the intimate Swan, with the audience on three sides.

In recent years the English theatre has moved well away from 'received pronunciation' when doing Shakespeare, a welcome development that is of particular benefit to *Henry IV, Part I*, where, as discussed in the Introduction, the north–south and English–Welsh divisions are so important. Michael Redgrave anticipated the trend in 1951, when he abandoned the stammer used by Hotspurs from Matheson Lang in 1896 to Laurence Olivier in 1945, and spoke in something like a Northumbrian accent, his burred 'r's contributing to the boisterousness of his portrayal. Nowadays it is the rare English production that does not exploit the varieties of speech that actors were once taught to suppress.

Anyone who performs one of Shakespeare's more popular plays is confronted with tradition – even if an actor is unfamiliar with previous Othellos or Rosalinds, many in the audience come to the theatre with a firm idea, however misguided, of what to expect. *Henry IV, Part I* is somewhat unusual in this regard; although it has a long performance history, there is surprisingly little real performance tradition, and some of the reasons why this is so are well worth considering by today's students of the play, including those involved in acting it.

The eighteenth and nineteenth centuries were the age
of the great actor-managers, who exercised nearly total
control over the repertory of the main English and
American theatres (until 1843 their power in London was
even greater, since only the patent houses, Drury Lane
and Covent Garden, were licensed by the crown to
perform plays). This was an actor's theatre, and later an
actor's and designer's theatre, in every respect. There
was no director – the idea that one person should be in
charge in order to create an artistically unified production was far off in the future – and the cast of a play
could change from night to night. All interest was on the
star parts and those who played them, and it is easy to
see why *Henry IV, Part I* held little interest for such
theatrical legends as David Garrick and Edmund Kean,
who both tried Hotspur briefly but soon gave it away.
The play is simply without a central role; Prince Hal
spends the most time onstage, but he has slightly fewer
lines than Falstaff, and only slightly more than Hotspur.

For such a famous play, there is an extraordinary
absence of 'big' dramatic moments by which actors,
especially those of the Romantic era, made their reputa-
tions. Samuel Taylor Coleridge's famous remark about
Edmund Kean, 'To see him act is like reading Shakespeare
by flashes of lightning', would never have been made had
Kean been playing Hotspur instead of Othello or Richard
III. The soliloquies we associate with the major tragic
figures are also missing; unless we include Falstaff's
discourses on honour, the play is without the introspec-
tive speeches the Romantics admired, and Falstaff is
hardly anyone's idea of a Romantic hero.

Sir John, of course, is one of the most loved (something very different from most lovable) characters in the
history of the theatre, but even here, that history does

not contain a great line of famous Falstaffs, actors who redefined the role until another came along to redefine it again, as so many have done with Hamlet or Shylock. Also, *The Merry Wives of Windsor*, the delightful comedy about Falstaff in love, was performed just as often in London throughout the eighteenth century, and the characterization of the two leading Falstaffs of the time, James Quin and John Henderson, would to some extent have been informed by both plays.

Even with all these qualifications, the high regard with which Quin in particular was held for his Falstaff is instructive to those confronting the role in the twenty-first century. Thomas Davies observed,

in scenes, where satire and sarcasm were poignant, he greatly excelled; particularly in the witty triumph over Bardolph's carbuncles, and the fooleries of the hostess. In the whole part he was animated, though not equally happy. His supercilious brow, in spite of assumed gaiety, sometimes unmasked the surliness of his disposition. (Salgādo, *Eyewitnesses*)

This 'intelligent and judicious' Falstaff was seen as more successful than the 'gay levity' of John Henderson, who was more the jolly old knight of Merrie England.

The most admired modern Falstaff, Ralph Richardson, was closer to Quin than to Henderson. Kenneth Tynan saw in his performance at the Old Vic in 1945:

. . . a Falstaff whose principal attribute was not his fatness but his knighthood. He was Sir John first, and Falstaff second . . . Richardson never rollicked or slobbered or staggered: it was not a sweaty fat man, but a dry and dignified one. As the great belly moved, step following step with great finesse lest it over-topple, the arms flapped fussily at the sides as if to paddle the body's bulk along. It was deliciously and subtly funny, not riotously so: from his height of pomp Falstaff was chuckling at himself: it was not we alone, laughing at him. (Tynan, *He That Plays the King*)

Most of the successful Falstaffs to follow Richardson, while finding their own, individual resonances, lent a certain measure of sadness and dignity to the part. At Stratford, in 1951, Anthony Quayle was a 'tuned-down' Falstaff, 'more than half aware that his standing with the Prince is in doubt' (*The Times*, 4 April 1951). Forty years later, on the same stage, Robert Stephens was 'like some fallen Lucifer with residual memories of a better life: when he finally vouchsafes to "live cleanly as a nobleman should do", you sense a poignant hunger for lost, aristocratic values' (Michael Billington, *Guardian*, 18 April 1991).

This emphasis, from Richardson onwards, on what might be called the 'serious' side of Falstaff derives as much from the circumstances of production as any individual choice of the actor: Richardson's Falstaff was the Falstaff of both parts of *Henry IV – Part II* opening a week after *Part I*. Since Barry Jackson did both plays in one day at the Birmingham Repertory in 1921, *Henry IV*, *Part I* has almost always been presented as part of a series, either a two-part play, a trilogy with the addition of *Henry V*, a tetralogy beginning with *Richard II*, or even, as in Franz Dingelstedt's Weimar production of 1864 and the English Shakespeare Company's world tours of *The Wars of the Roses* (1987–9), a series of eight plays compressed into seven – given in historical order, not the order in which they were written – from *Richard II* to *Richard III*, including the three parts of *Henry VI*.

For Falstaff, the two parts of *Henry IV* do make a coherent narrative, enabling and perhaps obliging the actor to mould a consistent characterization over both plays. *Part I* shows him not only surviving the battle of Shrewsbury, but departing triumphant, with hopes of a great reward. Alas, at the start of *Part II* he is impoverished and has effectively been banished from his 'Harry's company', as we learn when the Lord Chief Justice informs Falstaff that he is to go north to recruit soldiers: 'Well, the king hath severed you and Prince Harry' (I.2.204–5). The sadness of this separation does not suddenly hit Falstaff at the end of *Part II*, it is there from the beginning – what he fears now are poverty and old age.

The situation is different with Prince Hal: when a relatively unknown actor named Richard Burton appeared in both parts of *Henry IV* and *Henry V* at Stratford in 1951, his Hal of *Part I* was 'a troubled young man who stood apart from the Eastcheap crowd, eyeing them and already thinking ahead, uneasily, to the role he would eventually assume' (McMillin, *Shakespeare in Performance*). Burton's Hal was considered as much of a revelation as was Richardson's Falstaff six years earlier, and there is no denying that the most exciting actor to come along in a generation brought forward elements of *Part II* and *Henry V* into *Part I*. Even so, any actor, no matter how brilliant, will have difficulty in turning the two (or three) plays into a unified study about Henry V.

Falstaff's relationship with Hal may be consistently developed over the two plays but Hal's relationship with his father is not. Hal appears in only five of *Part II*'s nineteen scenes, and, as noted in the Introduction, the honour he gained at Shrewsbury seems to have been forgotten by everyone, including himself. He has nothing of any significance to do or say until he sees his sleeping father's crown on a pillow (IV.5.20–22); by then the play is nearly over. Hence, in order to perform the two parts of *Henry IV* as a work showing Hal's progress from wastrel to king, some serious rewriting needs to be done. In his 1986 production, later incorporated into *The Wars of the Roses*, Michael Bogdanov moved Falstaff's assertion that he killed Hotspur to the end of the play, after Hal reported Hotspur's death with a gesture to show his father that he was responsible for it. When John Woodvine then claimed, 'we rose both at an instant, and fought a long hour by Shrewsbury clock', the King believed it, and stalked off. Hal's alienation from his father at the start of *Part II* was thus made more credible, but at the expense of his having 'redeemed [his] lost opinion' by saving his father's life made meaningless, along with having the King suddenly appear a gullible fool.

Bogdanov took this idea from Orson Welles's film, *Chimes at Midnight* (Bogdanov and Pennington, *English Shakespeare Company*), a more radical intervention into both parts of *Henry IV*. Welles selected and rearranged passages (and some lines from *Richard II* and *Henry V*) to create a new, single 'text'. He was not the first to do this; in Germany Friedrich Ludwig Schröder staged a combined and reduced *Henry IV*, playing Falstaff himself, in 1778. Whatever the merits of Welles's film, or of the much-praised New York production of 2003, *Henry IV*, with Kevin Kline as Falstaff, the point remains that neither Welles nor Kline was performing in a Shakespeare play, or anything even resembling one. All of the lines might be Shakespeare's, but the characters are not, for characters do not exist outside the dramatic structure of the plays they inhabit, and that structure was completely discarded. The result may be wonderful, as *Chimes at Midnight* clearly is, but it needs to be approached on its own terms, not as a version of *Henry IV*, *Part I* or *Part II*.

Henry IV, Part I also provides great opportunities for the costume designer. To modern audiences, Elizabethan or medieval costumes usually provide little more than generalized quaintness – the personal qualities and social distinctions established by the clothes one wears, instantly recognizable in our own time, are not easily communicated. It is hard to see why anyone should worry about the Prince of Wales spending his time at the Boar's Head when it is a merry old Elizabethan inn full of seemingly good-natured Elizabethan folk. The Bogdanov production was at its most stunning in making the tavern a rough London pub of the 1980s, replete with bikers, punk rockers and seedy-looking men placing bets over the telephone – a dangerous place where real thieves, those who actually hurt people, congregate. The court scenes, which for the Elizabethans took place in the relatively recent past, also gained by being set in *our* relatively recent past of Victorian England. In the battle, where past and present come together, full medieval armour was worn, except by John Woodvine's splendid Falstaff, who donned modern fatigues.

The ever-growing number of Shakespeare festivals and Shakespearian companies all over the world guarantee that *Henry IV, Part I* will continue to be seen, usually as part of a series rather than on its own. There being only three female parts, one of whom speaks only Welsh, makes it a less attractive prospect to university drama departments, although the exclusion of women from their husbands' world 'Of prisoners' ransom, and of soldiers slain' (II.3.56) can be an affecting part of a production: at the Old Vic in 1945 Lady Percy exited with Hotspur at the end of Act II, scene 3, but then returned to join Lady Mortimer, alone onstage (McMillin, *Shakespeare in Performance*).

All in all, those in the performing arts and the audiences they serve should be grateful not only for *Henry IV, Part I*, but also for what it started, and for the perspicacity of the Elizabethans in knowing quality when they saw it. Had not *Part I* been a success, we would most probably be without the glories of Falstaff's visit to Justice Shallow's farm in *Part II*, the wonderful Ancient Pistol in *Part II* and *Henry V*, and the hilarity of Falstaff romancing Mistresses Ford and Page in both Shakespeare's *The Merry Wives of Windsor* and Otto Nicolai's opera *Die lustigen Weiber von Windsor* (1849). Most of all, there might have been no play to inspire Verdi, at the age of seventy-nine, to compose one last masterpiece. Apart from its own inherent quality, the descendants of *The History of Henry the Fourth; with the battle at Shrewsbury, between the King and Lord Henry Percy, surnamed Henry Hotspur of the North, With the humorous conceits of Sir John Falstaff* are enough to make it one of the greatest plays ever written.

Charles Edelman

Further Reading

For those who are relatively new to *Henry IV, Part I*, the most useful and interesting further reading, by far, is *Henry IV, Part II*, *Henry V* and, to a lesser extent, *The Merry Wives of Windsor*. Throughout its long critical history few writers have considered *Henry IV, Part I* in isolation, so relatively little will be gained from their commentary unless the reader is familiar with the other plays.

EDITIONS AND SOURCES

The most recent editions in the major Shakespeare series are splendid pieces of work: David Bevington's Oxford edition (1987), Herbert and Judith Weil's Cambridge edition (1997) and David Scott Kastan's Arden edition (2002) all offer stimulating introductions and wide-ranging commentary. Bevington is particularly interesting on the dramatic, philosophical and cultural traditions behind the play, the Weils excel on the play in performance and Kastan is both comprehensive and incisive on the Falstaff/Oldcastle controversy.

Barbara Hodgdon's edition (1997) for the Texts and Contexts series includes nearly three hundred pages of selections from the major sources and documents from Elizabethan times, comprising a large cultural map of which the play is a part. The New Variorum edition, edited by S. B. Hemingway (1936), is long out of print but available at many libraries – its collection of commentary and criticism makes it indispensable for any serious student of the play.

The Famous Victories of Henry V is printed along with the play *Sir John Oldcastle, Part I* in *The Oldcastle Controversy*, edited by Peter Corbin and Douglas Sedge (1991). Geoffrey Bullough's *Narrative and Dramatic Sources of Shakespeare*, vol. IV (1962) has *The Famous Victories* along with selections from Holinshed, Samuel Daniel's *The Civil Wars* (1595–1609) and other works Shakespeare is likely to have drawn from in composing the *Henry IV* plays.

ANTHOLOGIES AND COLLECTIONS

The best collection of criticism from the 1600s to the 1930s is the New Variorum, extended to the mid 1950s by G. Blakemore Evans with his 'Supplement to *Henry IV, Part I: A New Variorum Edition of Shakespeare*' (*Shakespeare Quarterly* 7, no. 3, 1956). Being one of Shakespeare's most popular plays in the seventeenth and eighteenth centuries, *Henry IV, Part I* is well represented in all six volumes of *Shakespeare: The Critical Heritage* (ed. Brian Vickers, 1974–81); Dr Johnson's commentary is most accessible in *Johnson on Shakespeare*, vol. 8 (ed. Arthur Sherbo, 1968); Jonathan Bate's *The Romantics on Shakespeare* (1992) is also well worth consulting. '*Henry IV, Parts I and II*': *A Casebook* (ed. G. K. Hunter, 1970) is valuable for both its selections, from Johnson to the

1960s, and Hunter's excellent introduction to them. David Bevington's *'Henry the Fourth, Parts I and II': Critical Essays* (1986) is comprehensive at 450 pages, and the works are judiciously chosen. Harold Bloom has given us two useful anthologies, *William Shakespeare's 'Henry IV, Part I'*, Modern Critical Interpretations series (1987) and *Major Literary Characters: Falstaff* (1992). Of the works discussed below, nearly all published before 1990 can be found in one or more of these collections.

CRITICAL WORKS

Some of the very best writing on *Henry IV, Part I* is from the eighteenth and nineteenth centuries; those who are interested in the most recent work are likely to get more out of it if they first read some of the early commentators, most of whom were concerned chiefly with Falstaff.

John Dryden (1668), Corbyn Morris (1744), Dr Johnson (1765) and Elizabeth Montague (1769) provide something of a prelude to Maurice Morgann's famous essay of 1777 on Falstaff's cowardice, fascinating not only in itself but also for the reactions it provoked, both for and against. More importantly, Morgann marks the beginning of 'character criticism', leading to the Romantic critics' assessment of Falstaff: Samuel Taylor Coleridge (1818) is particularly interesting in that he groups Sir John with two of Shakespeare's greatest villains, Iago and Richard III. William Hazlitt (1817) can find no moral objection to 'the most substantial comic character that ever was invented'; compared with Prince Hal, 'he is the better man of the two'. Like Hazlitt, A. C. Bradley ('The Rejection of Falstaff', *Oxford Lectures on Poetry* (1909)) is unable to forgive Hal for casting aside a friend whose 'essence' is 'the bliss of freedom'.

Two works of the 1940s brought about a radical shift in the critical discourse around the *Henry IV* plays. Although the title of Dover Wilson's book is *The Fortunes of Falstaff* (1943), he sees Hal as the main character in a two-part morality play, the action comprising a choice 'between Vanity and Government, taking the latter in its accepted Tudor meaning, which includes Chivalry or prowess in the field, the theme of Part I, and Justice, which is the theme of Part II'. Falstaff, the 'heir of traditional medieval "antics" like the Devil, the Vice, the Fool, Riot and Lord of Misrule', is seemingly a world away from the sentimental Falstaff of Bradley, but Wilson goes to great lengths to show that Falstaff did indeed recognize Hal and Poins at Gad's Hill.

The power and pervasiveness of E. M. W. Tillyard's *Shakespeare's History Plays* (1944) is demonstrated by the fact that even sixty years after it was written many critics still find a need to address Tillyard's conception of the histories, if only to denigrate it. The premise is well known: all ten English history plays form a single, unified historical poem around the idea of England as *Respublica*, held together by a desire for order and an abhorrence of rebellion. Like Dover Wilson, Tillyard regards *Henry IV, Parts I* and *II* as a single play 'built on the morality pattern', the first part depicting the choice confronting the Prince – as Tillyard always refers to him, never 'Hal' – between the exaggerated honour of Hotspur and the dishonour of Falstaff.

M. A. Shaaber, in 'The Unity of *Henry IV*' (*Adams Memorial Studies*, 1948, pp. 217–27), refutes the one-play notion, arguing that *Henry IV, Part I* is a play complete in itself. G. K. Hunter's essay, '*Henry IV* and the

Elizabethan Two-Part Play' (*Review of English Studies* 5 (1954), pp. 236–48), sees a thematic rather than narrative unity, the two plays working in parallel like a 'diptych'. Two years later Harold Jenkins proposed that Shakespeare started out intending to write one play, but changed his mind part of the way through – 'they are both one play and two' (*The Structural Problem in Shakespeare's 'Henry the Fourth'*, 1956).

Noting the parallels between the northern rebellion in the play and that of 1569, Lily B. Campbell's *Shakespeare's Histories, Mirrors of Elizabethan Policy* (1947) regards *Henry IV, Part I* as having more to do with late Tudor politics rather than those of the fourteenth and fifteenth centuries. But in order to make this the main concern of the play, she completely removes Falstaff from it, with the astonishing assertion that his scenes are 'comic interludes' that 'interrupt the continuity' of the two *Henry IV* plays. Tudor politics are also the theme of Stephen Greenblatt's widely read 'Invisible Bullets' (*Shakespearean Negotiations*, 1988), *Henry IV, Part I* being an example of how the Elizabethan theatre was a site of 'the circulation of social energy', where subversion was given expression in order to contain it.

As noted in both the Introduction and The Play in Performance, to regard *Henry IV, Part I* as part of a series is to direct attention away from Falstaff and towards Hal's progress from Eastcheap to the throne. Paul A. Jorgensen's 'Redeeming Time in Shakespeare's *Henry IV*' (*Tennessee Studies in Literature* 5 (1960), pp. 101–9) shows that this progress has as much to do with redemption as with honour; Sherman H. Hawkins argues that the two parts of *Henry IV* show Hal achieving the four Cardinal Virtues ('Virtue and Kingship in Shakespeare's *Henry IV*', *English Literary Renaissance* 5 (1975), pp. 313–43).

Hal's relationship with his 'two fathers', the King and Falstaff, is brilliantly interrogated by both A. D. Nuttall in *A New Mimesis: Shakespeare and the Representation of Reality* (1983) and David Bevington in *Shakespeare* (2002).

Falstaff criticism, while not as dominant as it once was, has nevertheless had some important contributions in the post-Tillyard era: two of the best-known works, and deservedly so, are W. H. Auden's 'The Prince's Dog' (*The Dyer's Hand and Other Essays*, 1948) and C. L. Barber's 'Rule and Misrule in *Henry IV*' (*Shakespeare's Festive Comedy*, 1959). To Auden, 'the better we come to know Falstaff, the clearer it becomes that the world of historical reality . . . is not a world which he can inhabit', while Barber sees in Sir John the Lord of Misrule, presiding over a Saturnalian Eastcheap. Brian Vickers expertly analyses Shakespeare's use of prose in creating in Falstaff a character whose world we enter 'as on a holiday' (*The Artistry of Shakespeare's Prose*, 1968); Sukunta Chaudhuri compares Falstaff's sceptical view of life with that of Montaigne and Rabelais (*Infirm Glory*, 1981); and finally there is Harold Bloom's tribute to Falstaff in *Shakespeare: The Invention of the Human* (1999), a delightful mixture of superb insight and sentimental nonsense.

The north–south divide in the play is illuminated by Graham Cattle in '"The Detested Blot": The Representation of Northern English in Shakespeare's *Henry IV, Part One*' (*Parergon* 13 (1995), pp. 25–32); Terence Hawkes, in *Shakespeare in the Present* (2002), offers an equally provocative discussion on the Welsh. In their feminist account of the histories, *Engendering a Nation* (1997), Jean E. Howard and Phyllis Rackin include an interesting chapter on the *Henry IV* plays, and Charles

Edelman's *Shakespeare's Military Language: A Dictionary* (2000) covers all aspects of Falstaff as an Elizabethan captain.

BIBLIOGRAPHIES, OTHER WORKS

The books and essays mentioned above represent a small fraction of the worthwhile commentary on *Henry IV, Part I*. Two excellent and relatively recent bibliographies cover many more works than can be listed here: Richard Dutton's chapter on the second tetralogy in *Shakespeare: A Bibliographical Guide* (ed. Stanley Wells, 1990), and *'Henry IV, Parts 1 and 2': An Annotated Bibliography*, collected by Catherine Gira and Adele Seeff (1994).

Works cited in the Introduction but not included in the above discussion are: Robert Berkelman, 'Lincoln's Interest in Shakespeare', *Shakespeare Quarterly* 2 (1951), pp. 303–12; Gordon Crosse, *Theatrical Diary: 1890–1953*, unpublished manuscript in the Shakespeare Library of the City of Birmingham Central Library, summarized in *Shakespearean Playgoing, 1890–1952* (1953); J. W. Fortescue, *A History of the British Army*, 13 vols. (1910–30), vol. 1; G. B. Harrison, *The Elizabethan Journals*, 2 vols. (1938), vol. 2; Machiavelli, *The Prince*, trans. N. H. Thomson (1919); Montaigne, *Essays*, trans. John Florio (repr. 1933); John Smythe, *Certain Discourses Military*, ed. J. R. Hale (1964); John Speed, *The Theatre of the Empire of Great Britain* (1612); and Anthony Wingfield, *A True Copy of a Discourse Written by a Gentleman Employed in the late Voyage of Spain and Portugal* (1589).

Works cited in The Play in Performance are: Michael

Bogdanov and Michael Pennington, *The English Shakespeare Company: The Story of the 'Wars of the Roses', 1986–1989* (1990); Scott McMillin, *Shakespeare in Performance: 'Henry IV, Part One'* (1991); Gāmini Salgādo, *Eyewitnesses of Shakespeare: First Hand Accounts of Performances 1590–1890* (1975); and Kenneth Tynan, *He That Plays the King: A View of the Theatre* (1950).

THE HISTORY OF
HENRY THE FOURTH

The Characters in the Play

The King's Party
KING HENRY IV, formerly Henry Bolingbroke, son of
    John of Gaunt
PRINCE HAL (Henry) of Wales, the King's eldest son
Lord John of LANCASTER, a younger son of King Henry
    IV
Earl of WESTMORLAND, kinsman by law to Henry IV
Sir Walter BLUNT

The Rebels
Henry Percy, Earl of NORTHUMBERLAND
Harry HOTSPUR, his son
LADY PERCY (Kate), Hotspur's wife, sister of Mortimer
Thomas Percy, Earl of WORCESTER
Edmund, Lord MORTIMER
Lady Mortimer, Mortimer's wife, daughter of Glendower
Owen GLENDOWER
Earl of DOUGLAS
Sir Richard VERNON
Richard Scroop, ARCHBISHOP of York
SIR MICHAEL, a member of the household of the
    Archbishop

Hal's Companions
Sir John FALSTAFF
POINS
BARDOLPH
PETO
Mistress Quickly, HOSTESS of the Tavern in Eastcheap
FRANCIS, a drawer
VINTNER

At Rochester
GADSHILL
FIRST CARRIER
SECOND CARRIER
CHAMBERLAIN
OSTLER
FIRST TRAVELLER
SECOND TRAVELLER

SERVANT
SHERIFF and officers
MESSENGERS
Lords and attendants
Soldiers

Enter the King, Lord John of Lancaster, Earl of
Westmorland, Sir Walter Blunt, with others

KING HENRY

So shaken as we are, so wan with care,
Find we a time for frighted peace to pant,
And breathe short-winded accents of new broils
To be commenced in strands afar remote.
No more the thirsty entrance of this soil
Shall daub her lips with her own children's blood,
No more shall trenching war channel her fields,
Nor bruise her flowerets with the armèd hoofs
Of hostile paces. Those opposèd eyes,
Which, like the meteors of a troubled heaven,   10
All of one nature, of one substance bred,
Did lately meet in the intestine shock
And furious close of civil butchery,
Shall now, in mutual well-beseeming ranks,
March all one way, and be no more opposed
Against acquaintance, kindred, and allies.
The edge of war, like an ill-sheathèd knife,
No more shall cut his master. Therefore friends,
As far as to the sepulchre of Christ –
Whose soldier now, under whose blessed cross   20
We are impressèd and engaged to fight –
Forthwith a power of English shall we levy,

Whose arms were moulded in their mother's womb
To chase these pagans in those holy fields
Over whose acres walked those blessèd feet,
Which fourteen hundred years ago were nailed
For our advantage on the bitter cross.
But this our purpose now is twelve month old,
And bootless 'tis to tell you we will go.
30   Therefor we meet not now. Then let me hear
Of you, my gentle cousin Westmorland,
What yesternight our Council did decree
In forwarding this dear expedience.

WESTMORLAND
My liege, this haste was hot in question,
And many limits of the charge set down
But yesternight, when all athwart there came
A post from Wales, loaden with heavy news,
Whose worst was that the noble Mortimer —
Leading the men of Herefordshire to fight
40   Against the irregular and wild Glendower —
Was by the rude hands of that Welshman taken,
A thousand of his people butcherèd,
Upon whose dead corpses there was such misuse,
Such beastly shameless transformation
By those Welshwomen done, as may not be
Without much shame retold or spoken of.

KING HENRY
It seems then that the tidings of this broil
Brake off our business for the Holy Land.

WESTMORLAND
This matched with other did, my gracious lord,
50   For more uneven and unwelcome news
Came from the north, and thus it did import.
On Holy-rood day, the gallant Hotspur there,
Young Harry Percy, and brave Archibald,
That ever valiant and approvèd Scot,

At Holmedon met, where they did spend
A sad and bloody hour —
As by discharge of their artillery,
And shape of likelihood, the news was told;
For he that brought them, in the very heat
And pride of their contention did take horse,   60
Uncertain of the issue any way.

KING HENRY
Here is a dear, a true industrious friend,
Sir Walter Blunt, new lighted from his horse,
Stained with the variation of each soil
Betwixt that Holmedon and this seat of ours,
And he hath brought us smooth and welcome news.
The Earl of Douglas is discomfited.
Ten thousand bold Scots, two-and-twenty knights,
Balked in their own blood, did Sir Walter see
On Holmedon's plains. Of prisoners Hotspur took   70
Mordake, Earl of Fife and eldest son
To beaten Douglas, and the Earl of Atholl,
Of Murray, Angus, and Menteith:
And is not this an honourable spoil?
A gallant prize? Ha, cousin, is it not?

WESTMORLAND   In faith,
It is a conquest for a prince to boast of.

KING HENRY
Yea, there thou makest me sad, and makest me sin
In envy that my Lord Northumberland
Should be the father to so blest a son:
A son who is the theme of honour's tongue,   80
Amongst a grove the very straightest plant,
Who is sweet Fortune's minion and her pride —
Whilst I by looking on the praise of him
See riot and dishonour stain the brow
Of my young Harry. O that it could be proved

That some night-tripping fairy had exchanged
In cradle-clothes our children where they lay,
And called mine Percy, his Plantagenet!
Then would I have his Harry, and he mine.
90   But let him from my thoughts. What think you, coz,
Of this young Percy's pride? The prisoners
Which he in this adventure hath surprised
To his own use he keeps, and sends me word
I shall have none but Mordake, Earl of Fife.

WESTMORLAND
This is his uncle's teaching. This is Worcester,
Malevolent to you in all aspects,
Which makes him prune himself, and bristle up
The crest of youth against your dignity.

KING HENRY
But I have sent for him to answer this,
100   And for this cause awhile we must neglect
Our holy purpose to Jerusalem.
Cousin, on Wednesday next our Council we
Will hold at Windsor, so inform the lords.
But come yourself with speed to us again,
For more is to be said and to be done
Than out of anger can be utterèd.

WESTMORLAND
I will, my liege.   *Exeunt*

I.2   *Enter Prince of Wales and Sir John Falstaff*
FALSTAFF Now Hal, what time of day is it lad?
PRINCE HAL Thou art so fat-witted with drinking of old
    sack, and unbuttoning thee after supper, and sleeping
    upon benches after noon, that thou hast forgotten to
    demand that truly which thou wouldst truly know.
    What a devil hast thou to do with the time of the day?

Unless hours were cups of sack, and minutes capons,
and clocks the tongues of bawds, and dials the signs of
leaping-houses, and the blessed sun himself a fair hot
wench in flame-coloured taffeta, I see no reason why   10
thou shouldst be so superfluous to demand the time of
the day.

FALSTAFF Indeed, you come near me now Hal, for we that
take purses go by the moon and the seven stars, and
not 'by Phoebus, he, that wandering knight so fair'.
And I prithee sweet wag, when thou art King, as God
save thy grace – majesty I should say, for grace thou
wilt have none –

PRINCE HAL What, none?

FALSTAFF No, by my troth, not so much as will serve to   20
be prologue to an egg and butter.

PRINCE HAL Well, how then? Come, roundly, roundly.

FALSTAFF Marry then, sweet wag, when thou art King let
not us that are squires of the night's body be called
thieves of the day's beauty. Let us be Diana's foresters,
gentlemen of the shade, minions of the moon. And let
men say we be men of good government, being governed
as the sea is, by our noble and chaste mistress the moon,
under whose countenance we steal.

PRINCE HAL Thou sayest well, and it holds well too, for   30
the fortune of us that are the moon's men doth ebb and
flow like the sea, being governed as the sea is, by the
moon. As for proof? Now, a purse of gold most reso-
lutely snatched on Monday night, and most dissolutely
spent on Tuesday morning, got with swearing 'Lay by!',
and spent with crying 'Bring in!', now in as low an ebb
as the foot of the ladder, and by and by in as high a flow
as the ridge of the gallows.

FALSTAFF By the Lord thou sayest true lad – and is not
my Hostess of the tavern a most sweet wench?   40

PRINCE HAL As the honey of Hybla, my old lad of the
  castle. And is not a buff jerkin a most sweet robe of
  durance?

FALSTAFF How now, how now, mad wag? What, in thy
  quips and thy quiddities? What a plague have I to do
  with a buff jerkin?

PRINCE HAL Why, what a pox have I to do with my
  Hostess of the tavern?

FALSTAFF Well, thou hast called her to a reckoning many
50 a time and oft.

PRINCE HAL Did I ever call for thee to pay thy part?

FALSTAFF No, I'll give thee thy due, thou hast paid all
  there.

PRINCE HAL Yea, and elsewhere, so far as my coin would
  stretch, and where it would not I have used my credit.

FALSTAFF Yea, and so used it that were it not here apparent that thou art heir apparent – but I prithee sweet
  wag, shall there be gallows standing in England when
  thou art King? And resolution thus fubbed as it is with
60 the rusty curb of old Father Antic the law? Do not thou
  when thou art King hang a thief.

PRINCE HAL No, thou shalt.

FALSTAFF Shall I? O rare! By the Lord, I'll be a brave
  judge!

PRINCE HAL Thou judgest false already! I mean thou shalt
  have the hanging of the thieves, and so become a
  rare hangman.

FALSTAFF Well, Hal, well! And in some sort it jumps
  with my humour – as well as waiting in the court, I can
70 tell you.

PRINCE HAL For obtaining of suits?

FALSTAFF Yea, for obtaining of suits, whereof the hangman hath no lean wardrobe. 'Sblood, I am as melancholy as a gib cat, or a lugged bear.

PRINCE HAL Or an old lion, or a lover's lute.

FALSTAFF Yea, or the drone of a Lincolnshire bagpipe.

PRINCE HAL What sayest thou to a hare, or the melancholy of Moorditch?

FALSTAFF Thou hast the most unsavoury similes, and art
indeed the most comparative rascalliest sweet young   80
prince. But Hal, I prithee trouble me no more with
vanity. I would to God thou and I knew where a commodity of good names were to be bought. An old lord of
the Council rated me the other day in the street about
you, sir, but I marked him not, and yet he talked very
wisely, but I regarded him not, and yet he talked wisely
– and in the street too.

PRINCE HAL Thou didst well, for wisdom cries out in the
streets and no man regards it.

FALSTAFF O, thou hast damnable iteration, and art   90
indeed able to corrupt a saint. Thou hast done much
harm upon me, Hal, God forgive thee for it. Before I
knew thee Hal, I knew nothing, and now am I, if a man
should speak truly, little better than one of the wicked.
I must give over this life, and I will give it over. By the
Lord, an I do not I am a villain. I'll be damned for
never a king's son in Christendom.

PRINCE HAL Where shall we take a purse tomorrow,
Jack?

FALSTAFF Zounds, where thou wilt lad, I'll make one; an   100
I do not, call me a villain and baffle me.

PRINCE HAL I see a good amendment of life in thee, from
praying to purse-taking.

FALSTAFF Why Hal, 'tis my vocation, Hal. 'Tis no sin
for a man to labour in his vocation.

Enter Poins

Poins! Now shall we know if Gadshill have set a
match! O, if men were to be saved by merit, what

hole in hell were hot enough for him? This is the most
omnipotent villain that ever cried 'Stand!' to a true man.

110 PRINCE HAL Good morrow, Ned.

POINS Good morrow, sweet Hal. What says Monsieur
Remorse? What says Sir John Sack – and Sugar? Jack!
How agrees the devil and thee about thy soul, that thou
soldest him on Good Friday last, for a cup of Madeira
and a cold capon's leg?

PRINCE HAL Sir John stands to his word, the devil shall
have his bargain, for he was never yet a breaker of
proverbs. He will give the devil his due.

POINS Then art thou damned for keeping thy word with
120 the devil.

PRINCE HAL Else he had been damned for cozening the
devil.

POINS But my lads, my lads, tomorrow morning, by four
o'clock early at Gad's Hill, there are pilgrims going to
Canterbury with rich offerings and traders riding to
London with fat purses. I have vizards for you all – you
have horses for yourselves. Gadshill lies tonight in
Rochester. I have bespoke supper tomorrow night in
Eastcheap. We may do it as secure as sleep. If you will
130 go, I will stuff your purses full of crowns. If you will
not, tarry at home and be hanged.

FALSTAFF Hear ye, Yedward, if I tarry at home and go
not, I'll hang you for going.

POINS You will, chops?

FALSTAFF Hal, wilt thou make one?

PRINCE HAL Who I? Rob? I a thief? Not I, by my faith.

FALSTAFF There's neither honesty, manhood, nor good
fellowship in thee, nor thou camest not of the blood
royal, if thou darest not stand for ten shillings.

140 PRINCE HAL Well then, once in my days I'll be a madcap.

FALSTAFF Why, that's well said.

PRINCE HAL Well, come what will, I'll tarry at home.

FALSTAFF By the Lord, I'll be a traitor then, when thou art King.

PRINCE HAL I care not.

POINS Sir John, I prithee leave the Prince and me alone. I will lay him down such reasons for this adventure that he shall go.

FALSTAFF Well, God give thee the spirit of persuasion, and him the ears of profiting, that what thou speakest may move, and what he hears may be believed, that the true prince may – for recreation sake – prove a false thief, for the poor abuses of the time want countenance. Farewell, you shall find me in Eastcheap.

PRINCE HAL Farewell, the latter spring! Farewell, All-hallown summer!   *Exit Falstaff*

POINS Now my good sweet honey lord, ride with us tomorrow. I have a jest to execute that I cannot manage alone. Falstaff, Bardolph, Peto, and Gadshill shall rob those men that we have already waylaid – yourself and I will not be there. And when they have the booty, if you and I do not rob them – cut this head off from my shoulders.

PRINCE HAL How shall we part with them in setting forth?

POINS Why, we will set forth before or after them, and appoint them a place of meeting – wherein it is at our pleasure to fail – and then will they adventure upon the exploit themselves, which they shall have no sooner achieved but we'll set upon them.

PRINCE HAL Yea, but 'tis like that they will know us by our horses, by our habits, and by every other appointment to be ourselves.

POINS Tut, our horses they shall not see, I'll tie them in

the wood. Our vizards we will change after we leave
them. And, sirrah, I have cases of buckram for the nonce,
to immask our noted outward garments.

PRINCE HAL Yea, but I doubt they will be too hard for
180   us.

POINS Well, for two of them, I know them to be as true-
bred cowards as ever turned back, and for the third, if
he fight longer than he sees reason, I'll forswear arms.
The virtue of this jest will be the incomprehensible lies
that this same fat rogue will tell us when we meet at
supper. How thirty at least he fought with, what wards,
what blows, what extremities he endured, and in the
reproof of this lives the jest.

PRINCE HAL Well, I'll go with thee. Provide us all things
190   necessary and meet me tomorrow night in Eastcheap.
There I'll sup. Farewell.

POINS Farewell, my lord.   *Exit*

PRINCE HAL
    I know you all, and will awhile uphold
    The unyoked humour of your idleness.
    Yet herein will I imitate the sun,
    Who doth permit the base contagious clouds
    To smother up his beauty from the world,
    That when he please again to be himself,
    Being wanted, he may be more wondered at
200   By breaking through the foul and ugly mists
    Of vapours that did seem to strangle him.
    If all the year were playing holidays,
    To sport would be as tedious as to work;
    But when they seldom come, they wished-for come,
    And nothing pleaseth but rare accidents.
    So when this loose behaviour I throw off,
    And pay the debt I never promisèd,
    By how much better than my word I am,

By so much shall I falsify men's hopes.
And like bright metal on a sullen ground,   210
My reformation, glittering o'er my fault,
Shall show more goodly, and attract more eyes
Than that which hath no foil to set it off.
I'll so offend, to make offence a skill,
Redeeming time when men think least I will.   *Exit*

Enter the King, Northumberland, Worcester,   I.3
Hotspur, Sir Walter Blunt, with others

KING HENRY
My blood hath been too cold and temperate,
Unapt to stir at these indignities,
And you have found me – for accordingly
You tread upon my patience. But be sure
I will from henceforth rather be myself,
Mighty, and to be feared, than my condition,
Which hath been smooth as oil, soft as young down,
And therefore lost that title of respect
Which the proud soul ne'er pays but to the proud.

WORCESTER
Our house, my sovereign liege, little deserves   10
The scourge of greatness to be used on it,
And that same greatness too which our own hands
Have helped to make so portly.

NORTHUMBERLAND   My lord –

KING HENRY
Worcester, get thee gone, for I do see
Danger and disobedience in thine eye.
O sir, your presence is too bold and peremptory,
And majesty might never yet endure
The moody frontier of a servant brow.
You have good leave to leave us. When we need

20   Your use and counsel we shall send for you.

                                        Exit Worcester

        (*To Northumberland*) You were about to speak.

NORTHUMBERLAND   Yea, my good lord.

        Those prisoners in your highness' name demanded,

        Which Harry Percy here at Holmedon took,

        Were, as he says, not with such strength denied

        As is delivered to your majesty.

        Either envy therefore, or misprision,

        Is guilty of this fault, and not my son.

HOTSPUR

        My liege, I did deny no prisoners.

        But I remember when the fight was done,

30   When I was dry with rage and extreme toil,

        Breathless and faint, leaning upon my sword,

        Came there a certain lord, neat and trimly dressed,

        Fresh as a bridegroom, and his chin new reaped

        Showed like a stubble-land at harvest-home.

        He was perfumèd like a milliner,

        And 'twixt his finger and his thumb he held

        A pouncet-box, which ever and anon

        He gave his nose, and took it away again –

        Who therewith angry, when it next came there,

40   Took it in snuff. And still he smiled and talked.

        And as the soldiers bore dead bodies by,

        He called them untaught knaves, unmannerly,

        To bring a slovenly unhandsome corpse

        Betwixt the wind and his nobility.

        With many holiday and lady terms

        He questioned me, amongst the rest demanded

        My prisoners in your majesty's behalf.

        I then, all smarting with my wounds being cold,

        To be so pestered with a popinjay,

50   Out of my grief and my impatience

Answered neglectingly, I know not what,
He should, or he should not, for he made me mad
To see him shine so brisk, and smell so sweet,
And talk so like a waiting-gentlewoman
Of guns, and drums, and wounds, God save the mark!
And telling me the sovereignest thing on earth
Was parmacity for an inward bruise,
And that it was great pity, so it was,
This villainous saltpetre should be digged
Out of the bowels of the harmless earth,   60
Which many a good tall fellow had destroyed
So cowardly, and but for these vile guns
He would himself have been a soldier.
This bald unjointed chat of his, my lord,
I answered indirectly, as I said,
And I beseech you, let not his report
Come current for an accusation
Betwixt my love and your high majesty.

BLUNT

The circumstance considered, good my lord,
Whate'er Lord Harry Percy then had said   70
To such a person, and in such a place,
At such a time, with all the rest retold,
May reasonably die, and never rise
To do him wrong, or any way impeach
What then he said, so he unsay it now.

KING HENRY

Why, yet he doth deny his prisoners,
But with proviso and exception,
That we at our own charge shall ransom straight
His brother-in-law, the foolish Mortimer,
Who, on my soul, hath wilfully betrayed   80
The lives of those that he did lead to fight
Against that great magician, damned Glendower,

Whose daughter, as we hear, that Earl of March
Hath lately married. Shall our coffers then
Be emptied to redeem a traitor home?
Shall we buy treason, and indent with fears
When they have lost and forfeited themselves?
No, on the barren mountains let him starve.
For I shall never hold that man my friend
90   Whose tongue shall ask me for one penny cost
To ransom home revolted Mortimer.

HOTSPUR
Revolted Mortimer!
He never did fall off, my sovereign liege,
But by the chance of war. To prove that true
Needs no more but one tongue for all those wounds,
Those mouthèd wounds, which valiantly he took,
When on the gentle Severn's sedgy bank,
In single opposition hand to hand,
He did confound the best part of an hour
100   In changing hardiment with great Glendower.
Three times they breathed, and three times did they drink
Upon agreement of swift Severn's flood,
Who then affrighted with their bloody looks
Ran fearfully among the trembling reeds,
And hid his crisp head in the hollow bank,
Bloodstainèd with these valiant combatants.
Never did bare and rotten policy
Colour her working with such deadly wounds,
Nor never could the noble Mortimer
110   Receive so many, and all willingly.
Then let not him be slandered with revolt.

KING HENRY
Thou dost belie him, Percy, thou dost belie him,
He never did encounter with Glendower.
I tell thee, he durst as well have met the devil alone

As Owen Glendower for an enemy.
Art thou not ashamed? But sirrah, henceforth
Let me not hear you speak of Mortimer.
Send me your prisoners with the speediest means –
Or you shall hear in such a kind from me
As will displease you. My Lord Northumberland: 120
We license your departure with your son.
Send us your prisoners, or you will hear of it.

                    Exit the King with Blunt and train

HOTSPUR
And if the devil come and roar for them
I will not send them. I will after straight
And tell him so, for I will ease my heart,
Albeit I make a hazard of my head.

NORTHUMBERLAND
What? Drunk with choler? Stay, and pause awhile,
Here comes your uncle.

    Enter Worcester

HOTSPUR   Speak of Mortimer?
Zounds, I will speak of him, and let my soul
Want mercy if I do not join with him.   130
Yea, on his part I'll empty all these veins
And shed my dear blood, drop by drop in the dust,
But I will lift the down-trod Mortimer
As high in the air as this unthankful King,
As this ingrate and cankered Bolingbroke.

NORTHUMBERLAND
Brother, the King hath made your nephew mad.

WORCESTER
Who struck this heat up after I was gone?

HOTSPUR
He will forsooth have all my prisoners,
And when I urged the ransom once again
Of my wife's brother, then his cheek looked pale,   140

And on my face he turned an eye of death,
Trembling even at the name of Mortimer.

WORCESTER
I cannot blame him. Was not he proclaimed,
By Richard that dead is, the next of blood?

NORTHUMBERLAND
He was, I heard the proclamation.
And then it was, when the unhappy King –
Whose wrongs in us God pardon! – did set forth
Upon his Irish expedition;
From whence he, intercepted, did return
150   To be deposed, and shortly murderèd.

WORCESTER
And for whose death we in the world's wide mouth
Live scandalized and foully spoken of.

HOTSPUR
But soft, I pray you, did King Richard then
Proclaim my brother Edmund Mortimer
Heir to the crown?

NORTHUMBERLAND He did, myself did hear it.

HOTSPUR
Nay then, I cannot blame his cousin King
That wished him on the barren mountains starve.
But shall it be that you that set the crown
Upon the head of this forgetful man,
160   And for his sake wear the detested blot
Of murderous subornation – shall it be
That you a world of curses undergo,
Being the agents, or base second means,
The cords, the ladder, or the hangman rather?
O pardon me, that I descend so low,
To show the line and the predicament
Wherein you range under this subtle King!
Shall it for shame be spoken in these days,

Or fill up chronicles in time to come,
That men of your nobility and power   170
Did gage them both in an unjust behalf –
As both of you, God pardon it, have done –
To put down Richard, that sweet lovely rose,
And plant this thorn, this canker Bolingbroke?
And shall it in more shame be further spoken,
That you are fooled, discarded, and shook off
By him for whom these shames ye underwent?
No, yet time serves wherein you may redeem
Your banished honours, and restore yourselves
Into the good thoughts of the world again: 180
Revenge the jeering and disdained contempt
Of this proud King, who studies day and night
To answer all the debt he owes to you,
Even with the bloody payment of your deaths.
Therefore, I say –

WORCESTER   Peace, cousin, say no more.
And now I will unclasp a secret book,
And to your quick-conceiving discontents
I'll read you matter deep and dangerous,
As full of peril and adventurous spirit
As to o'er-walk a current roaring loud   190
On the unsteadfast footing of a spear.

HOTSPUR
If he fall in, good night, or sink, or swim!
Send danger from the east unto the west,
So honour cross it from the north to south,
And let them grapple. O, the blood more stirs
To rouse a lion than to start a hare!

NORTHUMBERLAND
Imagination of some great exploit
Drives him beyond the bounds of patience.

HOTSPUR

    By heaven, methinks it were an easy leap
200   To pluck bright honour from the pale-faced moon,
    Or dive into the bottom of the deep,
    Where fathom-line could never touch the ground,
    And pluck up drownèd honour by the locks,
    So he that doth redeem her thence might wear
    Without corrival all her dignities.
    But out upon this half-faced fellowship!

WORCESTER

    He apprehends a world of figures here,
    But not the form of what he should attend.
    Good cousin, give me audience for a while.

HOTSPUR

210 I cry you mercy.

WORCESTER   Those same noble Scots
    That are your prisoners —

HOTSPUR   I'll keep them all!
    By God he shall not have a Scot of them,
    No, if a scot would save his soul he shall not.
    I'll keep them, by this hand!

WORCESTER   You start away,
    And lend no ear unto my purposes.
    Those prisoners you shall keep —

HOTSPUR   Nay, I will. That's flat!
    He said he would not ransom Mortimer,
    Forbade my tongue to speak of Mortimer,
    But I will find him when he lies asleep,
220   And in his ear I'll holla 'Mortimer!'
    Nay, I'll have a starling shall be taught to speak
    Nothing but 'Mortimer', and give it him
    To keep his anger still in motion.

WORCESTER

    Hear you, cousin, a word.

HOTSPUR

    All studies here I solemnly defy,

    Save how to gall and pinch this Bolingbroke.

    And that same sword-and-buckler Prince of Wales –

    But that I think his father loves him not

    And would be glad he met with some mischance –

    I would have him poisoned with a pot of ale.   230

WORCESTER

    Farewell, kinsman. I'll talk to you

    When you are better tempered to attend.

NORTHUMBERLAND

    Why, what a wasp-stung and impatient fool

    Art thou to break into this woman's mood,

    Tying thine ear to no tongue but thine own!

HOTSPUR

    Why, look you, I am whipped and scourged with rods,

    Nettled, and stung with pismires, when I hear

    Of this vile politician Bolingbroke.

    In Richard's time – what do you call the place?

    A plague upon it, it is in Gloucestershire.   240

    'Twas where the madcap Duke his uncle kept –

    His uncle York – where I first bowed my knee

    Unto this king of smiles, this Bolingbroke –

    'Sblood, when you and he came back from Ravens-

        purgh –

NORTHUMBERLAND

    At Berkeley Castle.

HOTSPUR

    You say true.

    Why, what a candy deal of courtesy

    This fawning greyhound then did proffer me!

    'Look when his infant fortune came to age',

    And 'gentle Harry Percy', and 'kind cousin'.   250

    O, the devil take such cozeners – God forgive me!

Good uncle, tell your tale. I have done.

WORCESTER

Nay, if you have not, to it again,
We will stay your leisure.

HOTSPUR   I have done, i'faith.

WORCESTER

Then once more to your Scottish prisoners.
Deliver them up without their ransom straight,
And make the Douglas' son your only mean
For powers in Scotland, which, for divers reasons
Which I shall send you written, be assured
260   Will easily be granted. (*To Northumberland*) You my lord,
Your son in Scotland being thus employed,
Shall secretly into the bosom creep
Of that same noble prelate well-beloved,
The Archbishop.

HOTSPUR   Of York, is it not?

WORCESTER   True, who bears hard
His brother's death at Bristol, the Lord Scroop.
I speak not this in estimation,
As what I think might be, but what I know
Is ruminated, plotted, and set down,
And only stays but to behold the face
270   Of that occasion that shall bring it on.

HOTSPUR

I smell it! Upon my life it will do well!

NORTHUMBERLAND

Before the game is afoot thou still lettest slip.

HOTSPUR

Why, it cannot choose but be a noble plot;
And then the power of Scotland, and of York,
To join with Mortimer, ha?

WORCESTER   And so they shall.

HOTSPUR

In faith it is exceedingly well aimed.

WORCESTER

And 'tis no little reason bids us speed,
To save our heads by raising of a head.
For, bear ourselves as even as we can,
The King will always think him in our debt,   280
And think we think ourselves unsatisfied,
Till he hath found a time to pay us home.
And see already how he doth begin
To make us strangers to his looks of love.

HOTSPUR

He does, he does, we'll be revenged on him.

WORCESTER

Cousin, farewell. No further go in this
Than I by letters shall direct your course.
When time is ripe, which will be suddenly,
I'll steal to Glendower, and Lord Mortimer,   290
Where you, and Douglas, and our powers at once,
As I will fashion it, shall happily meet
To bear our fortunes in our own strong arms,
Which now we hold at much uncertainty.

NORTHUMBERLAND

Farewell, good brother. We shall thrive, I trust.

HOTSPUR

Uncle, adieu. O, let the hours be short,
Till fields, and blows, and groans applaud our sport!

Exeunt

*

II.I   *Enter a Carrier with a lantern in his hand*

FIRST CARRIER Heigh-ho! An it be not four by the day
I'll be hanged. Charles's Wain is over the new chimney,
and yet our horse not packed. What, Ostler!

OSTLER (*within*) Anon, anon.

FIRST CARRIER I prithee, Tom, beat Cut's saddle, put a
few flocks in the point; poor jade is wrung in the withers
out of all cess.

Enter another Carrier

SECOND CARRIER Peas and beans are as dank here as a
dog, and that is the next way to give poor jades the bots.
10   This house is turned upside down since Robin Ostler
died.

FIRST CARRIER Poor fellow never joyed since the price of
oats rose, it was the death of him.

SECOND CARRIER I think this be the most villainous
house in all London road for fleas, I am stung like a
tench.

FIRST CARRIER Like a tench! By the mass, there is ne'er
a king Christian could be better bit than I have been
since the first cock.

20   SECOND CARRIER Why, they will allow us ne'er a
jordan, and then we leak in your chimney, and your
chamber-lye breeds fleas like a loach.

FIRST CARRIER What, Ostler! Come away, and be
hanged, come away!

SECOND CARRIER I have a gammon of bacon, and two
razes of ginger, to be delivered as far as Charing Cross.

FIRST CARRIER God's body! The turkeys in my pannier
are quite starved. What, Ostler! A plague on thee, hast
thou never an eye in thy head? Canst not hear? An
30   'twere not as good deed as drink to break the pate on
thee, I am a very villain. Come, and be hanged! Hast no
faith in thee?

Enter Gadshill

GADSHILL Good morrow, carriers, what's o'clock?

FIRST CARRIER I think it be two o'clock.

GADSHILL I prithee lend me thy lantern, to see my gelding in the stable.

FIRST CARRIER Nay, by God, soft! I know a trick worth two of that, i' faith.

GADSHILL I pray thee lend me thine.

SECOND CARRIER Ay, when? Canst tell? Lend me thy   40
lantern, quoth he! Marry I'll see thee hanged first.

GADSHILL Sirrah carrier, what time do you mean to come to London?

SECOND CARRIER Time enough to go to bed with a candle, I warrant thee! Come, neighbour Mugs, we'll call up the gentlemen, they will along with company, for they have great charge.   *Exeunt Carriers*

GADSHILL What ho! Chamberlain!

Enter Chamberlain

CHAMBERLAIN 'At hand, quoth pick-purse.'

GADSHILL That's even as fair as 'At hand, quoth the   50
chamberlain', for thou variest no more from picking of purses than giving direction doth from labouring. Thou layest the plot how.

CHAMBERLAIN Good morrow, Master Gadshill. It holds current that I told you yesternight. There's a franklin in the Weald of Kent hath brought three hundred marks with him in gold – I heard him tell it to one of his company last night at supper, a kind of auditor, one that hath abundance of charge too, God knows what. They are up already, and call for eggs and butter. They will   60
away presently.

GADSHILL Sirrah, if they meet not with Saint Nicholas' clerks, I'll give thee this neck.

CHAMBERLAIN No, I'll none of it, I pray thee keep that

for the hangman, for I know thou worshippest Saint
Nicholas, as truly as a man of falsehood may.

GADSHILL What talkest thou to me of the hangman? If I
hang, I'll make a fat pair of gallows. For if I hang, old
Sir John hangs with me, and thou knowest he is no
70   starveling. Tut, there are other Troyans that thou
dreamest not of, the which for sport sake are content to
do the profession some grace, that would, if matters
should be looked into, for their own credit sake make all
whole. I am joined with no foot-landrakers, no long-
staff sixpenny strikers, none of these mad mustachio
purple-hued maltworms, but with nobility and tran-
quillity, Burgomasters and great O-yeas, such as can
hold in, such as will strike sooner than speak, and speak
sooner than drink, and drink sooner than pray. And yet,
80   zounds, I lie, for they pray continually to their saint the
commonwealth, or rather not pray to her, but prey on
her, for they ride up and down on her, and make her
their boots.

CHAMBERLAIN What, the commonwealth their boots?
Will she hold out water in foul way?

GADSHILL She will, she will, justice hath liquored her.
We steal as in a castle, cock-sure. We have the receipt
of fern-seed, we walk invisible.

CHAMBERLAIN Nay, by my faith, I think you are more
90   beholding to the night than to fern-seed for your
walking invisible.

GADSHILL Give me thy hand, thou shalt have a share in
our purchase, as I am a true man.

CHAMBERLAIN Nay, rather let me have it as you are a
false thief.

GADSHILL Go to, *homo* is a common name to all men.
Bid the ostler bring my gelding out of the stable.
Farewell, you muddy knave.   *Exeunt*

Enter Prince and Poins   II.2

POINS Come, shelter, shelter! I have removed Falstaff's
horse, and he frets like a gummed velvet.

PRINCE HAL Stand close!

They hide

Enter Falstaff

FALSTAFF Poins! Poins, and be hanged! Poins!

PRINCE HAL (*coming forward*) Peace, ye fat-kidneyed
rascal, what a brawling dost thou keep!

FALSTAFF Where's Poins, Hal?

PRINCE HAL He is walked up to the top of the hill. I'll
go seek him.

He steps to one side

FALSTAFF I am accursed to rob in that thief's company.   10
The rascal hath removed my horse and tied him I know
not where. If I travel but four foot by the square further
afoot, I shall break my wind. Well, I doubt not but to
die a fair death for all this, if I scape hanging for killing
that rogue. I have forsworn his company hourly any
time this two-and-twenty years, and yet I am bewitched
with the rogue's company. If the rascal have not given
me medicines to make me love him, I'll be hanged. It
could not be else. I have drunk medicines. Poins! Hal!
A plague upon you both! Bardolph! Peto! I'll starve ere   20
I'll rob a foot further — an 'twere not as good a deed as
drink to turn true man, and to leave these rogues, I am
the veriest varlet that ever chewed with a tooth. Eight
yards of uneven ground is threescore-and-ten miles
afoot with me, and the stony-hearted villains know it
well enough. A plague upon it when thieves cannot be
true one to another!

They whistle

Whew! A plague upon you all. Give me my horse you
rogues, give me my horse and be hanged!

30 PRINCE HAL (*coming forward*) Peace, ye fat-guts, lie
    down, lay thine ear close to the ground and list if thou
    canst hear the tread of travellers.

    FALSTAFF Have you any levers to lift me up again, being
    down? 'Sblood, I'll not bear my own flesh so far afoot
    again for all the coin in thy father's exchequer. What a
    plague mean ye to colt me thus?

    PRINCE HAL Thou liest, thou art not colted, thou art
    uncolted.

    FALSTAFF I prithee good Prince Hal, help me to my
40 horse, good king's son.

    PRINCE HAL Out, ye rogue, shall I be your ostler?

    FALSTAFF Hang thyself in thine own heir-apparent
    garters! If I be taken, I'll peach for this. An I have not
    ballads made on you all, and sung to filthy tunes, let a
    cup of sack be my poison. When a jest is so forward –
    and afoot too – I hate it!

        Enter Gadshill, Bardolph, and Peto

    GADSHILL Stand!

    FALSTAFF So I do, against my will.

    POINS O, 'tis our setter, I know his voice. Bardolph, what
50 news?

    BARDOLPH Case ye, case ye, on with your vizards, there's
    money of the King's coming down the hill. 'Tis going to
    the King's exchequer.

    FALSTAFF You lie, ye rogue, 'tis going to the King's
    tavern.

    GADSHILL There's enough to make us all –

    FALSTAFF To be hanged.

    PRINCE HAL Sirs, you four shall front them in the narrow
    lane. Ned Poins and I will walk lower – if they scape
60 from your encounter, then they light on us.

    PETO How many be there of them?

    GADSHILL Some eight or ten.

FALSTAFF Zounds, will they not rob us?

PRINCE HAL What, a coward, Sir John Paunch?

FALSTAFF Indeed, I am not John of Gaunt your grandfather, but yet no coward, Hal.

PRINCE HAL Well, we leave that to the proof.

POINS Sirrah Jack, thy horse stands behind the hedge.
When thou needest him, there thou shalt find him. Fare-
well, and stand fast!   70

FALSTAFF Now cannot I strike him, if I should be hanged.

PRINCE HAL (*aside to Poins*) Ned, where are our dis-
guises?

POINS Here, hard by, stand close. *Exeunt Prince and Poins*

FALSTAFF Now, my masters, happy man be his dole, say
I. Every man to his business.
    Enter the Travellers

FIRST TRAVELLER Come, neighbour, the boy shall lead
our horses down the hill. We'll walk afoot awhile and
ease our legs.

THIEVES Stand!   80

SECOND TRAVELLER Jesus bless us!

FALSTAFF Strike, down with them, cut the villains'
throats! Ah, whoreson caterpillars, bacon-fed knaves,
they hate us youth! Down with them, fleece them!

FIRST TRAVELLER O, we are undone, both we and ours
for ever!

FALSTAFF Hang ye, gorbellied knaves, are ye undone?
No, ye fat chuffs, I would your store were here! On,
bacons, on! What, ye knaves, young men must live!
You are grandjurors, are ye? We'll jure ye, faith.   90
    Here they rob them and bind them
                                              Exeunt
    Enter the Prince and Poins, disguised

PRINCE HAL The thieves have bound the true men.
Now, could thou and I rob the thieves, and go merrily to

London, it would be argument for a week, laughter for a
month, and a good jest for ever.

POINS Stand close, I hear them coming.

They hide
Enter the thieves again

FALSTAFF Come my masters, let us share, and then to
horse before day. An the Prince and Poins be not two
arrant cowards there's no equity stirring. There's no
more valour in that Poins than in a wild duck.

As they are sharing the Prince and Poins set upon
them

100 PRINCE HAL Your money!

POINS Villains!

They all run away, and Falstaff after a blow or two
runs away too, leaving the booty behind them

PRINCE HAL

Got with much ease. Now merrily to horse.
The thieves are all scattered and possessed with fear
So strongly that they dare not meet each other.
Each takes his fellow for an officer!
Away, good Ned! Falstaff sweats to death,
And lards the lean earth as he walks along.
Were it not for laughing I should pity him.

POINS How the fat rogue roared!   *Exeunt*

II.3   *Enter Hotspur alone, reading a letter*

HOTSPUR *But for mine own part, my lord, I could be well*
contented to be there, in respect of the love I bear your
house.

He could be contented! Why is he not then? In respect
of the love he bears our house? He shows in this he
loves his own barn better than he loves our house. Let
me see some more.

The purpose you undertake is dangerous,
Why, that's certain. 'Tis dangerous to take a cold, to
sleep, to drink. But I tell you, my lord fool, out of this   10
nettle, danger, we pluck this flower, safety.
The purpose you undertake is dangerous, the friends you
have named uncertain, the time itself unsorted, and your
whole plot too light, for the counterpoise of so great an
opposition.
Say you so, say you so? I say unto you again, you are a
shallow cowardly hind, and you lie. What a lack-brain is
this! By the Lord, our plot is a good plot, as ever was
laid, our friends true and constant. A good plot, good
friends, and full of expectation. An excellent plot, very   20
good friends. What a frosty-spirited rogue is this! Why,
my Lord of York commends the plot, and the general
course of the action. Zounds, an I were now by this
rascal I could brain him with his lady's fan. Is there not
my father, my uncle, and myself? Lord Edmund
Mortimer, my Lord of York, and Owen Glendower? Is
there not besides the Douglas? Have I not all their
letters to meet me in arms by the ninth of the next
month, and are they not some of them set forward
already? What a pagan rascal is this, an infidel! Ha!   30
You shall see now in very sincerity of fear and cold heart
will he to the King, and lay open all our proceedings!
O, I could divide myself, and go to buffets, for moving
such a dish of skim milk with so honourable an action!
Hang him, let him tell the King, we are prepared. I will
set forward tonight.
     Enter his lady
How now, Kate? I must leave you within these two
hours.
LADY PERCY
     O my good lord, why are you thus alone?

40   For what offence have I this fortnight been
      A banished woman from my Harry's bed?
      Tell me, sweet lord, what is it that takes from thee
      Thy stomach, pleasure, and thy golden sleep?
      Why dost thou bend thine eyes upon the earth,
      And start so often when thou sittest alone?
      Why hast thou lost the fresh blood in thy cheeks,
      And given my treasures and my rights of thee
      To thick-eyed musing, and curst melancholy?
      In thy faint slumbers I by thee have watched
50   And heard thee murmur tales of iron wars,
      Speak terms of manage to thy bounding steed,
      Cry 'Courage! To the field!' And thou hast talked
      Of sallies, and retires, of trenches, tents,
      Of palisadoes, frontiers, parapets,
      Of basilisks, of cannon, culverin,
      Of prisoners' ransom, and of soldiers slain,
      And all the currents of a heady fight.
      Thy spirit within thee hath been so at war,
      And thus hath so bestirred thee in thy sleep,
60   That beads of sweat have stood upon thy brow
      Like bubbles in a late-disturbèd stream,
      And in thy face strange motions have appeared,
      Such as we see when men restrain their breath
      On some great sudden hest. O, what portents are these?
      Some heavy business hath my lord in hand,
      And I must know it, else he loves me not.

HOTSPUR
      What ho!
            Enter a Servant
                  Is Gilliams with the packet gone?
SERVANT He is, my lord, an hour ago.
HOTSPUR Hath Butler brought those horses from the
70   sheriff?

SERVANT One horse, my lord, he brought even now.

HOTSPUR What horse? A roan, a crop-ear is it not?

SERVANT

It is, my lord.

HOTSPUR   That roan shall be my throne.
Well, I will back him straight. O Esperance!
Bid Butler lead him forth into the park.

Exit Servant

LADY PERCY But hear you, my lord.

HOTSPUR What sayest thou, my lady?

LADY PERCY What is it carries you away?

HOTSPUR Why, my horse, my love, my horse.

LADY PERCY

Out, you mad-headed ape!   80
A weasel hath not such a deal of spleen
As you are tossed with. In faith,
I'll know your business, Harry, that I will.
I fear my brother Mortimer doth stir
About his title, and hath sent for you
To line his enterprise. But if you go —

HOTSPUR

So far afoot I shall be weary, love.

LADY PERCY

Come, come, you paraquito, answer me
Directly unto this question that I ask.
In faith, I'll break thy little finger, Harry,   90
An if thou wilt not tell me all things true.

HOTSPUR

Away,
Away, you trifler! Love! I love thee not,
I care not for thee, Kate? This is no world
To play with mammets, and to tilt with lips.
We must have bloody noses, and cracked crowns,
And pass them current too. God's me! My horse!

What sayst thou, Kate? What wouldst thou have with
    me?

LADY PERCY
    Do you not love me? Do you not indeed?
100   Well, do not then, for since you love me not
    I will not love myself. Do you not love me?
    Nay, tell me if you speak in jest or no?

HOTSPUR
    Come, wilt thou see me ride?
    And when I am a-horseback I will swear
    I love thee infinitely. But hark you, Kate,
    I must not have you henceforth question me
    Whither I go, nor reason whereabout.
    Whither I must, I must. And, to conclude,
    This evening must I leave you, gentle Kate.
110   I know you wise, but yet no farther wise
    Than Harry Percy's wife. Constant you are,
    But yet a woman. And for secrecy,
    No lady closer, for I well believe
    Thou wilt not utter – what thou dost not know.
    And so far will I trust thee, gentle Kate.

LADY PERCY
    How? So far?

HOTSPUR
    Not an inch further. But hark you, Kate,
    Whither I go, thither shall you go too.
    Today will I set forth, tomorrow you.
120   Will this content you, Kate?

LADY PERCY   It must, of force. *Exeunt*

II.4   *Enter Prince and Poins*

PRINCE HAL Ned, prithee come out of that fat room, and
    lend me thy hand to laugh a little.

POINS Where hast been, Hal?

PRINCE HAL With three or four loggerheads, amongst
three or fourscore hogsheads. I have sounded the very
bass string of humility. Sirrah, I am sworn brother to a
leash of drawers, and can call them all by their Christian
names, as Tom, Dick, and Francis. They take it already
upon their salvation that though I be but Prince of
Wales yet I am the king of courtesy, and tell me flatly I   10
am no proud Jack like Falstaff, but a Corinthian, a lad of
mettle, a good boy – by the Lord, so they call me! – and
when I am King of England I shall command all the
good lads in Eastcheap. They call drinking deep
'dyeing scarlet', and when you breathe in your watering
they cry 'Hem!' and bid you 'Play it off!' To conclude,
I am so good a proficient in one quarter of an hour that I
can drink with any tinker in his own language during my
life. I tell thee, Ned, thou hast lost much honour that
thou wert not with me in this action. But, sweet Ned –   20
to sweeten which name of Ned I give thee this pennyworth of sugar, clapped even now into my hand by an
underskinker, one that never spake other English in his
life than 'Eight shillings and sixpence', and 'You are
welcome', with this shrill addition, 'Anon, anon, sir!
Score a pint of bastard in the Half-moon!', or so. But
Ned, to drive away the time till Falstaff come – I
prithee do thou stand in some by-room while I question
my puny drawer to what end he gave me the sugar. And
do thou never leave calling 'Francis!', that his tale to me   30
may be nothing but 'Anon'. Step aside, and I'll show
thee a precedent.   *Exit Poins*

POINS (*within*) Francis!

PRINCE HAL Thou art perfect.

POINS (*within*) Francis!

    Enter Francis, a Drawer

FRANCIS Anon, anon, sir. Look down into the Pomgarnet, Ralph!

PRINCE HAL Come hither, Francis.

FRANCIS My lord?

40 PRINCE HAL How long hast thou to serve, Francis?

FRANCIS Forsooth, five years, and as much as to –

POINS (*within*) Francis!

FRANCIS Anon, anon, sir.

PRINCE HAL Five year! By'r lady, a long lease for the clinking of pewter. But Francis, darest thou be so valiant as to play the coward with thy indenture, and show it a fair pair of heels, and run from it?

FRANCIS O Lord, sir, I'll be sworn upon all the books in England, I could find in my heart –

50 POINS (*within*) Francis!

FRANCIS Anon, sir.

PRINCE HAL How old art thou, Francis?

FRANCIS Let me see, about Michaelmas next I shall be –

POINS (*within*) Francis!

FRANCIS Anon, sir – pray stay a little, my lord.

PRINCE HAL Nay but hark you, Francis, for the sugar thou gavest me, 'twas a pennyworth, was it not?

FRANCIS O Lord, I would it had been two!

PRINCE HAL I will give thee for it a thousand pound –
60 ask me when thou wilt, and thou shalt have it.

POINS (*within*) Francis!

FRANCIS Anon, anon.

PRINCE HAL Anon, Francis? No, Francis, but tomorrow, Francis. Or Francis, a-Thursday. Or indeed Francis, when thou wilt. But Francis!

FRANCIS My lord?

PRINCE HAL Wilt thou rob this leathern-jerkin, crystal-button, not-pated, agate-ring, puke-stocking, caddis-garter, smooth-tongue Spanish pouch?

FRANCIS O Lord, sir, who do you mean?   70

PRINCE HAL Why then your brown bastard is your only
    drink. For look you, Francis, your white canvas doublet
    will sully. In Barbary, sir, it cannot come to so much.

FRANCIS What, sir?

POINS (*within*) Francis!

PRINCE HAL Away, you rogue, dost thou not hear them
    call?

Here they both call him; the Drawer stands amazed,
not knowing which way to go
Enter Vintner

VINTNER What, standest thou still and hearest such a
    calling? Look to the guests within.   *Exit Francis*
    My lord, old Sir John with half-a-dozen more are at the   80
    door. Shall I let them in?

PRINCE HAL Let them alone awhile, and then open the
    door.   *Exit Vintner*
    Poins!

Enter Poins

POINS Anon, anon, sir.

PRINCE HAL Sirrah, Falstaff and the rest of the thieves
    are at the door. Shall we be merry?

POINS As merry as crickets, my lad. But hark ye, what
    cunning match have you made with this jest of the
    drawer? Come, what's the issue?   90

PRINCE HAL I am now of all humours that have showed
    themselves humours since the old days of goodman
    Adam to the pupil age of this present twelve o'clock at
    midnight.

Enter Francis

    What's o'clock, Francis?

FRANCIS Anon, anon, sir.   *Exit*

PRINCE HAL That ever this fellow should have fewer
    words than a parrot, and yet the son of a woman! His

industry is up-stairs and down-stairs, his eloquence the
100   parcel of a reckoning. I am not yet of Percy's mind, the
Hotspur of the north, he that kills me some six or seven
dozen of Scots at a breakfast, washes his hands, and says
to his wife, 'Fie upon this quiet life, I want work.' 'O
my sweet Harry,' says she, 'how many hast thou killed
today?' 'Give my roan horse a drench,' says he, and
answers, 'Some fourteen,' an hour after, 'a trifle, a
trifle.' I prithee call in Falstaff. I'll play Percy, and that
damned brawn shall play Dame Mortimer his wife.
'Rivo!' says the drunkard. Call in Ribs, call in Tallow!

   Enter Falstaff, Gadshill, Bardolph, and Peto;
   followed by Francis, with wine

110 POINS Welcome, Jack, where hast thou been?

FALSTAFF A plague of all cowards, I say, and a vengeance
too, marry and amen! Give me a cup of sack, boy. Ere I
lead this life long, I'll sew nether-stocks, and mend
them and foot them too. A plague of all cowards! Give
me a cup of sack, rogue. Is there no virtue extant?

   He drinks

PRINCE HAL Didst thou never see Titan kiss a dish of
butter – pitiful-hearted Titan! – that melted at the sweet
tale of the sun's? If thou didst, then behold that
compound.

120 FALSTAFF You rogue, here's lime in this sack too. There
is nothing but roguery to be found in villainous man, yet
a coward is worse than a cup of sack with lime in it. A
villainous coward! Go thy ways, old Jack, die when thou
wilt. If manhood, good manhood, be not forgot upon
the face of the earth, then am I a shotten herring. There
lives not three good men unhanged in England, and one
of them is fat, and grows old. God help the while, a bad
world I say. I would I were a weaver: I could sing
psalms – or anything. A plague of all cowards, I say still.

PRINCE HAL How now, woolsack, what mutter you?   130

FALSTAFF A king's son! If I do not beat thee out of thy kingdom with a dagger of lath, and drive all thy subjects afore thee like a flock of wild geese, I'll never wear hair on my face more. You, Prince of Wales!

PRINCE HAL Why, you whoreson round man, what's the matter?

FALSTAFF Are not you a coward? Answer me to that – and Poins there?

POINS Zounds, ye fat paunch, an ye call me coward by the Lord I'll stab thee.   140

FALSTAFF I call thee coward? I'll see thee damned ere I call thee coward, but I would give a thousand pound I could run as fast as thou canst. You are straight enough in the shoulders, you care not who sees your back. Call you that backing of your friends? A plague upon such backing, give me them that will face me! Give me a cup of sack! I am a rogue if I drunk today.

PRINCE HAL O villain! Thy lips are scarce wiped since thou drunkest last.

FALSTAFF All is one for that. (*He drinks*) A plague of all   150
cowards, still say I.

PRINCE HAL What's the matter?

FALSTAFF What's the matter? There be four of us here have taken a thousand pound this day morning.

PRINCE HAL Where is it, Jack, where is it?

FALSTAFF Where is it? Taken from us it is. A hundred upon poor four of us.

PRINCE HAL What, a hundred, man?

FALSTAFF I am a rogue if I were not at half-sword with a dozen of them two hours together. I have scaped by   160
miracle. I am eight times thrust through the doublet, four through the hose, my buckler cut through and through, my sword hacked like a handsaw – *ecce*

signum! I never dealt better since I was a man. All would
not do. A plague of all cowards! Let them speak. If they
speak more or less than truth, they are villains and the
sons of darkness.

PRINCE HAL Speak, sirs, how was it?

GADSHILL We four set upon some dozen –

170 FALSTAFF Sixteen at least, my lord.

GADSHILL And bound them.

PETO No, no, they were not bound.

FALSTAFF You rogue, they were bound, every man of
them, or I am a Jew else: an Ebrew Jew.

GADSHILL As we were sharing, some six or seven fresh
men set upon us –

FALSTAFF And unbound the rest, and then come in the
other.

PRINCE HAL What, fought you with them all?

180 FALSTAFF All? I know not what you call all, but if I
fought not with fifty of them I am a bunch of radish. If
there were not two or three and fifty upon poor old
Jack, then am I no two-legg'd creature.

PRINCE HAL Pray God you have not murdered some of
them.

FALSTAFF Nay, that's past praying for, I have peppered
two of them. Two I am sure I have paid, two rogues in
buckram suits. I tell thee what, Hal, if I tell thee a lie,
spit in my face, call me horse. Thou knowest my old

190 ward – here I lay, and thus I bore my point. Four rogues
in buckram let drive at me –

PRINCE HAL What, four? Thou saidst but two even now.

FALSTAFF Four, Hal, I told thee four.

POINS Ay, ay, he said four.

FALSTAFF These four came all afront, and mainly thrust
at me. I made me no more ado, but took all their seven
points in my target, thus!

PRINCE HAL Seven? Why, there were but four even
 now.

FALSTAFF In buckram?   200

POINS Ay, four, in buckram suits.

FALSTAFF Seven, by these hilts, or I am a villain else.

PRINCE HAL Prithee let him alone, we shall have more
 anon.

FALSTAFF Dost thou hear me, Hal?

PRINCE HAL Ay, and mark thee too, Jack.

FALSTAFF Do so, for it is worth the listening to. These
 nine in buckram that I told thee of —

PRINCE HAL So, two more already.

FALSTAFF Their points being broken —   210

POINS Down fell their hose.

FALSTAFF — began to give me ground. But I followed me
 close, came in, foot and hand, and, with a thought,
 seven of the eleven I paid.

PRINCE HAL O monstrous! Eleven buckram men grown
 out of two!

FALSTAFF But as the devil would have it, three mis-
 begotten knaves in Kendal green came at my back and
 let drive at me, for it was so dark, Hal, that thou couldst
 not see thy hand.   220

PRINCE HAL These lies are like their father that begets
 them, gross as a mountain, open, palpable. Why, thou
 clay-brained guts, thou knotty-pated fool, thou whoreson obscene greasy tallow-catch —

FALSTAFF What, art thou mad? Art thou mad? Is not the
 truth the truth?

PRINCE HAL Why, how couldst thou know these men in
 Kendal green when it was so dark thou couldst not see
 thy hand? Come, tell us your reason. What sayest thou
 to this?   230

POINS Come, your reason, Jack, your reason!

FALSTAFF What, upon compulsion? Zounds, an I were
at the strappado, or all the racks in the world, I would
not tell you on compulsion. Give you a reason on compulsion? If reasons were as plentiful as blackberries, I
would give no man a reason upon compulsion, I.

PRINCE HAL I'll be no longer guilty of this sin. This
sanguine coward, this bed-presser, this horse-back-
breaker, this huge hill of flesh —

240 FALSTAFF 'Sblood, you starveling, you elf-skin, you dried
neat's-tongue, you bull's-pizzle, you stock-fish! O for
breath to utter what is like thee! You tailor's-yard, you
sheath, you bow-case, you vile standing tuck!

PRINCE HAL Well, breathe awhile, and then to it again,
and when thou hast tired thyself in base comparisons
hear me speak but this.

POINS Mark, Jack!

PRINCE HAL We two saw you four set on four, and bound
them and were masters of their wealth — mark now how a
250 plain tale shall put you down. Then did we two set on
you four, and, with a word, out-faced you from your
prize, and have it, yea, and can show it you here in the
house. And Falstaff, you carried your guts away as
nimbly, with as quick dexterity, and roared for mercy,
and still run and roared, as ever I heard bull-calf. What
a slave art thou to hack thy sword as thou hast done, and
then say it was in fight! What trick, what device, what
starting-hole canst thou now find out, to hide thee from
this open and apparent shame?

260 POINS Come, let's hear Jack, what trick hast thou now?

FALSTAFF By the Lord, I knew ye as well as he that made
ye. Why, hear you, my masters, was it for me to kill the
heir apparent? Should I turn upon the true prince?
Why, thou knowest I am as valiant as Hercules. But
beware instinct. The lion will not touch the true prince.

Instinct is a great matter. I was now a coward on
instinct. I shall think the better of myself, and thee,
during my life – I for a valiant lion, and thou for a true
prince. But by the Lord lads, I am glad you have the
money! Hostess, clap to the doors! Watch tonight, pray   270
tomorrow! Gallants, lads, boys, hearts of gold, all the
titles of good fellowship come to you! What, shall we be
merry? Shall we have a play extempore?

PRINCE HAL Content, and the argument shall be thy
running away.

FALSTAFF Ah, no more of that Hal, an thou lovest me.
    Enter Hostess

HOSTESS O Jesu, my lord the Prince!

PRINCE HAL How now, my lady the Hostess, what
sayest thou to me?

HOSTESS Marry my lord, there is a nobleman of the court   280
at door would speak with you. He says he comes from
your father.

PRINCE HAL Give him as much as will make him a royal
man and send him back again to my mother.

FALSTAFF What manner of man is he?

HOSTESS An old man.

FALSTAFF What doth gravity out of his bed at midnight?
Shall I give him his answer?

PRINCE HAL Prithee do, Jack.

FALSTAFF Faith, and I'll send him packing.   *Exit*   290

PRINCE HAL Now, sirs, by'r lady, you fought fair, so did
you, Peto, so did you, Bardolph. You are lions too, you
ran away upon instinct, you will not touch the true
prince, no fie!

BARDOLPH Faith, I ran when I saw others run.

PRINCE HAL Faith, tell me now in earnest, how came
Falstaff's sword so hacked?

PETO Why, he hacked it with his dagger, and said he

would swear truth out of England but he would make
300   you believe it was done in fight, and persuaded us to do
the like.

BARDOLPH Yea, and to tickle our noses with spear-grass,
to make them bleed, and then to beslubber our garments
with it, and swear it was the blood of true men. I did
that I did not this seven year before: I blushed to hear
his monstrous devices.

PRINCE HAL O villain, thou stolest a cup of sack eighteen
years ago, and wert taken with the manner, and ever
since thou hast blushed extempore. Thou hadst fire and
310   sword on thy side, and yet thou rannest away. What
instinct hadst thou for it?

BARDOLPH My lord, do you see these meteors? Do you
behold these exhalations?

PRINCE HAL I do.

BARDOLPH What think you they portend?

PRINCE HAL Hot livers, and cold purses.

BARDOLPH Choler, my lord, if rightly taken.

PRINCE HAL No, if rightly taken, halter.

    Enter Falstaff

Here comes lean Jack, here comes bare-bone. How now
320   my sweet creature of bombast, how long is't ago, Jack,
since thou sawest thine own knee?

FALSTAFF My own knee? When I was about thy years,
Hal, I was not an eagle's talon in the waist – I could have
crept into any alderman's thumb-ring. A plague of
sighing and grief, it blows a man up like a bladder.
There's villainous news abroad. Here was Sir John
Bracy from your father. You must to the court in the
morning. That same mad fellow of the north, Percy,
and he of Wales that gave Amamon the bastinado, and
330   made Lucifer cuckold, and swore the devil his true

liegeman upon the cross of a Welsh hook – what a
plague call you him?

POINS O, Glendower.

FALSTAFF Owen, Owen, the same. And his son-in-law
Mortimer, and old Northumberland, and that sprightly
Scot of Scots, Douglas, that runs a-horseback up a hill
perpendicular –

PRINCE HAL He that rides at high speed, and with his
pistol kills a sparrow flying.

FALSTAFF You have hit it. 340

PRINCE HAL So did he never the sparrow.

FALSTAFF Well, that rascal hath good mettle in him, he
will not run.

PRINCE HAL Why, what a rascal art thou then, to praise
him so for running!

FALSTAFF A-horseback, ye cuckoo, but afoot he will not
budge a foot.

PRINCE HAL Yes, Jack, upon instinct.

FALSTAFF I grant ye, upon instinct. Well, he is there too,
and one Mordake, and a thousand blue-caps more. 350
Worcester is stolen away tonight. Thy father's beard is
turned white with the news. You may buy land now as
cheap as stinking mackerel.

PRINCE HAL Why then, it is like if there come a hot June,
and this civil buffeting hold, we shall buy maidenheads
as they buy hob-nails, by the hundreds.

FALSTAFF By the mass, lad, thou sayest true, it is like we
shall have good trading that way. But tell me, Hal, art
not thou horrible afeard? Thou being heir apparent,
could the world pick thee out three such enemies again, 360
as that fiend Douglas, that spirit Percy, and that devil
Glendower? Art thou not horribly afraid? Doth not thy
blood thrill at it?

PRINCE HAL Not a whit, i'faith, I lack some of thy instinct.

FALSTAFF Well, thou wilt be horribly chid tomorrow when thou comest to thy father. If thou love me, practise an answer.

PRINCE HAL Do thou stand for my father and examine
370 me upon the particulars of my life.

FALSTAFF Shall I? Content! This chair shall be my state, this dagger my sceptre, and this cushion my crown.

PRINCE HAL Thy state is taken for a joint-stool, thy golden sceptre for a leaden dagger, and thy precious rich crown for a pitiful bald crown.

FALSTAFF Well, an the fire of grace be not quite out of thee, now shalt thou be moved. Give me a cup of sack to make my eyes look red, that it may be thought I have wept, for I must speak in passion, and I will do it in
380 King Cambyses' vein.

PRINCE HAL Well, here is my leg.

FALSTAFF And here is my speech. Stand aside, nobility.

HOSTESS O Jesu, this is excellent sport, i'faith.

FALSTAFF

Weep not, sweet Queen, for trickling tears are vain.

HOSTESS O the Father, how he holds his countenance!

FALSTAFF

For God's sake, lords, convey my tristful Queen,
For tears do stop the floodgates of her eyes.

HOSTESS O Jesu, he doth it as like one of these harlotry players as ever I see!

390 FALSTAFF Peace, good pint-pot, peace, good tickle-brain.

(*as* KING)

Harry, I do not only marvel where thou spendest thy time, but also how thou art accompanied. For though the camomile, the more it is trodden on the faster it grows, yet youth, the more it is wasted the sooner it wears. That thou art my son I have partly thy mother's word, partly my own opinion, but chiefly a villainous trick of thine eye, and a foolish hanging of thy nether lip, that doth warrant me. If then thou be son to me – here lies the point – why, being son to me, art thou so pointed at? Shall the blessed sun of heaven prove a micher, and eat blackberries? A question not to be asked. Shall the son of England prove a thief, and take purses? A question to be asked. There is a thing, Harry, which thou hast often heard of, and it is known to many in our land by the name of pitch. This pitch – as ancient writers do report – doth defile, so doth the company thou keepest. For, Harry, now I do not speak to thee in drink, but in tears; not in pleasure, but in passion; not in words only, but in woes also. And yet there is a virtuous man whom I have often noted in thy company, but I know not his name.

PRINCE HAL (*as himself*)
  What manner of man, an it like your Majesty?

FALSTAFF (*as* KING)
  A goodly portly man, i'faith, and a corpulent; of a cheerful look, a pleasing eye, and a most noble carriage; and, as I think, his age some fifty, or by'r lady inclining to threescore. And now I remember me, his name is Falstaff. If that man should be lewdly given, he deceiveth me, for, Harry, I see virtue in his looks. If then the tree may be known by the fruit, as the fruit by the tree, then peremptorily I speak it, there is virtue in that Falstaff. Him keep with, the rest banish. And tell me now, thou naughty varlet, tell me where hast thou been this month?

PRINCE HAL Dost thou speak like a king? Do thou stand for me, and I'll play my father.

FALSTAFF Depose me? If thou dost it half so gravely, so majestically, both in word and matter, hang me up by the heels for a rabbit-sucker, or a poulter's hare.

PRINCE HAL Well, here I am set.

FALSTAFF And here I stand. Judge, my masters.

PRINCE HAL (*as* KING)

Now, Harry, whence come you?

FALSTAFF (*as* HAL)

430   My noble lord, from Eastcheap.

PRINCE HAL (*as* KING)

The complaints I hear of thee are grievous.

FALSTAFF (*as* HAL)

'Sblood, my lord, they are false!

Nay, I'll tickle ye for a young prince, i'faith.

PRINCE HAL (*as* KING)

Swearest thou, ungracious boy? Henceforth ne'er look on me.
Thou art violently carried away from grace. There is a devil
haunts thee in the likeness of an old fat man, a tun of man is
thy companion. Why dost thou converse with that trunk of
humours, that bolting-hutch of beastliness, that swollen
parcel of dropsies, that huge bombard of sack, that stuffed
440   cloak-bag of guts, that roasted Manningtree ox with the
pudding in his belly, that reverend Vice, that grey Iniquity,
that Father Ruffian, that Vanity in years? Wherein is he
good, but to taste sack and drink it? Wherein neat and
cleanly, but to carve a capon and eat it? Wherein cunning,
but in craft? Wherein crafty, but in villainy? Wherein
villainous, but in all things? Wherein worthy, but in nothing?

FALSTAFF (*as* HAL)

I would your grace would take me with you. Whom means
your grace?

PRINCE HAL (*as* KING)

That villainous abominable misleader of youth, Falstaff,
450   that old white-bearded Satan.

FALSTAFF (*as* HAL)

My lord, the man I know.

PRINCE HAL (*as* KING)
    I know thou dost.
FALSTAFF (*as* HAL)
    But to say I know more harm in him than in myself were to
    say more than I know. That he is old, the more the pity, his
    white hairs do witness it, but that he is, saving your rever-
    ence, a whoremaster, that I utterly deny. If sack and sugar
    be a fault, God help the wicked! If to be old and merry be a
    sin, then many an old host that I know is damned. If to be
    fat be to be hated, then Pharaoh's lean kine are to be loved.
    No, my good lord! Banish Peto, banish Bardolph, banish   460
    Poins – but for sweet Jack Falstaff, kind Jack Falstaff, true
    Jack Falstaff, valiant Jack Falstaff – and therefore more
    valiant, being as he is old Jack Falstaff – banish not him thy
    Harry's company, banish not him thy Harry's company.
    Banish plump Jack, and banish all the world.
PRINCE HAL (*as* KING)
    I do, I will.
        A knocking heard
                        Exeunt Hostess, Francis and Bardolph
        Enter Bardolph, running
BARDOLPH O my lord, my lord, the sheriff with a most
    monstrous watch is at the door.
FALSTAFF Out, ye rogue! Play out the play! I have much
    to say in the behalf of that Falstaff.   470
        Enter the Hostess
HOSTESS O Jesu, my lord, my lord!
PRINCE HAL Heigh, heigh, the devil rides upon a fiddle-
    stick. What's the matter?
HOSTESS The sheriff and all the watch are at the door.
    They are come to search the house. Shall I let them in?
FALSTAFF Dost thou hear, Hal? Never call a true piece of
    gold a counterfeit. Thou art essentially made without
    seeming so.

PRINCE HAL And thou a natural coward without in-
480 stinct.

FALSTAFF I deny your major. If you will deny the sheriff,
so; if not, let him enter. If I become not a cart as well as
another man, a plague on my bringing up! I hope I shall
as soon be strangled with a halter as another.

PRINCE HAL Go hide thee behind the arras. The rest,
walk up above. Now, my masters, for a true face, and
good conscience.

FALSTAFF Both which I have had, but their date is out,
and therefore I'll hide me.

Exeunt all but the Prince and Peto

490 PRINCE HAL Call in the Sheriff.

Enter Sheriff and the Carrier

Now, master Sheriff, what is your will with me?

SHERIFF
First, pardon me, my lord. A hue and cry
Hath followed certain men unto this house.

PRINCE HAL
What men?

SHERIFF
One of them is well known my gracious lord,
A gross fat man.

CARRIER   As fat as butter.

PRINCE HAL
The man I do assure you is not here,
For I myself at this time have employed him.
And Sheriff, I will engage my word to thee,
500 That I will by tomorrow dinner-time
Send him to answer thee, or any man,
For anything he shall be charged withal.
And so let me entreat you leave the house.

SHERIFF
I will, my lord. There are two gentlemen

Have in this robbery lost three hundred marks.

PRINCE HAL

It may be so. If he have robbed these men
He shall be answerable. And so, farewell.

SHERIFF

Good night, my noble lord.

PRINCE HAL

I think it is good morrow, is it not?

SHERIFF

Indeed, my lord, I think it be two o'clock.   510

Exit with Carrier

PRINCE HAL This oily rascal is known as well as Paul's.
Go call him forth.

PETO Falstaff! Fast asleep behind the arras, and snorting
like a horse.

PRINCE HAL Hark how hard he fetches breath. Search
his pockets.

Peto searcheth his pockets, and findeth certain papers

What hast thou found?

PETO Nothing but papers, my lord.

PRINCE HAL Let's see what they be, read them.

PETO *Item a capon* *2s. 2d.*   520
Item sauce .... *4d.*
Item sack two gallons .... *5s. 8d.*
Item anchovies and sack after supper .. *2s. 6d.*
Item bread .... *ob.*

PRINCE HAL O monstrous! But one halfpennyworth of
bread to this intolerable deal of sack? What there is else
keep close, we'll read it at more advantage. There let him
sleep till day. I'll to the court in the morning. We must
all to the wars, and thy place shall be honourable. I'll
procure this fat rogue a charge of foot, and I know his   530
death will be a march of twelve score. The money shall

be paid back again with advantage. Be with me betimes
in the morning, and so, good morrow, Peto.

PETO Good morrow, good my lord.   *Exeunt*

*

III.I   *Enter Hotspur, Worcester, Lord Mortimer, Owen*
               Glendower

MORTIMER
     These promises are fair, the parties sure,
     And our induction full of prosperous hope.

HOTSPUR
     Lord Mortimer, and cousin Glendower, will you sit down?
     And uncle Worcester. A plague upon it!
     I have forgot the map.

GLENDOWER   No, here it is.
     Sit, cousin Percy, sit – good cousin Hotspur –
     For by that name as oft as Lancaster doth speak of you
     His cheek looks pale, and with a rising sigh
     He wisheth you in heaven.

HOTSPUR   And you in hell,
10   As oft as he hears Owen Glendower spoke of.

GLENDOWER
     I cannot blame him. At my nativity
     The front of heaven was full of fiery shapes,
     Of burning cressets, and at my birth
     The frame and huge foundation of the earth
     Shaked like a coward.

HOTSPUR   Why, so it would have done
     At the same season if your mother's cat
     Had but kittened, though yourself had never been born.

GLENDOWER
     I say the earth did shake when I was born.

HOTSPUR
    And I say the earth was not of my mind,
    If you suppose as fearing you it shook.   20
GLENDOWER
    The heavens were all on fire, the earth did tremble –
HOTSPUR
    O, then the earth shook to see the heavens on fire,
    And not in fear of your nativity.
    Diseasèd nature oftentimes breaks forth
    In strange eruptions, oft the teeming earth
    Is with a kind of colic pinched and vexed
    By the imprisoning of unruly wind
    Within her womb, which for enlargement striving
    Shakes the old beldam earth, and topples down
    Steeples and moss-grown towers. At your birth   30
    Our grandam earth, having this distemperature,
    In passion shook.
GLENDOWER   Cousin, of many men
    I do not bear these crossings. Give me leave
    To tell you once again that at my birth
    The front of heaven was full of fiery shapes,
    The goats ran from the mountains, and the herds
    Were strangely clamorous to the frighted fields.
    These signs have marked me extraordinary,
    And all the courses of my life do show
    I am not in the roll of common men.   40
    Where is he living, clipped in with the sea
    That chides the banks of England, Scotland, Wales,
    Which calls me pupil or hath read to me?
    And bring him out that is but woman's son
    Can trace me in the tedious ways of art,
    And hold me pace in deep experiments.
HOTSPUR
    I think there's no man speaks better Welsh.

I'll to dinner.

MORTIMER

Peace, cousin Percy, you will make him mad.

GLENDOWER

50   I can call spirits from the vasty deep.

HOTSPUR

Why, so can I, or so can any man:

But will they come when you do call for them?

GLENDOWER

Why, I can teach you, cousin, to command the devil.

HOTSPUR

And I can teach thee, coz, to shame the devil

By telling truth. Tell truth, and shame the devil.

If thou have power to raise him, bring him hither,

And I'll be sworn I have power to shame him hence.

O, while you live, tell truth, and shame the devil!

MORTIMER

Come, come, no more of this unprofitable chat.

GLENDOWER

60   Three times hath Henry Bolingbroke made head

Against my power, thrice from the banks of Wye

And sandy-bottomed Severn have I sent him

Bootless home, and weather-beaten back.

HOTSPUR

Home without boots, and in foul weather too!

How scapes he agues, in the devil's name?

GLENDOWER

Come, here is the map, shall we divide our right

According to our threefold order taken?

MORTIMER

The Archdeacon hath divided it

Into three limits very equally.

70   England, from Trent and Severn hitherto,

By south and east is to my part assigned.
All westward, Wales beyond the Severn shore,
And all the fertile land within that bound,
To Owen Glendower. And, dear coz, to you
The remnant northward lying off from Trent.
And our indentures tripartite are drawn,
Which being sealed interchangeably —
A business that this night may execute —
Tomorrow, cousin Percy, you and I
And my good Lord of Worcester will set forth   80
To meet your father and the Scottish power,
As is appointed us, at Shrewsbury.
My father Glendower is not ready yet,
Nor shall we need his help these fourteen days.
(*To Glendower*) Within that space you may have drawn
      together
Your tenants, friends, and neighbouring gentlemen.

GLENDOWER
A shorter time shall send me to you, lords,
And in my conduct shall your ladies come,
From whom you now must steal and take no leave,
For there will be a world of water shed   90
Upon the parting of your wives and you.

HOTSPUR
Methinks my moiety, north from Burton here,
In quantity equals not one of yours.
See how this river comes me cranking in,
And cuts me from the best of all my land
A huge half-moon, a monstrous cantle out.
I'll have the current in this place dammed up,
And here the smug and silver Trent shall run
In a new channel fair and evenly.
It shall not wind with such a deep indent,   100

To rob me of so rich a bottom here.

GLENDOWER
Not wind? It shall, it must — you see it doth.

MORTIMER
Yea,
But mark how he bears his course, and runs me up
With like advantage on the other side,
Gelding the opposèd continent as much
As on the other side it takes from you.

WORCESTER
Yea, but a little charge will trench him here,
And on this north side win this cape of land,
And then he runs straight and even.

HOTSPUR
I'll have it so, a little charge will do it.

GLENDOWER
I'll not have it altered.

HOTSPUR   Will not you?

GLENDOWER
No, nor you shall not.

HOTSPUR   Who shall say me nay?

GLENDOWER
Why, that will I.

HOTSPUR
Let me not understand you then, speak it in Welsh.

GLENDOWER
I can speak English, lord, as well as you,
For I was trained up in the English court,
Where being but young I framèd to the harp
Many an English ditty lovely well,
And gave the tongue a helpful ornament —
A virtue that was never seen in you.

HOTSPUR
Marry and I am glad of it with all my heart!

I had rather be a kitten and cry 'mew'
Than one of these same metre ballad-mongers.
I had rather hear a brazen canstick turned,
Or a dry wheel grate on the axle-tree,
And that would set my teeth nothing on edge,
Nothing so much as mincing poetry.
'Tis like the forced gait of a shuffling nag.

GLENDOWER

Come, you shall have Trent turned.   130

HOTSPUR

I do not care, I'll give thrice so much land
To any well-deserving friend.
But in the way of bargain, mark ye me,
I'll cavil on the ninth part of a hair.
Are the indentures drawn? Shall we be gone?

GLENDOWER

The moon shines fair, you may away by night.
I'll haste the writer, and withal
Break with your wives of your departure hence.
I am afraid my daughter will run mad,
So much she doteth on her Mortimer.   *Exit*   140

MORTIMER

Fie, cousin Percy, how you cross my father!

HOTSPUR

I cannot choose. Sometime he angers me
With telling me of the moldwarp and the ant,
Of the dreamer Merlin and his prophecies,
And of a dragon and a finless fish,
A clip-winged griffin and a moulten raven,
A couching lion and a ramping cat,
And such a deal of skimble-skamble stuff
As puts me from my faith. I tell you what –
He held me last night at least nine hours   150
In reckoning up the several devils' names

That were his lackeys. I cried 'Hum', and 'Well, go to!'
But marked him not a word. O, he is as tedious
As a tired horse, a railing wife,
Worse than a smoky house. I had rather live
With cheese and garlic in a windmill, far,
Than feed on cates and have him talk to me
In any summer house in Christendom.

MORTIMER

In faith, he is a worthy gentleman,
160   Exceedingly well read, and profited
In strange concealments, valiant as a lion,
And wondrous affable, and as bountiful
As mines of India. Shall I tell you, cousin?
He holds your temper in a high respect
And curbs himself even of his natural scope
When you come 'cross his humour, faith he does.
I warrant you that man is not alive
Might so have tempted him as you have done
Without the taste of danger and reproof.
170   But do not use it oft, let me entreat you.

WORCESTER

In faith, my lord, you are too wilful-blame,
And since your coming hither have done enough
To put him quite besides his patience.
You must needs learn, lord, to amend this fault.
Though sometimes it show greatness, courage, blood –
And that's the dearest grace it renders you –
Yet oftentimes it doth present harsh rage,
Defect of manners, want of government,
Pride, haughtiness, opinion, and disdain,
180   The least of which haunting a nobleman
Loseth men's hearts and leaves behind a stain
Upon the beauty of all parts besides,
Beguiling them of commendation.

HOTSPUR

    Well, I am schooled – good manners be your speed!

    Here come our wives, and let us take our leave.

    Enter Glendower with the ladies

MORTIMER

    This is the deadly spite that angers me,

    My wife can speak no English, I no Welsh.

GLENDOWER

    My daughter weeps, she'll not part with you,

    She'll be a soldier too, she'll to the wars.

MORTIMER

    Good father, tell her that she and my aunt Percy   190

    Shall follow in your conduct speedily.

    Glendower speaks to her in Welsh, and she answers him

    in the same

GLENDOWER She is desperate here, a peevish, self-willed

    harlotry, one that no persuasion can do good upon.

    The lady speaks in Welsh

MORTIMER

    I understand thy looks, that pretty Welsh

    Which thou pourest down from these swelling heavens

    I am too perfect in, and but for shame

    In such a parley should I answer thee.

    The lady speaks again in Welsh

    I understand thy kisses, and thou mine,

    And that's a feeling disputation,

    But I will never be a truant, love,   200

    Till I have learnt thy language, for thy tongue

    Makes Welsh as sweet as ditties highly penned,

    Sung by a fair queen in a summer's bower

    With ravishing division to her lute.

GLENDOWER

    Nay, if you melt, then will she run mad.

    The lady speaks again in Welsh

MORTIMER

O, I am ignorance itself in this!

GLENDOWER

She bids you on the wanton rushes lay you down,
And rest your gentle head upon her lap,
And she will sing the song that pleaseth you,
210   And on your eyelids crown the god of sleep,
Charming your blood with pleasing heaviness,
Making such difference 'twixt wake and sleep
As is the difference betwixt day and night,
The hour before the heavenly-harnessed team
Begins his golden progress in the east.

MORTIMER

With all my heart I'll sit and hear her sing,
By that time will our book I think be drawn.

GLENDOWER

Do so, and those musicians that shall play to you
Hang in the air a thousand leagues from hence,
220   And straight they shall be here. Sit, and attend.

HOTSPUR

Come, Kate, thou art perfect in lying down.
Come, quick, quick, that I may lay my head in thy lap.

LADY PERCY Go, ye giddy goose.

The music plays

HOTSPUR

Now I perceive the devil understands Welsh,
And 'tis no marvel he is so humorous,
By'r lady, he is a good musician.

LADY PERCY

Then should you be nothing but musical,
For you are altogether governed by humours.
Lie still, ye thief, and hear the lady sing in Welsh.

230   HOTSPUR I had rather hear Lady my brach howl in Irish.

LADY PERCY Wouldst thou have thy head broken?

HOTSPUR No.

LADY PERCY Then be still.

HOTSPUR Neither, 'tis a woman's fault.

LADY PERCY Now, God help thee!

HOTSPUR To the Welsh lady's bed.

LADY PERCY What's that?

HOTSPUR Peace, she sings.

    Here the lady sings a Welsh song

  Come, Kate, I'll have your song too.

LADY PERCY Not mine, in good sooth.   240

HOTSPUR Not yours, in good sooth! Heart, you swear like
  a comfit-maker's wife – 'Not you, in good sooth!', and
  'As true as I live!', and 'As God shall mend me!', and
  'As sure as day!' –
  And givest such sarcenet surety for thy oaths
  As if thou never walkest further than Finsbury.
  Swear me, Kate, like a lady as thou art,
  A good mouth-filling oath, and leave 'In sooth',
  And such protest of pepper-gingerbread,
  To velvet-guards, and Sunday citizens.   250
  Come, sing.

LADY PERCY I will not sing.

HOTSPUR 'Tis the next way to turn tailor, or be redbreast
  teacher. An the indentures be drawn I'll away within
  these two hours. And so, come in when ye will.   *Exit*

GLENDOWER
  Come, come, Lord Mortimer, you are as slow
  As hot Lord Percy is on fire to go.
  By this our book is drawn – we'll but seal,
  And then to horse immediately.

MORTIMER   With all my heart.

                                 Exeunt

III.2   *Enter the King, Prince of Wales, and others*
KING HENRY
    Lords, give us leave. The Prince of Wales and I
    Must have some private conference – but be near at hand,
    For we shall presently have need of you.
                          Exeunt Lords
    I know not whether God will have it so
    For some displeasing service I have done,
    That in his secret doom out of my blood
    He'll breed revengement and a scourge for me.
    But thou dost in thy passages of life
    Make me believe that thou art only marked
10   For the hot vengeance and the rod of heaven,
    To punish my mistreadings. Tell me else,
    Could such inordinate and low desires,
    Such poor, such bare, such lewd, such mean attempts,
    Such barren pleasures, rude society,
    As thou art matched withal, and grafted to,
    Accompany the greatness of thy blood
    And hold their level with thy princely heart?
PRINCE HAL
    So please your majesty, I would I could
    Quit all offences with as clear excuse
20   As well as I am doubtless I can purge
    Myself of many I am charged withal.
    Yet such extenuation let me beg
    As, in reproof of many tales devised,
    Which oft the ear of greatness needs must hear,
    By smiling pickthanks, and base newsmongers,
    I may for some things true, wherein my youth
    Hath faulty wandered and irregular,
    Find pardon on my true submission.
KING HENRY
    God pardon thee! Yet let me wonder, Harry,

At thy affections, which do hold a wing   30
Quite from the flight of all thy ancestors.
Thy place in Council thou hast rudely lost,
Which by thy younger brother is supplied,
And art almost an alien to the hearts
Of all the court and princes of my blood.
The hope and expectation of thy time
Is ruined, and the soul of every man
Prophetically do forethink thy fall.
Had I so lavish of my presence been,
So common-hackneyed in the eyes of men,   40
So stale and cheap to vulgar company,
Opinion, that did help me to the crown,
Had still kept loyal to possession,
And left me in reputeless banishment,
A fellow of no mark nor likelihood.
By being seldom seen, I could not stir
But like a comet I was wondered at,
That men would tell their children, 'This is he!'
Others would say, 'Where, which is Bolingbroke?'
And then I stole all courtesy from heaven,   50
And dressed myself in such humility
That I did pluck allegiance from men's hearts,
Loud shouts and salutations from their mouths,
Even in the presence of the crownèd King.
Thus did I keep my person fresh and new,
My presence, like a robe pontifical,
Ne'er seen but wondered at, and so my state,
Seldom, but sumptuous, showed like a feast,
And won by rareness such solemnity.
The skipping King, he ambled up and down,   60
With shallow jesters, and rash bavin wits,
Soon kindled and soon burnt, carded his state,
Mingled his royalty with capering fools,

Had his great name profanèd with their scorns,
And gave his countenance against his name
To laugh at gibing boys, and stand the push
Of every beardless vain comparative,
Grew a companion to the common streets,
Enfeoffed himself to popularity,
70   That, being daily swallowed by men's eyes,
They surfeited with honey, and began
To loathe the taste of sweetness, whereof a little
More than a little is by much too much.
So, when he had occasion to be seen,
He was but as the cuckoo is in June,
Heard, not regarded; seen, but with such eyes
As, sick and blunted with community,
Afford no extraordinary gaze,
Such as is bent on sun-like majesty
80   When it shines seldom in admiring eyes,
But rather drowsed and hung their eyelids down,
Slept in his face, and rendered such aspect
As cloudy men use to their adversaries,
Being with his presence glutted, gorged, and full.
And in that very line, Harry, standest thou,
For thou hast lost thy princely privilege
With vile participation. Not an eye
But is a-weary of thy common sight,
Save mine, which hath desired to see thee more,
90   Which now doth that I would not have it do,
Make blind itself with foolish tenderness.

PRINCE HAL
I shall hereafter, my thrice-gracious lord,
Be more myself.

KING HENRY   For all the world
As thou art to this hour was Richard then

When I from France set foot at Ravenspurgh,
And even as I was then is Percy now.
Now by my sceptre, and my soul to boot,
He hath more worthy interest to the state
Than thou the shadow of succession.
For of no right, nor colour like to right,   100
He doth fill fields with harness in the realm,
Turns head against the lion's armèd jaws,
And being no more in debt to years than thou
Leads ancient lords and reverend bishops on
To bloody battles, and to bruising arms.
What never-dying honour hath he got
Against renownèd Douglas! Whose high deeds,
Whose hot incursions and great name in arms,
Holds from all soldiers chief majority
And military title capital   110
Through all the kingdoms that acknowledge Christ.
Thrice hath this Hotspur, Mars in swaddling clothes,
This infant warrior, in his enterprises
Discomfited great Douglas, taken him once,
Enlargèd him, and made a friend of him,
To fill the mouth of deep defiance up,
And shake the peace and safety of our throne.
And what say you to this? Percy, Northumberland,
The Archbishop's Grace of York, Douglas, Mortimer,
Capitulate against us and are up.   120
But wherefore do I tell these news to thee?
Why, Harry, do I tell thee of my foes,
Which art my nearest and dearest enemy?
Thou that art like enough, through vassal fear,
Base inclination, and the start of spleen,
To fight against me under Percy's pay,
To dog his heels, and curtsy at his frowns,

To show how much thou art degenerate.

PRINCE HAL

Do not think so, you shall not find it so;
130   And God forgive them that so much have swayed
Your majesty's good thoughts away from me!
I will redeem all this on Percy's head,
And in the closing of some glorious day
Be bold to tell you that I am your son,
When I will wear a garment all of blood,
And stain my favours in a bloody mask,
Which, washed away, shall scour my shame with it.
And that shall be the day, whene'er it lights,
That this same child of honour and renown,
140   This gallant Hotspur, this all-praisèd knight,
And your unthought-of Harry chance to meet.
For every honour sitting on his helm,
Would they were multitudes, and on my head
My shames redoubled. For the time will come
That I shall make this northern youth exchange
His glorious deeds for my indignities.
Percy is but my factor, good my lord,
To engross up glorious deeds on my behalf,
And I will call him to so strict account
150   That he shall render every glory up,
Yea, even the slightest worship of his time,
Or I will tear the reckoning from his heart.
This in the name of God I promise here,
The which if He be pleased I shall perform,
I do beseech your majesty may salve
The long-grown wounds of my intemperance.
If not, the end of life cancels all bonds,
And I will die a hundred thousand deaths
Ere break the smallest parcel of this vow.

KING HENRY
    A hundred thousand rebels die in this.   160
    Thou shalt have charge and sovereign trust herein.
      Enter Blunt
    How now, good Blunt? Thy looks are full of speed.

BLUNT
    So hath the business that I come to speak of.
    Lord Mortimer of Scotland hath sent word
    That Douglas and the English rebels met
    The eleventh of this month at Shrewsbury.
    A mighty and a fearful head they are,
    If promises be kept on every hand,
    As ever offered foul play in a state.

KING HENRY
    The Earl of Westmorland set forth today,   170
    With him my son, Lord John of Lancaster,
    For this advertisement is five days old.
    On Wednesday next, Harry, you shall set forward.
    On Thursday we ourselves will march.
    Our meeting is Bridgnorth, and, Harry, you
    Shall march through Gloucestershire, by which account,
    Our business valued, some twelve days hence
    Our general forces at Bridgnorth shall meet.
    Our hands are full of business, let's away,
    Advantage feeds him fat while men delay.   *Exeunt*   180

      Enter Falstaff and Bardolph   **III.3**

FALSTAFF Bardolph, am I not fallen away vilely since this
last action? Do I not bate? Do I not dwindle? Why, my
skin hangs about me like an old lady's loose gown. I am
withered like an old apple-john. Well, I'll repent, and
that suddenly, while I am in some liking. I shall be out
of heart shortly, and then I shall have no strength to

repent. An I have not forgotten what the inside of a
church is made of, I am a peppercorn, a brewer's horse.
The inside of a church! Company, villainous company,
10 hath been the spoil of me.

BARDOLPH Sir John, you are so fretful you cannot live
long.

FALSTAFF Why, there is it. Come, sing me a bawdy song,
make me merry. I was as virtuously given as a gentleman need to be. Virtuous enough. Swore little. Diced
not above seven times a week. Went to a bawdy-house
not above once in a quarter – of an hour. Paid money
that I borrowed – three or four times. Lived well, and in
good compass: and now I live out of all order, out of all
20 compass.

BARDOLPH Why, you are so fat, Sir John, that you must
needs be out of all compass, out of all reasonable compass, Sir John.

FALSTAFF Do thou amend thy face, and I'll amend my
life. Thou art our admiral, thou bearest the lantern in
the poop, but 'tis in the nose of thee. Thou art the
Knight of the Burning Lamp.

BARDOLPH Why, Sir John, my face does you no harm.

FALSTAFF No, I'll be sworn, I make as good use of it as
30 many a man doth of a death's-head, or a *memento mori*.
I never see thy face but I think upon hell-fire, and Dives
that lived in purple: for there he is in his robes, burning,
burning. If thou wert any way given to virtue, I would
swear by thy face. My oath should be 'By this fire, that's
God's angel!' But thou art altogether given over, and
wert indeed, but for the light in thy face, the son of
utter darkness. When thou rannest up Gad's Hill in the
night to catch my horse, if I did not think thou hadst
been an *ignis fatuus*, or a ball of wildfire, there's no

purchase in money. O, thou art a perpetual triumph, an   40
everlasting bonfire-light! Thou hast saved me a thousand
marks in links and torches, walking with thee in the
night betwixt tavern and tavern. But the sack that thou
hast drunk me would have bought me lights as good
cheap at the dearest chandler's in Europe. I have
maintained that salamander of yours with fire any time
this two-and-thirty years, God reward me for it!

BARDOLPH 'Sblood, I would my face were in your belly!

FALSTAFF God-a-mercy! So should I be sure to be heart-
burnt.   50

Enter Hostess

How now, dame Partlet the hen, have you enquired yet
who picked my pocket?

HOSTESS Why, Sir John, what do you think, Sir John, do
you think I keep thieves in my house? I have searched, I
have enquired, so has my husband, man by man, boy by
boy, servant by servant – the tithe of a hair was never
lost in my house before.

FALSTAFF Ye lie, hostess. Bardolph was shaved and lost
many a hair, and I'll be sworn my pocket was picked.
Go to, you are a woman, go!   60

HOSTESS Who, I? No, I defy thee! God's light, I was
never called so in mine own house before.

FALSTAFF Go to, I know you well enough.

HOSTESS No, Sir John, you do not know me, Sir John, I
know you, Sir John, you owe me money, Sir John, and
now you pick a quarrel to beguile me of it. I bought you
a dozen of shirts to your back.

FALSTAFF Dowlas, filthy dowlas. I have given them away
to bakers' wives. They have made bolters of them.

HOSTESS Now as I am a true woman, holland of eight   70
shillings an ell! You owe money here besides, Sir John,

for your diet, and by-drinkings, and money lent you,
four-and-twenty pound.

FALSTAFF He had his part of it, let him pay.

HOSTESS He? Alas, he is poor, he hath nothing.

FALSTAFF How? Poor? Look upon his face. What call you
rich? Let them coin his nose, let them coin his
cheeks, I'll not pay a denier. What, will you make a
younker of me? Shall I not take mine ease in mine inn
but I shall have my pocket picked? I have lost a seal-
ring of my grandfather's worth forty mark.

HOSTESS O Jesu, I have heard the Prince tell him I know
not how oft, that that ring was copper.

FALSTAFF How? The Prince is a Jack, a sneak-up.
'Sblood, an he were here I would cudgel him like a dog
if he would say so.

Enter the Prince marching, with Peto, and Falstaff
meets him, playing upon his truncheon like a fife

How now, lad? Is the wind in that door, i'faith, must
we all march?

BARDOLPH Yea, two and two, Newgate fashion.

HOSTESS My lord, I pray you hear me.

PRINCE HAL What sayest thou, Mistress Quickly? How
doth thy husband? I love him well, he is an honest man.

HOSTESS Good my lord, hear me.

FALSTAFF Prithee let her alone, and list to me.

PRINCE HAL What sayest thou, Jack?

FALSTAFF The other night I fell asleep here, behind the
arras, and had my pocket picked. This house is turned
bawdy-house, they pick pockets.

PRINCE HAL What didst thou lose, Jack?

FALSTAFF Wilt thou believe me, Hal, three or four bonds
of forty pound apiece, and a seal-ring of my grandfather's.

PRINCE HAL A trifle, some eightpenny matter.

HOSTESS So I told him, my lord, and I said I heard your
grace say so. And, my lord, he speaks most vilely of you,
like a foul-mouthed man as he is, and said he would
cudgel you.

PRINCE HAL What! He did not?

HOSTESS There's neither faith, truth, nor womanhood in
me else.   110

FALSTAFF There's no more faith in thee than in a stewed
prune, nor no more truth in thee than in a drawn fox —
and for womanhood, Maid Marian may be the deputy's
wife of the ward to thee. Go, you thing, go!

HOSTESS Say, what thing, what thing?

FALSTAFF What thing? Why, a thing to thank God on.

HOSTESS I am no thing to thank God on, I would thou
shouldst know it, I am an honest man's wife, and setting
thy knighthood aside, thou art a knave to call me so.

FALSTAFF Setting thy womanhood aside, thou art a beast   120
to say otherwise.

HOSTESS Say, what beast, thou knave, thou?

FALSTAFF What beast? Why — an otter.

PRINCE HAL An otter, Sir John? Why an otter?

FALSTAFF Why? She's neither fish nor flesh, a man knows
not where to have her.

HOSTESS Thou art an unjust man in saying so, thou or
any man knows where to have me, thou knave, thou.

PRINCE HAL Thou sayest true, Hostess, and he slanders
thee most grossly.   130

HOSTESS So he doth you, my lord, and said this other day
you owed him a thousand pound.

PRINCE HAL Sirrah, do I owe you a thousand pound?

FALSTAFF A thousand pound, Hal? A million, thy love is
worth a million, thou owest me thy love.

HOSTESS Nay my lord, he called you Jack, and said he
would cudgel you.

FALSTAFF Did I, Bardolph?

BARDOLPH Indeed, Sir John, you said so.

140 FALSTAFF Yea, if he said my ring was copper.

PRINCE HAL I say 'tis copper, darest thou be as good as
thy word now?

FALSTAFF Why Hal, thou knowest as thou art but man I
dare, but as thou art prince, I fear thee as I fear the
roaring of the lion's whelp.

PRINCE HAL And why not as the lion?

FALSTAFF The King himself is to be feared as the lion.
Dost thou think I'll fear thee as I fear thy father? Nay,
an I do, I pray God my girdle break.

150 PRINCE HAL O, if it should, how would thy guts fall
about thy knees! But sirrah, there's no room for faith,
truth, nor honesty in this bosom of thine. It is all filled
up with guts and midriff. Charge an honest woman with
picking thy pocket? Why, thou whoreson impudent
embossed rascal, if there were anything in thy pocket
but tavern reckonings, memorandums of bawdy-
houses, and one poor pennyworth of sugar-candy to
make thee long-winded, if thy pocket were enriched
with any other injuries but these, I am a villain. And yet
160 you will stand to it, you will not pocket up wrong! Art
thou not ashamed?

FALSTAFF Dost thou hear, Hal? Thou knowest in the
state of innocency Adam fell, and what should poor
Jack Falstaff do in the days of villainy? Thou seest I
have more flesh than another man, and therefore more
frailty. You confess then, you picked my pocket?

PRINCE HAL It appears so by the story.

FALSTAFF Hostess, I forgive thee, go make ready
breakfast, love thy husband, look to thy servants,
170 cherish thy guests, thou shalt find me tractable to any

honest reason, thou seest I am pacified still – nay
prithee be gone.   *Exit Hostess*
Now, Hal, to the news at court: for the robbery, lad,
how is that answered?

PRINCE HAL O my sweet beef, I must still be good angel
to thee – the money is paid back again.

FALSTAFF O, I do not like that paying back, 'tis a double
labour.

PRINCE HAL I am good friends with my father and may
do anything.   180

FALSTAFF Rob me the exchequer the first thing thou
dost, and do it with unwashed hands too.

BARDOLPH Do, my lord.

PRINCE HAL I have procured thee, Jack, a charge of foot.

FALSTAFF I would it had been of horse. Where shall I
find one that can steal well? O for a fine thief of the age
of two-and-twenty or thereabouts! I am heinously un-
provided. Well, God be thanked for these rebels, they
offend none but the virtuous. I laud them, I praise them.

PRINCE HAL Bardolph!   190

BARDOLPH My lord?

PRINCE HAL
Go bear this letter to Lord John of Lancaster,
To my brother John, this to my Lord of Westmorland.
                                        Exit Bardolph
Go, Peto, to horse, to horse, for thou and I
Have thirty miles to ride yet ere dinner-time.
                                          Exit Peto
Jack, meet me tomorrow in the Temple hall
At two o'clock in the afternoon.
There shalt thou know thy charge, and there receive
Money and order for their furniture.
The land is burning, Percy stands on high,   200

And either we or they must lower lie.   *Exit*

FALSTAFF

Rare words! Brave world! Hostess, my breakfast, come!

O, I could wish this tavern were my drum.   *Exit*

*

IV. I   *Enter Hotspur, Worcester, and Douglas*

HOTSPUR

Well said, my noble Scot! If speaking truth

In this fine age were not thought flattery,

Such attribution should the Douglas have

As not a soldier of this season's stamp

Should go as general current through the world.

By God, I cannot flatter, I do defy

The tongues of soothers, but a braver place

In my heart's love hath no man than yourself.

Nay, task me to my word, approve me, lord.

DOUGLAS

10   Thou art the king of honour.

No man so potent breathes upon the ground

But I will beard him.

HOTSPUR   Do so, and 'tis well.

        Enter one with letters

What letters hast thou there? – I can but thank you.

MESSENGER

These letters come from your father.

HOTSPUR

Letters from him? Why comes he not himself?

MESSENGER

He cannot come, my lord, he is grievous sick.

HOTSPUR

Zounds, how has he the leisure to be sick

In such a justling time? Who leads his power?
Under whose government come they along?

MESSENGER
His letters bear his mind, not I, my lord.   20

WORCESTER
I prithee tell me, doth he keep his bed?

MESSENGER
He did, my lord, four days ere I set forth,
And at the time of my departure thence
He was much feared by his physicians.

WORCESTER
I would the state of time had first been whole
Ere he by sickness had been visited.
His health was never better worth than now.

HOTSPUR
Sick now? Droop now? This sickness doth infect
The very life-blood of our enterprise.
'Tis catching hither, even to our camp.   30
He writes me here that inward sickness –
And that his friends by deputation could not
So soon be drawn, nor did he think it meet
To lay so dangerous and dear a trust
On any soul removed but on his own.
Yet doth he give us bold advertisement
That with our small conjunction we should on,
To see how fortune is disposed to us.
For, as he writes, there is no quailing now,
Because the King is certainly possessed   40
Of all our purposes. What say you to it?

WORCESTER
Your father's sickness is a maim to us.

HOTSPUR
A perilous gash, a very limb lopped off –
And yet, in faith, it is not! His present want

Seems more than we shall find it. Were it good
To set the exact wealth of all our states
All at one cast? To set so rich a main
On the nice hazard of one doubtful hour?
It were not good, for therein should we read
50   The very bottom and the soul of hope,
The very list, the very utmost bound
Of all our fortunes.

DOUGLAS

Faith, and so we should, where now remains
A sweet reversion – we may boldly spend
Upon the hope of what is to come in.
A comfort of retirement lives in this.

HOTSPUR

A rendezvous, a home to fly unto,
If that the devil and mischance look big
Upon the maidenhead of our affairs.

WORCESTER

60   But yet I would your father had been here.
The quality and hair of our attempt
Brooks no division. It will be thought,
By some that know not why he is away,
That wisdom, loyalty, and mere dislike
Of our proceedings kept the Earl from hence.
And think how such an apprehension
May turn the tide of fearful faction,
And breed a kind of question in our cause.
For well you know we of the offering side
70   Must keep aloof from strict arbitrement,
And stop all sight-holes, every loop from whence
The eye of reason may pry in upon us.
This absence of your father's draws a curtain
That shows the ignorant a kind of fear
Before not dreamt of.

HOTSPUR   You strain too far.
  I rather of his absence make this use.
  It lends a lustre and more great opinion,
  A larger dare to our great enterprise,
  Than if the Earl were here. For men must think
  If we without his help can make a head   80
  To push against a kingdom, with his help
  We shall o'erturn it topsy-turvy down.
  Yet all goes well, yet all our joints are whole.

DOUGLAS
  As heart can think. There is not such a word
  Spoke of in Scotland as this term of fear.
    Enter Sir Richard Vernon

HOTSPUR
  My cousin Vernon! Welcome, by my soul!

VERNON
  Pray God my news be worth a welcome, lord.
  The Earl of Westmorland seven thousand strong
  Is marching hitherwards, with him Prince John.

HOTSPUR
  No harm, what more?

VERNON   And further, I have learned,   90
  The King himself in person is set forth,
  Or hitherwards intended speedily,
  With strong and mighty preparation.

HOTSPUR
  He shall be welcome too. Where is his son,
  The nimble-footed madcap Prince of Wales,
  And his comrades that daffed the world aside
  And bid it pass?

VERNON   All furnished, all in arms,
  All plumed like estridges that with the wind
  Bated, like eagles having lately bathed,
  Glittering in golden coats like images,   100

As full of spirit as the month of May,
And gorgeous as the sun at midsummer,
Wanton as youthful goats, wild as young bulls.
I saw young Harry with his beaver on,
His cuishes on his thighs, gallantly armed,
Rise from the ground like feathered Mercury,
And vaulted with such ease into his seat
As if an angel dropped down from the clouds
To turn and wind a fiery Pegasus,
110 And witch the world with noble horsemanship.

HOTSPUR
No more, no more! Worse than the sun in March,
This praise doth nourish agues. Let them come!
They come like sacrifices in their trim,
And to the fire-eyed maid of smoky war
All hot and bleeding will we offer them.
The mailèd Mars shall on his altar sit
Up to the ears in blood. I am on fire
To hear this rich reprisal is so nigh,
And yet not ours! Come, let me taste my horse,
120 Who is to bear me like a thunderbolt
Against the bosom of the Prince of Wales.
Harry to Harry shall, hot horse to horse,
Meet and ne'er part till one drop down a corpse.
O that Glendower were come!

VERNON   There is more news.
I learned in Worcester as I rode along
He cannot draw his power this fourteen days.

DOUGLAS
That's the worst tidings that I hear of yet.

WORCESTER
Ay, by my faith, that bears a frosty sound.

HOTSPUR
What may the King's whole battle reach unto?

VERNON
  To thirty thousand.
HOTSPUR   Forty let it be.   130
  My father and Glendower being both away,
  The powers of us may serve so great a day.
  Come, let us take a muster speedily.
  Doomsday is near. Die all, die merrily.
DOUGLAS
  Talk not of dying, I am out of fear
  Of death or death's hand for this one half year.

Exeunt

        Enter Falstaff and Bardolph   IV.2
FALSTAFF Bardolph, get thee before to Coventry. Fill me
  a bottle of sack. Our soldiers shall march through. We'll
  to Sutton Coldfield tonight.
BARDOLPH Will you give me money, captain?
FALSTAFF Lay out, lay out.
BARDOLPH This bottle makes an angel.
FALSTAFF And if it do, take it for thy labour – and if it
  make twenty, take them all, I'll answer the coinage. Bid
  my lieutenant Peto meet me at town's end.
BARDOLPH I will, captain. Farewell.   *Exit* 10
FALSTAFF If I be not ashamed of my soldiers, I am a
  soused gurnet. I have misused the King's press damnably. I have got in exchange of a hundred and fifty
  soldiers three hundred and odd pounds. I press me
  none but good householders, yeomen's sons, enquire
  me out contracted bachelors, such as had been asked
  twice on the banns, such a commodity of warm slaves as
  had as lief hear the devil as a drum, such as fear the
  report of a caliver worse than a struck fowl or a hurt wild
  duck. I pressed me none but such toasts-and-butter,   20

with hearts in their bellies no bigger than pins' heads,
and they have bought out their services. And now my
whole charge consists of ancients, corporals, lieutenants,
gentlemen of companies – slaves as ragged as Lazarus in
the painted cloth, where the glutton's dogs licked his
sores. And such as indeed were never soldiers, but discarded unjust serving-men, younger sons to younger
brothers, revolted tapsters, and ostlers trade-fallen, the
cankers of a calm world and a long peace, ten times more
dishonourable-ragged than an old fazed ancient. And
such have I to fill up the rooms of them as have bought
out their services, that you would think that I had a
hundred and fifty tattered prodigals lately come from
swine-keeping, from eating draff and husks. A mad
fellow met me on the way, and told me I had unloaded
all the gibbets and pressed the dead bodies. No eye hath
seen such scarecrows. I'll not march through Coventry
with them, that's flat. Nay, and the villains march wide
betwixt the legs as if they had gyves on, for indeed I had
the most of them out of prison. There's not a shirt and a
half in all my company, and the half shirt is two napkins
tacked together and thrown over the shoulders like a
herald's coat without sleeves. And the shirt to say the
truth stolen from my host at Saint Albans, or the red-
nose innkeeper of Daventry. But that's all one, they'll
find linen enough on every hedge.

Enter the Prince and the Lord of Westmorland

PRINCE HAL How now, blown Jack? How now, quilt?

FALSTAFF What, Hal! How now, mad wag? What a devil
dost thou in Warwickshire? My good Lord of Westmorland, I cry you mercy, I thought your honour had
already been at Shrewsbury.

WESTMORLAND Faith, Sir John, 'tis more than time that
I were there, and you too, but my powers are there

already. The King I can tell you looks for us all, we must
away all night.

FALSTAFF Tut, never fear me, I am as vigilant as a cat to
steal cream.

PRINCE HAL I think, to steal cream indeed, for thy theft
hath already made thee butter. But tell me, Jack, whose
fellows are these that come after?   60

FALSTAFF Mine, Hal, mine.

PRINCE HAL I did never see such pitiful rascals.

FALSTAFF Tut, tut, good enough to toss, food for powder, food for powder, they'll fill a pit as well as better.
Tush, man, mortal men, mortal men.

WESTMORLAND Ay, but Sir John, methinks they are
exceeding poor and bare, too beggarly.

FALSTAFF Faith, for their poverty I know not where they
had that. And for their bareness I am sure they never
learned that of me.   70

PRINCE HAL No, I'll be sworn, unless you call three
fingers in the ribs bare. But sirrah, make haste. Percy
is already in the field.   *Exit*

FALSTAFF What, is the King encamped?

WESTMORLAND He is, Sir John, I fear we shall stay too
long.   *Exit*

FALSTAFF Well,
To the latter end of a fray, and the beginning of a feast
Fits a dull fighter and a keen guest.   *Exit*

Enter Hotspur, Worcester, Douglas, Vernon   IV.3

HOTSPUR
We'll fight with him tonight.

WORCESTER   It may not be.

DOUGLAS
You give him then advantage.

VERNON   Not a whit.

HOTSPUR

Why say you so, looks he not for supply?

VERNON

So do we.

HOTSPUR   His is certain, ours is doubtful.

WORCESTER

Good cousin, be advised, stir not tonight.

VERNON

Do not, my lord.

DOUGLAS   You do not counsel well.

You speak it out of fear and cold heart.

VERNON

Do me no slander, Douglas. By my life,
And I dare well maintain it with my life,
If well-respected honour bid me on,
I hold as little counsel with weak fear
As you, my lord, or any Scot that this day lives.
Let it be seen tomorrow in the battle
Which of us fears.

DOUGLAS   Yea, or tonight.

VERNON   Content.

HOTSPUR

Tonight, say I.

VERNON

Come, come, it may not be. I wonder much,
Being men of such great leading as you are,
That you foresee not what impediments
Drag back our expedition. Certain horse
Of my cousin Vernon's are not yet come up,
Your uncle Worcester's horse came but today,
And now their pride and mettle is asleep,
Their courage with hard labour tame and dull,
That not a horse is half the half himself.

HOTSPUR

So are the horses of the enemy
In general journey-bated and brought low.
The better part of ours are full of rest.

WORCESTER

The number of the King exceedeth ours.
For God's sake, cousin, stay till all come in.
        The trumpet sounds a parley
        Enter Sir Walter Blunt

BLUNT

I come with gracious offers from the King,   30
If you vouchsafe me hearing and respect.

HOTSPUR

Welcome, Sir Walter Blunt: and would to God
You were of our determination!
Some of us love you well, and even those some
Envy your great deservings and good name,
Because you are not of our quality,
But stand against us like an enemy.

BLUNT

And God defend but still I should stand so,
So long as out of limit and true rule
You stand against anointed majesty.   40
But to my charge. The King hath sent to know
The nature of your griefs, and whereupon
You conjure from the breast of civil peace
Such bold hostility, teaching his duteous land
Audacious cruelty. If that the King
Have any way your good deserts forgot,
Which he confesseth to be manifold,
He bids you name your griefs, and with all speed
You shall have your desires with interest
And pardon absolute for yourself, and these   50
Herein misled by your suggestion.

HOTSPUR

    The King is kind, and well we know the King
    Knows at what time to promise, when to pay.
    My father, and my uncle, and myself
    Did give him that same royalty he wears,
    And when he was not six-and-twenty strong,
    Sick in the world's regard, wretched and low,
    A poor unminded outlaw sneaking home,
    My father gave him welcome to the shore.
60   And when he heard him swear and vow to God
    He came but to be Duke of Lancaster,
    To sue his livery, and beg his peace
    With tears of innocency and terms of zeal,
    My father, in kind heart and pity moved,
    Swore him assistance, and performed it too.
    Now when the lords and barons of the realm
    Perceived Northumberland did lean to him,
    The more and less came in with cap and knee,
    Met him in boroughs, cities, villages,
70   Attended him on bridges, stood in lanes,
    Laid gifts before him, proffered him their oaths,
    Gave him their heirs as pages, followed him
    Even at the heels in golden multitudes.
    He presently, as greatness knows itself,
    Steps me a little higher than his vow
    Made to my father while his blood was poor
    Upon the naked shore at Ravenspurgh;
    And now forsooth takes on him to reform
    Some certain edicts and some strait decrees
80   That lie too heavy on the commonwealth,
    Cries out upon abuses, seems to weep
    Over his country's wrongs – and by this face,
    This seeming brow of justice, did he win
    The hearts of all that he did angle for.

Proceeded further – cut me off the heads
Of all the favourites that the absent King
In deputation left behind him here,
When he was personal in the Irish war.

BLUNT

Tut, I came not to hear this.

HOTSPUR   Then to the point.

In short time after he deposed the King,   90
Soon after that deprived him of his life,
And in the neck of that tasked the whole state.
To make that worse, suffered his kinsman March –
Who is, if every owner were well placed,
Indeed his King – to be engaged in Wales,
There without ransom to lie forfeited.
Disgraced me in my happy victories,
Sought to entrap me by intelligence,
Rated mine uncle from the Council-board,
In rage dismissed my father from the court,   100
Broke oath on oath, committed wrong on wrong,
And in conclusion drove us to seek out
This head of safety, and withal to pry
Into his title, the which we find
Too indirect for long continuance.

BLUNT

Shall I return this answer to the King?

HOTSPUR

Not so, Sir Walter. We'll withdraw awhile.
Go to the King, and let there be impawned
Some surety for a safe return again,
And in the morning early shall mine uncle   110
Bring him our purposes – and so, farewell.

BLUNT

I would you would accept of grace and love.

HOTSPUR
    And may be so we shall.
BLUNT   Pray God you do.   *Exeunt*

IV.4   *Enter the Archbishop of York and Sir Michael*
ARCHBISHOP
    Hie, good Sir Michael, bear this sealèd brief
    With wingèd haste to the Lord Marshal,
    This to my cousin Scroop, and all the rest
    To whom they are directed. If you knew
    How much they do import you would make haste.
SIR MICHAEL
    My good lord,
    I guess their tenor.
ARCHBISHOP   Like enough you do.
    Tomorrow, good Sir Michael, is a day
    Wherein the fortune of ten thousand men
10   Must bide the touch. For, sir, at Shrewsbury,
    As I am truly given to understand,
    The King with mighty and quick-raisèd power
    Meets with Lord Harry, and I fear, Sir Michael,
    What with the sickness of Northumberland,
    Whose power was in the first proportion,
    And what with Owen Glendower's absence thence,
    Who with them was a rated sinew too,
    And comes not in, o'er-ruled by prophecies,
    I fear the power of Percy is too weak
20   To wage an instant trial with the King.
SIR MICHAEL
    Why, my good lord, you need not fear,
    There is Douglas, and Lord Mortimer.
ARCHBISHOP
    No, Mortimer is not there.

SIR MICHAEL

But there is Mordake, Vernon, Lord Harry Percy,
And there is my Lord of Worcester, and a head
Of gallant warriors, noble gentlemen.

ARCHBISHOP

And so there is. But yet the King hath drawn
The special head of all the land together.
The Prince of Wales, Lord John of Lancaster,
The noble Westmorland, and warlike Blunt,   30
And many more corrivals and dear men
Of estimation and command in arms.

SIR MICHAEL

Doubt not, my lord, they shall be well opposed.

ARCHBISHOP

I hope no less, yet needful 'tis to fear,
And to prevent the worst, Sir Michael, speed.
For if Lord Percy thrive not, ere the King
Dismiss his power he means to visit us,
For he hath heard of our confederacy,
And 'tis but wisdom to make strong against him.
Therefore make haste – I must go write again   40
To other friends. And so, farewell, Sir Michael.

                                                    Exeunt

                              *

         Enter the King, Prince of Wales, Lord John   V.I
         of Lancaster, Sir Walter Blunt, Falstaff

KING HENRY

How bloodily the sun begins to peer
Above yon bulky hill! The day looks pale
At his distemperature.

PRINCE HAL   The southern wind

Doth play the trumpet to his purposes,
And by his hollow whistling in the leaves
Foretells a tempest and a blustering day.

KING HENRY

Then with the losers let it sympathize,
For nothing can seem foul to those that win.

The trumpet sounds
Enter Worcester and Vernon

How now, my Lord of Worcester! 'Tis not well

10   That you and I should meet upon such terms
As now we meet. You have deceived our trust,
And made us doff our easy robes of peace
To crush our old limbs in ungentle steel.
This is not well, my lord, this is not well.
What say you to it? Will you again unknit
The churlish knot of all-abhorrèd war,
And move in that obedient orb again
Where you did give a fair and natural light,
And be no more an exhaled meteor,

20   A prodigy of fear, and a portent
Of broachèd mischief to the unborn times?

WORCESTER

Hear me, my liege.
For mine own part I could be well content
To entertain the lag end of my life
With quiet hours. For I protest
I have not sought the day of this dislike.

KING HENRY

You have not sought it? How comes it, then?

FALSTAFF Rebellion lay in his way, and he found it.

PRINCE HAL Peace, chewet, peace!

WORCESTER

30   It pleased your majesty to turn your looks
Of favour from myself, and all our house,

And yet I must remember you, my lord,
We were the first and dearest of your friends.
For you my staff of office did I break
In Richard's time, and posted day and night
To meet you on the way, and kiss your hand,
When yet you were in place and in account
Nothing so strong and fortunate as I.
It was myself, my brother, and his son,
That brought you home, and boldly did outdare   40
The dangers of the time. You swore to us,
And you did swear that oath at Doncaster,
That you did nothing purpose 'gainst the state,
Nor claim no further than your new-fallen right,
The seat of Gaunt, dukedom of Lancaster.
To this we swore our aid. But in short space
It rained down fortune showering on your head,
And such a flood of greatness fell on you,
What with our help, what with the absent King,
What with the injuries of a wanton time,   50
The seeming sufferances that you had borne,
And the contrarious winds that held the King
So long in his unlucky Irish wars
That all in England did repute him dead.
And from this swarm of fair advantages
You took occasion to be quickly wooed
To gripe the general sway into your hand,
Forget your oath to us at Doncaster,
And being fed by us, you used us so
As that ungentle gull the cuckoo's bird   60
Useth the sparrow – did oppress our nest,
Grew by our feeding to so great a bulk
That even our love durst not come near your sight
For fear of swallowing. But with nimble wing
We were enforced for safety sake to fly

Out of your sight, and raise this present head,
Whereby we stand opposèd by such means
As you yourself have forged against yourself,
By unkind usage, dangerous countenance,
70   And violation of all faith and troth
Sworn to us in your younger enterprise.

KING HENRY

These things indeed you have articulate,
Proclaimed at market crosses, read in churches,
To face the garment of rebellion
With some fine colour that may please the eye
Of fickle changelings and poor discontents,
Which gape and rub the elbow at the news
Of hurlyburly innovation.
And never yet did insurrection want
80   Such water-colours to impaint his cause,
Nor moody beggars starving for a time
Of pell-mell havoc and confusion.

PRINCE HAL

In both your armies there is many a soul
Shall pay full dearly for this encounter
If once they join in trial. Tell your nephew,
The Prince of Wales doth join with all the world
In praise of Henry Percy. By my hopes,
This present enterprise set off his head,
I do not think a braver gentleman,
90   More active-valiant or more valiant-young,
More daring or more bold, is now alive
To grace this latter age with noble deeds.
For my part, I may speak it to my shame,
I have a truant been to chivalry,
And so I hear he doth account me too.
Yet this before my father's majesty —
I am content that he shall take the odds

Of his great name and estimation,
And will, to save the blood on either side,
Try fortune with him in a single fight.   100

KING HENRY

And, Prince of Wales, so dare we venture thee,
Albeit considerations infinite
Do make against it. No, good Worcester, no,
We love our people well, even those we love
That are misled upon your cousin's part,
And will they take the offer of our grace,
Both he, and they, and you, yea, every man
Shall be my friend again, and I'll be his.
So tell your cousin, and bring me word
What he will do. But if he will not yield,   110
Rebuke and dread correction wait on us,
And they shall do their office. So, be gone.
We will not now be troubled with reply.
We offer fair, take it advisedly.

Exeunt Worcester and Vernon

PRINCE HAL

It will not be accepted, on my life.
The Douglas and the Hotspur both together
Are confident against the world in arms.

KING HENRY

Hence, therefore, every leader to his charge,
For on their answer will we set on them,
And God befriend us as our cause is just!   120

Exeunt all but the Prince and Falstaff

FALSTAFF Hal, if thou see me down in the battle and
bestride me, so. 'Tis a point of friendship.

PRINCE HAL Nothing but a Colossus can do thee that
friendship. Say thy prayers, and farewell.

FALSTAFF I would 'twere bed-time, Hal, and all well.

PRINCE HAL Why, thou owest God a death.   *Exit*

FALSTAFF 'Tis not due yet – I would be loath to pay him
before his day. What need I be so forward with him that
calls not on me? Well, 'tis no matter, honour pricks
130   me on. Yea, but how if honour prick me off when I
come on, how then? Can honour set to a leg? No. Or
an arm? No. Or take away the grief of a wound? No.
Honour hath no skill in surgery then? No. What is
honour? A word. What is in that word honour? What is
that honour? Air. A trim reckoning! Who hath it? He
that died a'Wednesday. Doth he feel it? No. Doth he
hear it? No. 'Tis insensible, then? Yea, to the dead.
But will it not live with the living? No. Why? Detraction will not suffer it. Therefore I'll none of it. Honour
140   is a mere scutcheon – and so ends my catechism. *Exit*

V.2   *Enter Worcester and Sir Richard Vernon*

WORCESTER
    O no, my nephew must not know, Sir Richard,
    The liberal and kind offer of the King.
VERNON
    'Twere best he did.
WORCESTER   Then are we all undone.
    It is not possible, it cannot be,
    The King should keep his word in loving us.
    He will suspect us still, and find a time
    To punish this offence in other faults.
    Supposition all our lives shall be stuck full of eyes,
    For treason is but trusted like the fox,
10   Who, never so tame, so cherished and locked up,
    Will have a wild trick of his ancestors.
    Look how we can or sad or merrily,
    Interpretation will misquote our looks,
    And we shall feed like oxen at a stall,

The better cherished still the nearer death.
My nephew's trespass may be well forgot,
It hath the excuse of youth and heat of blood,
And an adopted name of privilege —
A hare-brained Hotspur, governed by a spleen.
All his offences live upon my head   20
And on his father's. We did train him on,
And, his corruption being taken from us,
We as the spring of all shall pay for all.
Therefore, good cousin, let not Harry know
In any case the offer of the King.

VERNON
Deliver what you will; I'll say 'tis so.
Here comes your cousin.

    Enter Hotspur and Douglas

HOTSPUR   My uncle is returned;
Deliver up my Lord of Westmorland.
Uncle, what news?

WORCESTER
The King will bid you battle presently.   30

DOUGLAS
Defy him by the Lord of Westmorland.

HOTSPUR
Lord Douglas, go you and tell him so.

DOUGLAS
Marry, and shall, and very willingly.   *Exit*

WORCESTER
There is no seeming mercy in the King.

HOTSPUR
Did you beg any? God forbid!

WORCESTER
I told him gently of our grievances,
Of his oath-breaking — which he mended thus,
By now forswearing that he is forsworn.

He calls us rebels, traitors, and will scourge
40   With haughty arms this hateful name in us.
        Enter Douglas

DOUGLAS

Arm, gentlemen, to arms! For I have thrown
A brave defiance in King Henry's teeth,
And Westmorland that was engaged did bear it,
Which cannot choose but bring him quickly on.

WORCESTER

The Prince of Wales stepped forth before the King,
And, nephew, challenged you to single fight.

HOTSPUR

O, would the quarrel lay upon our heads,
And that no man might draw short breath today
But I and Harry Monmouth! Tell me, tell me,
50   How showed his tasking? Seemed it in contempt?

VERNON

No, by my soul, I never in my life
Did hear a challenge urged more modestly,
Unless a brother should a brother dare
To gentle exercise and proof of arms.
He gave you all the duties of a man,
Trimmed up your praises with a princely tongue,
Spoke your deserving like a chronicle,
Making you ever better than his praise
By still dispraising praise valued with you,
60   And, which became him like a prince indeed,
He made a blushing cital of himself,
And chid his truant youth with such a grace
As if he mastered there a double spirit
Of teaching and of learning instantly.
There did he pause. But let me tell the world –
If he outlive the envy of this day,
England did never owe so sweet a hope

So much misconstrued in his wantonness.

HOTSPUR

Cousin, I think thou art enamourèd
On his follies! Never did I hear   70
Of any prince so wild a liberty.
But be he as he will, yet once ere night
I will embrace him with a soldier's arm,
That he shall shrink under my courtesy.
Arm, arm with speed! And fellows, soldiers, friends,
Better consider what you have to do
Than I that have not well the gift of tongue
Can lift your blood up with persuasion.

Enter a Messenger

FIRST MESSENGER My lord, here are letters for you.

HOTSPUR I cannot read them now.   80

O gentlemen, the time of life is short!
To spend that shortness basely were too long
If life did ride upon a dial's point,
Still ending at the arrival of an hour.
And if we live, we live to tread on kings,
If die, brave death when princes die with us!
Now, for our consciences, the arms are fair
When the intent of bearing them is just.

Enter another Messenger

SECOND MESSENGER

My lord, prepare, the King comes on apace.

HOTSPUR

I thank him that he cuts me from my tale,   90
For I profess not talking. Only this —
Let each man do his best. And here draw I
A sword whose temper I intend to stain
With the best blood that I can meet withal
In the adventure of this perilous day.
Now, Esperance! Percy! and set on!

Sound all the lofty instruments of war,
And by that music let us all embrace,
For, heaven to earth, some of us never shall
100   A second time do such a courtesy.
          Here they embrace, the trumpets sound   Exeunt

V.3   *The King enters with his power. Alarum to the*
              battle. Then enter Douglas, and Sir Walter Blunt,
              disguised as the King

BLUNT
      What is thy name that in the battle thus
      Thou crossest me? What honour dost thou seek
      Upon my head?
DOUGLAS   Know then my name is Douglas,
      And I do haunt thee in the battle thus
      Because some tell me that thou art a king.
BLUNT
      They tell thee true.
DOUGLAS
      The Lord of Stafford dear today hath bought
      Thy likeness, for instead of thee, King Harry,
      This sword hath ended him: so shall it thee
10   Unless thou yield thee as my prisoner.
BLUNT
      I was not born a yielder, thou proud Scot,
      And thou shalt find a king that will revenge
      Lord Stafford's death.
          They fight; Douglas kills Blunt
          Then enter Hotspur
HOTSPUR
      O Douglas, hadst thou fought at Holmedon thus
      I never had triumphed upon a Scot.

DOUGLAS
  All's done, all's won. Here breathless lies the King.
HOTSPUR Where?
DOUGLAS Here.
HOTSPUR
  This, Douglas? No, I know this face full well.
  A gallant knight he was, his name was Blunt,   20
  Semblably furnished like the King himself.
DOUGLAS
  A fool go with thy soul, whither it goes!
  A borrowed title hast thou bought too dear.
  Why didst thou tell me that thou wert a king?
HOTSPUR
  The King hath many marching in his coats.
DOUGLAS
  Now, by my sword, I will kill all his coats!
  I'll murder all his wardrobe, piece by piece,
  Until I meet the King.
HOTSPUR   Up and away!
  Our soldiers stand full fairly for the day.   *Exeunt*
    Alarum. Enter Falstaff alone
FALSTAFF Though I could scape shot-free at London, I   30
  fear the shot here, here's no scoring but upon the pate.
  Soft! Who are you? Sir Walter Blunt — there's honour
  for you! Here's no vanity! I am as hot as molten lead,
  and as heavy too. God keep lead out of me, I need no
  more weight than mine own bowels. I have led my
  ragamuffins where they are peppered. There's not three
  of my hundred-and-fifty left alive — and they are for the
  town's end, to beg during life. But who comes here?
    Enter the Prince
PRINCE HAL
  What, standest thou idle here? Lend me thy sword.
  Many a nobleman lies stark and stiff   40

Under the hoofs of vaunting enemies,
Whose deaths are yet unrevenged. I prithee
Lend me thy sword.

FALSTAFF O Hal, I prithee give me leave to breathe awhile. Turk Gregory never did such deeds in arms as I have done this day. I have paid Percy, I have made him sure.

PRINCE HAL
He is indeed, and living to kill thee.
I prithee lend me thy sword.

50 FALSTAFF Nay, before God, Hal, if Percy be alive thou gets not my sword, but take my pistol if thou wilt.

PRINCE HAL Give it me. What, is it in the case?

FALSTAFF Ay, Hal, 'tis hot, 'tis hot. There's that will sack a city.

The Prince draws it out, and finds it to be a bottle of sack

PRINCE HAL
What, is it a time to jest and dally now?

He throws the bottle at him   *Exit*

FALSTAFF Well, if Percy be alive, I'll pierce him. If he do come in my way, so. If he do not, if I come in his willingly, let him make a carbonado of me. I like not such grinning honour as Sir Walter hath. Give me life, 60 which if I can save, so. If not, honour comes unlooked for, and there's an end.   *Exit*

V.4   *Alarum. Excursions. Enter the King, the Prince, Lord John of Lancaster, Earl of Westmorland*

KING HENRY
I prithee, Harry, withdraw thyself, thou bleedest too much.
Lord John of Lancaster, go you with him.

LANCASTER

  Not I, my lord, unless I did bleed too.

PRINCE HAL

  I beseech your majesty, make up,

  Lest your retirement do amaze your friends.

KING HENRY

  I will do so. My Lord of Westmorland,

  Lead him to his tent.

WESTMORLAND

  Come, my lord, I'll lead you to your tent.

PRINCE HAL

  Lead me, my lord? I do not need your help,

  And God forbid a shallow scratch should drive   10

  The Prince of Wales from such a field as this,

  Where stained nobility lies trodden on,

  And rebels' arms triumph in massacres!

LANCASTER

  We breathe too long: come, cousin Westmorland,

  Our duty this way lies: for God's sake, come.

                    Exeunt Lancaster and Westmorland

PRINCE HAL

  By God, thou hast deceived me, Lancaster,

  I did not think thee lord of such a spirit:

  Before, I loved thee as a brother, John,

  But now I do respect thee as my soul.

KING HENRY

  I saw him hold Lord Percy at the point   20

  With lustier maintenance than I did look for

  Of such an ungrown warrior.

PRINCE HAL   O, this boy

  Lends mettle to us all!   *Exit*

    Enter Douglas

DOUGLAS

  Another king! They grow like Hydra's heads.

I am the Douglas, fatal to all those
That wear those colours on them. What art thou
That counterfeitest the person of a king?

KING HENRY

The King himself, who, Douglas, grieves at heart
So many of his shadows thou hast met,
30   And not the very King. I have two boys
Seek Percy and thyself about the field,
But seeing thou fallest on me so luckily
I will assay thee, and defend thyself.

DOUGLAS

I fear thou art another counterfeit,
And yet, in faith, thou bearest thee like a king –
But mine I am sure thou art, whoe'er thou be,
And thus I win thee.

They fight, the King being in danger; enter
Prince of Wales

PRINCE HAL

Hold up thy head, vile Scot, or thou art like
Never to hold it up again! The spirits
40   Of valiant Shirley, Stafford, Blunt are in my arms.
It is the Prince of Wales that threatens thee,
Who never promiseth but he means to pay.

They fight; Douglas flees

Cheerly, my lord, how fares your grace?
Sir Nicholas Gawsey hath for succour sent,
And so hath Clifton – I'll to Clifton straight.

KING HENRY

Stay and breathe a while.
Thou hast redeemed thy lost opinion,
And showed thou makest some tender of my life
In this fair rescue thou hast brought to me.

PRINCE HAL

50   O God, they did me too much injury

That ever said I hearkened for your death.
If it were so, I might have let alone
The insulting hand of Douglas over you,
Which would have been as speedy in your end
As all the poisonous potions in the world,
And saved the treacherous labour of your son.

KING HENRY

Make up to Clifton, I'll to Sir Nicholas Gawsey. *Exit*
   Enter Hotspur

HOTSPUR

If I mistake not, thou art Harry Monmouth.

PRINCE HAL

Thou speakest as if I would deny my name.

HOTSPUR

My name is Harry Percy.

PRINCE HAL   Why then I see   60
A very valiant rebel of the name.
I am the Prince of Wales, and think not, Percy,
To share with me in glory any more.
Two stars keep not their motion in one sphere,
Nor can one England brook a double reign
Of Harry Percy and the Prince of Wales.

HOTSPUR

Nor shall it, Harry, for the hour is come
To end the one of us; and would to God
Thy name in arms were now as great as mine.

PRINCE HAL

I'll make it greater ere I part from thee,   70
And all the budding honours on thy crest
I'll crop to make a garland for my head.

HOTSPUR

I can no longer brook thy vanities.
   They fight

Enter Falstaff

FALSTAFF Well said, Hal! To it, Hal! Nay, you shall find
    no boy's play here, I can tell you.

    *Enter Douglas; he fighteth with Falstaff, who falls
    down as if he were dead*

                               Exit Douglas

    The Prince mortally wounds Hotspur

HOTSPUR

    O Harry, thou hast robbed me of my youth!
    I better brook the loss of brittle life
    Than those proud titles thou hast won of me.
    They wound my thoughts worse than thy sword my flesh.
80   But thoughts, the slaves of life, and life, time's fool,
    And time, that takes survey of all the world,
    Must have a stop. O, I could prophesy,
    But that the earthy and cold hand of death
    Lies on my tongue. No, Percy, thou art dust,
    And food for –

                                   He dies

PRINCE HAL

    For worms, brave Percy. Fare thee well, great heart!
    Ill-weaved ambition, how much art thou shrunk.
    When that this body did contain a spirit,
    A kingdom for it was too small a bound.
90   But now two paces of the vilest earth
    Is room enough. This earth that bears thee dead
    Bears not alive so stout a gentleman.
    If thou wert sensible of courtesy
    I should not make so dear a show of zeal,
    But let my favours hide thy mangled face,
    And even in thy behalf I'll thank myself
    For doing these fair rites of tenderness.
    Adieu, and take thy praise with thee to heaven!

Thy ignominy sleep with thee in the grave,
But not remembered in thy epitaph.   100

He spieth Falstaff on the ground
What, old acquaintance, could not all this flesh
Keep in a little life? Poor Jack, farewell!
I could have better spared a better man.
O, I should have a heavy miss of thee
If I were much in love with vanity.
Death hath not struck so fat a deer today,
Though many dearer, in this bloody fray.
Embowelled will I see thee by and by,
Till then in blood by noble Percy lie.   *Exit*

Falstaff riseth up

FALSTAFF Embowelled? If thou embowel me today, I'll   110
give you leave to powder me and eat me too tomorrow.
'Sblood, 'twas time to counterfeit, or that hot termagant
Scot had paid me, scot and lot too. Counterfeit? I lie,
I am no counterfeit. To die is to be a counterfeit, for he
is but the counterfeit of a man who hath not the life of
a man. But to counterfeit dying, when a man thereby
liveth, is to be no counterfeit, but the true and perfect
image of life indeed. The better part of valour is discretion, in the which better part I have saved my life.
Zounds, I am afraid of this gunpowder Percy, though he   120
be dead. How if he should counterfeit too and rise? By
my faith, I am afraid he would prove the better counterfeit. Therefore I'll make him sure, yea, and I'll swear I
killed him. Why may not he rise as well as I? Nothing
confutes me but eyes, and nobody sees me. Therefore,
sirrah (*stabbing him*), with a new wound in your thigh,
come you along with me.

He takes up Hotspur on his back
Enter Prince and John of Lancaster

PRINCE HAL
Come, brother John, full bravely hast thou fleshed
Thy maiden sword.

LANCASTER   But soft, whom have we here?
130   Did you not tell me this fat man was dead?

PRINCE HAL
I did, I saw him dead,
Breathless and bleeding on the ground. Art thou alive?
Or is it fantasy that plays upon our eyesight?
I prithee speak, we will not trust our eyes
Without our ears. Thou art not what thou seemest.

FALSTAFF No, that's certain, I am not a double-man. But
if I be not Jack Falstaff, then am I a Jack. There is
Percy!
     He throws the body down
If your father will do me any honour, so. If not, let him
140   kill the next Percy himself. I look to be either earl or
duke, I can assure you.

PRINCE HAL Why, Percy I killed myself, and saw thee
dead.

FALSTAFF Didst thou? Lord, Lord, how this world is
given to lying! I grant you I was down, and out of
breath, and so was he, but we rose both at an instant,
and fought a long hour by Shrewsbury clock. If I may
be believed, so. If not, let them that should reward
valour bear the sin upon their own heads. I'll take it
150   upon my death, I gave him this wound in the thigh. If
the man were alive, and would deny it, zounds, I would
make him eat a piece of my sword.

LANCASTER This is the strangest tale that ever I heard.

PRINCE HAL This is the strangest fellow, brother John.
Come, bring your luggage nobly on your back.
(*Aside to Falstaff*) For my part, if a lie may do thee grace,
I'll gild it with the happiest terms I have.

A retreat is sounded
The trumpet sounds retreat, the day is ours.
Come, brother, let us to the highest of the field,
To see what friends are living, who are dead.   160
            Exeunt Prince of Wales and Lancaster
FALSTAFF I'll follow, as they say, for reward. He that
rewards me, God reward him! If I do grow great, I'll
grow less, for I'll purge, and leave sack, and live
cleanly as a nobleman should do.
                    Exit, bearing off the body

The trumpets sound. Enter the King, Prince of Wales,   V.5
Lord John of Lancaster, Earl of Westmorland, with
Worcester and Vernon prisoners
KING HENRY
Thus ever did rebellion find rebuke.
Ill-spirited Worcester, did not we send grace,
Pardon, and terms of love to all of you?
And wouldst thou turn our offers contrary?
Misuse the tenor of thy kinsman's trust?
Three knights upon our party slain today,
A noble earl, and many a creature else
Had been alive this hour
If like a Christian thou hadst truly borne
Betwixt our armies true intelligence.   10
WORCESTER
What I have done my safety urged me to,
And I embrace this fortune patiently,
Since not to be avoided it falls on me.
KING HENRY
Bear Worcester to the death, and Vernon too.
Other offenders we will pause upon.
                    Exeunt Worcester and Vernon

How goes the field?

PRINCE HAL
The noble Scot, Lord Douglas, when he saw
The fortune of the day quite turned from him,
The noble Percy slain, and all his men
20   Upon the foot of fear, fled with the rest,
And falling from a hill he was so bruised
That the pursuers took him. At my tent
The Douglas is – and I beseech your grace
I may dispose of him.

KING HENRY   With all my heart.

PRINCE HAL
Then, brother John of Lancaster, to you
This honourable bounty shall belong.
Go to the Douglas and deliver him
Up to his pleasure, ransomless and free.
His valours shown upon our crests today
30   Have taught us how to cherish such high deeds,
Even in the bosom of our adversaries.

LANCASTER
I thank your grace for this high courtesy,
Which I shall give away immediately.

KING HENRY
Then this remains, that we divide our power.
You, son John, and my cousin Westmorland,
Towards York shall bend you with your dearest speed
To meet Northumberland and the prelate Scroop,
Who, as we hear, are busily in arms.
Myself and you, son Harry, will towards Wales,
40   To fight with Glendower and the Earl of March.
Rebellion in this land shall lose his sway,
Meeting the check of such another day,
And since this business so fair is done,
Let us not leave till all our own be won.   *Exeunt*

An Account of the Text

When we read a book in a certain edition we expect every copy of that edition to be identical. If a dozen people were each to use a copy of this edition of *Henry IV*, *Part I* for study or in preparing a production of the play, they would rightly expect the same words to appear in the same places in each person's copy. The content of books can change from edition to edition, and that of newspapers invariably does, but sometimes books will go through edition after edition without any changes being made, other than the date of the edition, repeating even errors that are obvious.

This edition of Shakespeare's play differs from versions prepared by other editors. The arrangement of the contents and the editorial comment will be expected to be different, but it may come as a surprise that the words of the play itself are sometimes different from those in other editions. The text given here is similar to that in the edition prepared by A. R. Humphreys in 1960, rather less like that published in 1946 by John Dover Wilson, and quite different from the version printed in the collected edition of Shakespeare's plays published nine years after his death. Some of the changes reflect different approaches to modernization. The 1598 edition prints 'coarse' at IV.1.123 but the Arden editor spells this 'corse', whereas it is fully modernized to 'corpse' in this edition. Some changes are the result of different ways of adapting Elizabethan punctuation to modern needs. Only occasionally is meaning affected in *Henry IV*, *Part I*. All editors find it necessary to change the names of the speakers at II.4.168, 169, 171 and 175 from those given in 1598. Many editors consider that 'Oneyres'

(II.1.77) needs amendment. This kind of variation is not the product of editorial pedantry. Each editor has tried to provide his readers with what Shakespeare intended to be his *First Part of King Henry the Fourth* in a way that will be comprehensible to them. But the editor has then to work out what Shakespeare did intend. *Henry IV, Part I*, like many plays of the period, was published in different versions that might or might not represent its author's intention, and copies of the same edition read differently in places because in Shakespeare's time printing often began before proofs were read.

As our knowledge of Shakespeare's plays, and the ways in which they were printed, has grown, it has become possible, despite many frustrations and uncertainties, to present texts which are believed to be closer to what Shakespeare wrote than those published a decade or a century ago, or even than those published in his own lifetime. This is not as surprising as it might seem, for the texts of works by modern authors are not always printed as they have directed.

Obviously an editor's problem is more difficult when he cannot know at first hand what an author intended. Nowadays most authors have some say in the printing of their work. What they say may not be noted, or the author may have said different things on different occasions so that the resulting editions are not always readily reconcilable, or the author may not have noticed errors made in printing or reproduced from his original.

It cannot be taken for granted that an author saw his work through the press in Shakespeare's day, and it has long been asserted that most dramatists, and Shakespeare especially, had little control over the printing of their work. So inaccurate are even the best early editions of some of Shakespeare's plays that scholars have felt reluctant to believe that such a genius could have been so careless of his reputation. One contemporary of Shakespeare, Thomas Heywood, in an epistle printed with his play *The English Traveller* in 1633, stated that actors were averse to the publication of those of his plays which were still in the repertoire because they 'think it against their peculiar profit to have them come into print'. In the prologue to his delightfully named play, *If You Know Not Me*

You Know Nobody (1637), he maintained that a quarter of a century earlier this play had been pirated (published without authority): 'some by Stenography drew the plot: put it in print: (scarce one word true)'. Evidence of this kind, and our knowledge that the law of copyright did not then protect authors to the extent it does now, have given the impression that dramatists had little control over the publication of their plays.

On the other hand, Thomas Heywood also tells us, in an address to the reader published in 1608 with his play *The Rape of Lucrece*, that some playwrights sold their work twice, first to a company of actors and then to a printer. In recent years close examination of various kinds of evidence, including plays themselves, has shown that more dramatists than was once thought likely read proofs of their plays and sometimes even added material to them for the benefit of their readers. Thus it has been suggested that Shakespeare too might have been more active in the publication of his plays than was once thought.

It seems to me that the printer's copy used for the publication of *Henry IV, Part I* in 1598 was in Shakespeare's handwriting and that he may have slightly revised it for this purpose. There is no evidence that he did more than that.

The first complete version of *Henry IV, Part I* that has come down to us is the first Quarto, of 1598 (Q1). It is called a quarto because the individual sheets used to make up the book were each folded twice to give four leaves (eight pages). In 1867 it was reported that a single sheet of a slightly earlier version had been found in the binding of an Italian grammar published over three hundred years earlier (though obviously bound later). This fragment is called Q0. From the similarity of type used it seems to have been printed by the same printer, Peter Short, as Q1. Q1 has one line more on each page than Q0 and these extra lines made it possible to print Q1 much more economically, saving not only two leaves required for these extra lines but also the paper for the blank leaves that would usually be used with these additional pages. For these and other reasons Q1 is thought to be a reprint of Q0.

Each of the succeeding five Quartos was printed from its predecessor and one cannot take very seriously the claim on the title page of Q2 that it has been 'Newly corrected by

W. Shakespeare'. Then, in 1623, Shakespeare's plays were gathered together and printed in what has come to be called the Folio (F). Later Quartos introduced colloquial contractions, and the Folio introduces, among other things, act divisions, the purging of oaths (in belated accordance with an Act of Parliament passed in 1606), and a very small number of interesting amendments. In addition, 'Bardolph' usually replaced 'Bardol'. The only other text of the period is a handwritten version, the Dering Manuscript, which is made up from both parts of *Henry IV*, evidently for a private performance.

It is known that some literary works were prepared by their authors in different versions on, or for, different occasions. We know that Thomas Middleton, a contemporary of Shakespeare, wrote different versions of his play *A Game at Chess*; these versions, in his own handwriting, have come down to us. Furthermore, these versions coexist – one does not replace the other.

It has recently been argued from evidence of this kind that different versions of words and lines in Shakespeare's plays may be Shakespearian – that though some variant forms result from the errors of scribes or the men who set the type, we ought to take into account the possibility that Shakespeare, like Middleton and others, may have produced more than one 'final' version of his work. If this argument is correct, then an editor has to choose between correct and incorrect readings and also between different authorial versions. When looked at in isolation the choice between these readings may be slight, but cumulatively the effect can be significant. For example, the tone of *Henry IV, Part I* differs quite surprisingly if an editor (or director) chooses colloquial instead of formal readings.

Some editors have considered that when the text for the Folio was prepared, Q5 (upon which it was certainly based) was corrected from the prompt book that had been used in the Globe Theatre. If this were so, it is very surprising that so *few* changes were made. Indeed, all the changes introduced could have been made without reference to any other manuscript. If the prompt book had been used, we should expect amplified stage directions; the supply of those missing (rather than their *omission*); the correction of long-standing errors; and perhaps the restoration of 'fat' at II.2.109, a word omitted in all editions after Qo. It has been argued that Shakespeare would naturally have written colloquially (especially in prose passages) and that a pedantic scribe or compositor was responsible for expanding many colloquialisms. But there is no necessity for even such a line as 'All is one for that' (II.4.150) to be made colloquial, for it is at least as dramatically effective in its context that 'All' should be stressed as it is to say 'All's one for that'. If such pedantry were practised, it is remarkable that so many colloquial contractions were allowed to stand, and even in F there are many places where contractions are not used. Furthermore, these colloquial contractions do not all appear for the first time in F but are introduced gradually, quarto by quarto. It seems more likely that as compositors said lines over to themselves – carrying them in their heads as they set the type – they themselves colloquialized the lines. Contractions, incidentally, require less work to set, and speed is always an attraction to compositors.

As it stands, Q1 does not read like an acting script. It lacks, for example, certain entrances and exits; a few, if unimportant, speech-prefixes are inexact; and there are references to non-existent characters. It is likely that from Shakespeare's manuscript he, or someone else, prepared a version for use as the theatrical prompt book, tidying up details in order to make the play suitable for performance. This copy would be sent to the Master of the Revels, Edmund Tilney, who was required to authorize plays for performance – that is, act as censor. Although the manuscript believed to have been used for the first edition of the play was not entirely suitable for performance as it stood, it was in very much better order than is usually the case in copy of this kind – much better than that used for *Henry IV, Part II* for example.

We are here in the field of conjecture (as is everyone endeavouring to solve this problem), but it may be helpful to imagine what occurred when objections were raised to the use of the name of Oldcastle in *Henry IV, Part I* (see Introduction, pp. xxxv–xxxvi), and perhaps also to the use of the names 'Harvey' and 'Russell' which seem originally to have been

used for 'Bardolph' and 'Peto'. ('Harvey' and 'Russell' survive
in QI at I.2.160.) There existed a prompt-book manuscript
and the manuscript on which it was based. Changes had to
be made in the prompt book at once and this task would, it
seems to me, have been given to the author, who might be
expected to provide alternative names and would be the person
most familiar with the text, and thus most able to make the
necessary changes rapidly. Later, when printing was proposed,
a manuscript would have to be provided. Even if the play
was not then being performed, it is unlikely that the prompt
book would be released, because it would contain the precious
authorization for performance; and, in any case, the text we
have is not prepared for performance. In order to avoid giving
offence by the use of the name 'Oldcastle' it would be necessary to amend the earlier manuscript or to make a copy of
either the manuscript or the prompt book. This work could
have been done by a scribe or by Shakespeare.

A scribe, one imagines, would need the prompt book before
him to see what changes were necessary, and these would be
hard to miss if they stood out like the emendations in the
prompt book of Massinger's *Believe as You List* (which has
come down to us). It is not unreasonable to suggest that if a
scribe had collated this manuscript with the prompt book,
though he would doubtless have made errors, he might have
been expected to make a more thorough job of the entries
and exits than is the case. I imagine, therefore, that Shakespeare
himself made the emendations in his own manuscript and, simultaneously, tidied up most of the speech-prefixes. That is, he
changed chiefly what was obvious (for example, speech-
prefixes) but missed what wasn't, such as the prefix '*Per.*' (Percy)
instead of '*Hot.*' (Hotspur) in IV.1, the reference to Harvey
and Russell at I.2.160, the three speeches attributed to Russell
in II.4 and the entries and exits already lacking.

Thus I believe (for there is no certainty) that the manuscript used in 1598 by Peter Short, the printer, was in
Shakespeare's handwriting and that there is a reasonable likelihood that he revised it slightly for publication; and, furthermore, that no later edition, or the Dering Manuscript, has any
authority, though these versions contain occasional acceptable

guesses. It seems to me improbable that the existence of full and elided expressions represents alternative readings both having Shakespeare's authority.

How far can we rely upon Peter Short's workmanship? There are two emendations that appear in F ('President' – for 'precedent' – at II.4.32 and 'cantle' at III.1.96) and one in the Dering Manuscript ('tristful' at II.4.386) that every editor is grateful for. Some editors make use of more readings from editions published after Q1 than do others, but on the whole Q1 gives the impression of being a very reliable edition. Its printer, Peter Short, was very respectable. He printed Foxe's *Acts and Monuments* for the Company of Stationers, and a number of works by St Augustine, Bede and Thomas à Kempis, by Lodge, Drayton and Garnier; music by Farnaby, Morley and Dowland; Daniel's *Civil Wars* (a source of *Henry IV, Part I*); Meres's *Palladis Tamia* (which quotes a line from *Henry IV, Part I*, though they were published in the same year); as well as two plays with Shakespearian associations, *The Taming of a Shrew* (in two editions) and *The True Tragedy of Richard Duke of York*; and editions of Shakespeare's *Venus and Adonis* and *The Rape of Lucrece*.

In the past decade or so editors have devoted particular attention to what went on in Elizabethan printing-houses. Efforts have been made by a variety of techniques to identify the work and habits of those who set type, the aim being to evolve techniques that are objective and demonstrable in order that the editor's subjective impressions shall not unduly influence his decisions. The application of such techniques to Q1 of *Henry IV, Part I* virtually proves what might be guessed from the publication of a second edition (Q1) within a few months of the first (Q0), and it also reveals an unusual printing procedure.

There are still words in English which may, allowably, be spelt in different ways. In consequence, printing-houses must decide whether, for example, they will favour endings in '-ise' or '-ize', and whether they will spell 'judgement' as 'judgment'. In Elizabethan times spelling was far more variable. In Q1 of *Henry IV, Part I* we have, for example, 'tongue', 'toung' and 'tong'. It is sometimes possible to distinguish between the men who set type by examining the way they spelt. There are many difficulties: some compositors did not stick to preferred spellings; some altered spellings to make words fit the length of line required; sometimes they adopted spellings from the copy they were setting, especially in line-for-line reprints like Q1.

The problem is made difficult, wellnigh impossible indeed, in *Henry IV, Part I* because we have only eight pages of Q0 (too small a sample in this case to make precise discrimination possible) and Q1 reveals a bewildering variation of spellings. In the part we can check, we can see that whoever set Q1 changed 'enough' in Q0 to 'inough' on two occasions; changed 'tongue' to 'toung', 'all' to 'al' – and 'al' to 'all'! Six times -ie endings were changed to -y endings – and six times exactly the opposite change was made. Either one or two men could have set Q1 so far as the evidence of spellings alone is concerned. What is clear is that though spellings were altered, Q1 follows Q0 remarkably faithfully by the standards of Elizabethan dramatic printing. A slight error is corrected ('my' is changed to 'mine') and one word, 'fat' at II.2.109, is erroneously omitted.

Of the other editorial techniques applied, only one produced useful information. At the top of each page of Q1 of *Henry IV, Part I* the play's title is given in the form *The History | of Henry the fourth* (spelt in a variety of ways). It was customary for such 'running heads' to be transferred, after they had been used with one set of type, to another set of pages. Whereas the type for the text had to be broken up to be used again, the type for running heads could be kept standing. In Q1 of *Henry IV, Part I* four pages of type were printed simultaneously on *one side* of a large sheet of paper. This required four running heads – two for *The History* and two for *of Henry the fourth*. After the first four pages had been printed on one side of the large sheet, the four pages that backed on to them had to be printed on the other side. This, when folded twice, gave eight pages of text (four leaves). It was (and is) possible to use the same running heads for both sides of the sheet, but it seems likely that it was more economical of time to arrange two sets of four running heads, each set forming a 'skeleton'. Studies of printed books of the late Elizabethan period have indicated that normal practice was for these skeletons to be used alternately.

It so happens that in Q1 not only are the running heads spelt in different ways but some of the pieces of type can be individually identified and it is thus possible to demonstrate that Q1 uses eight titles, making two distinct skeletons. But, instead of being used alternately, one is used twice, then the other occurs twice, and so on. As the whole point of making up two skeletons is to use them alternately, why did Short's men do this?

In all the other plays Short printed before 1598, whether quartos or octavos, only one skeleton is used for each text. Though the evidence is slight, a single skeleton seems to have been used for the fragment we have of Q0. The effect of using two skeletons in this manner in Q1 is as if *two* compositors had set the type, each one using a single skeleton for the pages he set, and each man setting an alternate eight pages. What we normally expect when two men set type for a quarto is the use of four skeletons (as for *Hamlet* in 1604). The implications are modest but support an editor's reliance on Q0 and Q1.

It will be remembered that Q0 and Q1 do not show as much colloquial elision as later Quartos and F and that it has been agreed by some editors the lack of colloquialism in Q1 was caused by a pedantic compositor. Certainly we can say that Q1 follows Q0 exactly. Furthermore, lines where colloquial elision occurs in later quartos and F, where past forms of verbs are wrongly left unelided, and lines in Q1 which might have been adapted to suit the metre, are evenly distributed between the two men conjectured to have set Q1. We can reasonably assume that what we have in Q1 almost certainly represents the copy provided for these two compositors – that is, Q0. Unfortunately we cannot extract as much information as we should like about Q0 from the fragment that has come down to us. We can but wonder if whoever set the type was as accurate as his colleagues who set Q1, if, indeed, he was not one of them.

That Short took the, for him, unusual step of putting two men to set the type for Q1 confirms what we might guess:

that there was a heavy demand for the play and he was anxious
to publish it quickly. (It is the only play by Shakespeare of
which two editions were published in the same year – and a
third appeared in the following year.) Yet the evidence we
have shows no sign of carelessness or undue haste on the part
of the compositors. It would seem that Short's compositors were
competent craftsmen who followed their copy with care –
much more than can be said for the compositor who set the
greater part of *Henry IV, Part I* in F. Until further evidence
comes to light we must put our trust in the 1598 editions of
Henry IV, Part I, and we may do so, I believe, with some
confidence.

Postscript, 1996

John Jowett and his scrutinizer, Stanley Wells, offer a detailed
analysis of the play in *A Textual Companion* to the Oxford
Shakespeare, ed. Stanley Wells and Gary Taylor (1987). They
agree that Q is derived from a scribal transcript but point to
usages that were not Shakespeare's. I did not rule out the
possibility of Shakespeare being the scribe (p. 114), but I find
their evidence convincing. This edition uses the original names
for Falstaff, Bardolph and Peto – Sir John Oldcastle, Harvey
and Russell. At II.1.77, for 'Oneyres' in Qo, Q1 and F, they
find my reading, 'O-yeas', 'attractive as far as it goes' but it
fails to provide a title and necessitates an unlikely conjectural
spelling. They propose 'Oiezres', which, though a nonce-word,
has in '"Oiez" . . . a recognized spelling variant, and the addition of the suffix "-res" gives both a closer analogy with
"Burgomasters" and a more directly applicable sense' (see note
to II.1.76/689).

A few years after editing this edition I suggested how
printing techniques might have been transferred from Valentine
Simmes's printing-house to Peter Short's, in particular the
use of two-skeleton forme printing used in setting *Henry IV,
Part I*, Q1 ('The Selection and Presentation of Bibliographical
Evidence', *Analytical & Enumerative Bibliography* 1 (1977), pp.
101–36). In 'The Use of Headlines: Peter Short's Shakespearian
Quartos, *1 Henry IV* and *Richard III*', Susan Zimmerman

argued (convincingly, I think) against automatically establishing correlations between compositors and presswork in
general and in Peter Short's house in particular (*The Library*
VI, 7 (1985), pp. 217–55). Fredson Bowers discussed
'Establishing Shakespeare's Text: Poins and Peto in *1 Henry
IV*' in *Studies in Bibliography* 34 (1981), pp. 189–98, and Gilian
West considered '"Titan", "Onyers", and Other Difficulties in
the Text of *1 Henry IV*' in *Shakespeare Quarterly* 34 (1983),
pp. 330–33.

COLLATIONS

The lists that follow are *selective*. Except where a passage has
been relineated for the first time in this edition, relineation
(usually of prose to verse) is not noted; nor are changes in
punctuation, and minor variants that are undisputed. The long
s used in printing the early texts (ſ) is replaced here by modern
s (except where long s affects the reading).

1

The first word or phrase is that given in this edition; the word
or phrase after the square bracket is what is given by Q1, in
its original spelling. Most of the changes are modern forms
of archaic words.

I.1

    4 strands] stronds
    43 corpses] corpes

I.2

    33 moon. As for proof? Now,] moone, as for proofe.
       Now
    136 Who I? Rob? I a thief?] Who I rob, I a thiefe?
       (*Most editors read* Who, I rob? I a thief?)

I.3

    43 corpse] coarse (*and at* IV.1.123)

II.1

    18 Christian] christen

56 Weald] wilde
77 O-yeas] Oneyres (*see Commentary*)

II.2

46 Bardolph, and Peto] *not in* Qo (*see Commentary at* II.2.0)

II.3

94 Kate?] Kate (*see Commentary*)

III.2

59 won] wan

III.3

132 owed] ought

IV.2

3 Sutton Coldfield] Sutton cop-hill

V.3

42 Whose deaths . . . prithee] *taken as verse;* Lend me *follows* preethe *in* Q1.

2

The following readings have been adopted from editions other than Qo and Q1. Only the more interesting changes, and any that could be considered significant from the early Quartos and F, are included. The first word or phrase is that given in this text. It is followed by a square bracket and sometimes the source of the emendation. Usually where no source is named, the emendation is the work of an eighteenth-century editor, e.g. Capell, Theobald, Hanmer or Steevens. The second word or phrase quoted is the reading of Q1 unless a statement to the contrary appears.

I.1

0 *Sir Walter Blunt*] *added from Dering MS*
30 Therefor] *A. R. Humphreys*; Therefore
62 a dear] deere
75–6 In faith, | It is] In faith it is. *spoken by King*

I.2

79 similes] Q5; smiles
80 sweet] sweer (*the error in* Q1 *not noted elsewhere*)
160 Falstaff] Falstalffe (*and frequently*)

Bardolph, Peto] Haruey Rossill (*see An Account of the Text, above*)

I.3

95 tongue for] tongue: for
199 HOTSPUR] Q5; *omitted from Q0 and Q1*
260 granted. (*To Northumberland*) You my lord,]
granted you my Lord.

II.2

12 square] squire
109 fat] *omitted from F and from all early Quartos except Q0*

II.3

50 thee] the
72 A roan] Q3; Roane

II.4

6 bass string] *G. L. Kittredge*; base string
7 Christian] Q5; christen
32 precedent] F (President); present
168 PRINCE HAL] *Prince F; Gad.*
169, 171, 175 GADSHILL] *Gad. F; Ross.* (*See An Account of the Text above*)
240 elf-skin] Q3 (elfskin); elfskin Q1; *many editors emend the reading of Q1 to eel-skin (see Commentary)*
386 tristful] *Dering MS*; trustful
394 yet] Q3; so

III.1

96 cantle] F; scantle

III.3

56 tithe] tight

IV.1

20 I, my lord] I my mind
55 is] F; tis
108 dropped] Q2 (dropt); drop
126 cannot] Q5; can
127 yet] Q5; it

V.2

3 undone] Q5; vnder one

V.3

22 A fool] Ah foole
36 ragamuffins] rag of Muffins

V.4

67 Nor] F; Now
91 thee] the
164 nobleman] Q4; noble man

3

The short list that follows gives a few of the more interesting
readings that have not been adopted in this edition. The Commentary at II.1.77 and II.4.240 might also be consulted in this
connection. The reading of the present text is given first.

I.1

16 allies] all eyes Q4

I.3

233 wasp-stung] waspe-tongue Q2

II.2

34 my] Q0; mine Q1

II.4

122 lime in it] in't *uncorrected* F; lime *corrected* F. *The Folio
compositor missed out the word* lime *when he set this
passage and the result was nonsense. To make sense
(but not quite that of the original) without readjusting
all the type that followed in order to take in an extra
word*, in't *was simply replaced by* lime.

333 O, Glendower] Q2; O Glendower Q1; Owen
Glendower *Dering MS*

III.2

156 intemperance] intemperature F

Claimants to the Throne of England after the Deposition of Richard II

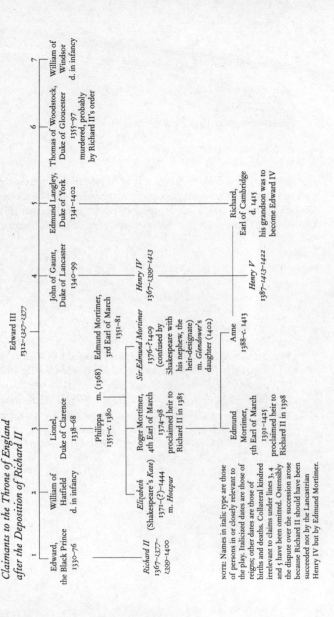

Edward III
1312–1327–1377

1	2	3	4	5	6	7
Edward, the Black Prince 1330–76	William of Hatfield d. in infancy	Lionel, Duke of Clarence 1338–68	John of Gaunt, Duke of Lancaster 1340–99	Edmund Langley, Duke of York 1341–1402	Thomas of Woodstock, Duke of Gloucester 1355–97 murdered, probably by Richard II's order	William of Windsor d. in infancy

Richard II 1367–*1377*–*1399*–1400

Philippa 1355–c. 1380   m. (1368)   Edmund Mortimer, 3rd Earl of March 1351–81

Henry IV 1367–*1399*–*1413*

Richard, Earl of Cambridge d. 1415 his grandson was to become Edward IV

Elizabeth (Shakespeare's *Kate*) 1371–(?)–1444 m. *Hotspur*

Roger Mortimer, 4th Earl of March 1374–98 proclaimed heir to Richard II in 1385

Sir Edmund Mortimer 1376–?1409 (confused by Shakespeare with his nephew, the heir-designate) m. *Glendower's* daughter (1402)

Henry V 1387–*1413*–*1422*

Edmund Mortimer, 5th Earl of March 1391–1425 proclaimed heir to Richard II in 1398

Anne 1388–c. 1413

NOTE: Names in italic type are those of persons in or closely relevant to the play. Italicized dates are those of reigns; other dates are those of births and deaths. Collateral kindred irrelevant to claims under lines 3, 4 and 5 have been omitted. Ostensibly the dispute over the succession arose because Richard II should have been succeeded not by the Lancastrian Henry IV but by Edmund Mortimer.

Commentary

Q1 refers to the first Quarto (1598), Q0 to an earlier fragment and Q2, Q3, etc. to later Quarto texts. F refers to the Folio text of 1623. Biblical references are to the Bishops' Bible (1568), the official English translation of Elizabeth's reign.

I.1

Shakespeare does not give locations for any of the scenes in *Henry IV, Part I* and Q1 is not even divided into scenes and acts. Such divisions, and insistence on places of action, impose a formal and rigid structure which the play does not have. The transition from scene to scene in Elizabethan drama was rapid and informal and many modern productions have, with advantage, adopted a similar method of presenting plays of this period. What we need to know about location in *Henry IV, Part I* is told us in the play itself, either by direct statement — thus we know the robbery takes place at Gad's Hill and that the character Gadshill 'lies tonight in Rochester' (I.2.127–8), indicating the location of II.1 — or, less precisely, by the style of the language. So we can gather as much as we need to know about the situation of the action from the play itself. It has been customary in the past, particularly in the eighteenth century, for editors to obtain possible locations from external sources. Thus III.1 has sometimes been placed in the Archdeacon's House in Bangor, North Wales, because the historian Holinshed records that the 'tripartite indenture' was sealed there by the principal rebels. Such particularity is perhaps more distracting than helpful.

1 *we*: The nation and the King himself.

2 *frighted peace to pant*: Peace, like an animal terrified in the chase, needs to recover strength. The play concerning the deposition of Henry's predecessor, *Richard II*, concluded with the outbreak of civil strife and reports of the unruly behaviour of Henry's son, Prince Hal. These events are recalled in this opening scene.

3 *accents*: Words, discussion.
broils: Battles, warfare.

4 *strands*: Shores, lands.

5–6 *No more the thirsty entrance . . . children's blood*: The fratricidal strife following the deposition of Richard is foretold by Carlisle in *Richard II*, IV.1.115–49, and by Richard himself, III.3.85–100. The King concludes his prophecy with a warning that seems from Henry's statement to have been fulfilled:

> Ten thousand bloody crowns of mothers' sons
> Shall . . . bedew
> Her pastor's grass with faithful English blood.

The idea of the earth as a thirsty mouth may have been suggested to Shakespeare by Genesis 4:11, where the earth is said to have 'opened her mouth to receive thy brother's blood from thy hand'.

6 *daub*: Paint, defile.

7 *trenching*: Cutting, wounding.

8 *flowerets*: It has been customary to indicate elisions by an apostrophe in texts of Shakespeare produced since the eighteenth century. Thus the *flourets* of Q1 has been represented as 'flow'rets'. With the exception of 'e'er' and 'ne'er', which have established for themselves an existence of their own, at least in verse, this practice has not been followed in this edition. A major virtue of the English language is its infinite variety of

stress. It is possible to vary the number of syllables in
the iambic pentameter (a line not originally designed
for the English language) to give a wide range of effects.
This Shakespeare knew and any competent actor can
demonstrate. It has been thought more helpful to a
modern reader to print the words fully and to rely upon
actors and actresses to give the amount of stress and
the degree of elision necessary to the line as required
by the context. (See also note on V.2.32.)

9 *opposèd eyes*: The eyes of conflicting forces. These, after
being likened to meteors, are not thought of simply as
gazing at each other but actually meeting in the *furious
close of civil butchery* (13).

10 *meteors of a troubled heaven*: Shakespeare frequently
relates human action to cosmic harmony and disturb-
ance. Meteors had for Elizabethans something of the
mystery and variable properties that some people nowadays associate with unidentified flying objects of other
kinds. They might be associated with rain, hail, snow,
wind, thunder or lightning, and they suggested the
involvement of other worlds in human affairs. (See also
the note on I.2.195.)

12 *intestine*: Internal.

13 *close*: Engagement.

19 *As far as to the sepulchre of Christ*: At the very end of
Richard II Henry vows to 'make a voyage to the Holy
Land | To wash this blood off from my guilty hand'
for the part he played in Richard's murder. Shakespeare
here recalls that vow but in doing so brings the proposed
crusade forward from the end of Henry's reign, when
plans were made for this expedition, to the early months
of his reign. This strengthens the sense of continua-
tion from the end of Richard's reign, and as line 28 of
this scene reveals, Shakespeare seemed anxious to avoid
there being too great a gap in time between the two
plays, presumably to be able to stress the relationship,
dramatic and historic, of cause and effect.

21 *impressèd*: Conscripted, bound (by his vow).

28 *twelve month old*: Two years had, in fact, elapsed

between Richard's murder in February 1400 and the
battle of Holmedon (see note to 55).

29 *bootless*: Useless.

30 *Therefor*: For that purpose.

31 *Of*: From.

33 *dear expedience*: Cherished and urgent expedition.

34 *hot in question*: Urgently before us, actively debated.

35 *limits of the charge set down*: Many duties and commands
had been assigned.

36 *all athwart*: Across (our purpose), thwartingly.

37 *post*: Messenger.

38 *Mortimer*: There were two Edmund Mortimers: one,
Hotspur's brother-in-law; the other, that Edmund's
nephew. These two men were confused by Shakespeare
(and see also the notes to I.3.79, 83).

40 *irregular and wild Glendower*: The description hardly
accords with the man who, he tells us, *was trained up
in the English court* and was capable of framing *to the
harp* | *Many an English ditty lovely well* (III.1.117–19)!
irregular: As in guerrilla warfare, and possibly also
glancing at Glendower's conduct.

41 *rude*: Uncivilized.

47 *broil*: Quarrel, strife.

52 *Holy-rood day*: Holy-cross day (14 September).

53 *Archibald*: Douglas's full title was Archibald, 4th Earl
of Douglas.

55 *Holmedon*: That is, Humbleton, Northumberland,
though the battle is also known as Homildon Hill. It
took place nearly three months after Mortimer's defeat
but Shakespeare brings the events together for dramatic
effect. (Curiously the Scots were beaten at Nesbit on
the day Mortimer lost to Glendower.)

57 *artillery*: Westmorland means gunpowder artillery (as
indicated by II.3.55), although the artillery actually
employed at the battle was bow and arrow. See
Introduction, p.xxviii.

58 *shape of likelihood*: The way events were shaping.

63 *Sir Walter Blunt*: The news was brought by Nicholas
Merbury, who received a grant of £40 a year for this

service. By assuming Blunt to be the messenger (no
name is given by Holinshed), Shakespeare is able to
draw attention to the King's dependence on Blunt,
which will be of some importance in IV.3 and V.3. (See
also the note to IV.3.30.)

66 *smooth*: Pleasant.

68 *two-and-twenty*: Three-and-twenty according to Holinshed.

69 *Balked in their own blood*: A balk is the ridge left between
two furrows in ploughing. The bodies fell in blood-
stained rows. Cf. the use of *trenching war channel her
fields* at 7.

71 *Mordake*: Murdoch Stewart was the eldest son of
Robert, Duke of Albany, Regent of Scotland. Shakespeare's error stems from a misplaced comma in his
source, Holinshed.

73 *Menteith*: Not a separate individual but one of
Mordake's titles.

75 *A gallant prize*: As we are told that Blunt left the battle
at its climax – the *pride of their contention* (60) – it is
a little odd that he should know the final outcome in
such detail. It is also a little strange that the King should
have spoken of the urgent preparations for an expedition to the Holy Land, though it is now evident he
knew of trouble in the North. At first sight this might
seem like duplicity but, though Hotspur had refused to
give up his prisoners, the King could hardly have
expected that this would lead to civil war. It is the tidings
from Wales, which the King did not know, that cause
him to break off the crusade (as is precisely stated at
47–8). This victory is, then, a gallant prize, securing
rather than threatening the safety of the country (that
is, England, not Great Britain). By 99–101 Percy has
become an excuse for delay.

82 *minion*: Darling.

86–7 *exchanged . . . our children*: Shakespeare frequently makes
radical changes in the ages of his characters. At this
time, Hotspur was thirty-eight, Henry three years
younger, and Hal only fifteen. What is of greater interest

than these minor distortions of fact is the way in which
Shakespeare uses age. He not only makes comparison
frequently between youth and age, but will make some
characters seem to age more rapidly than others. Richard
II was only three months older than Henry IV, yet the
former ages much more rapidly than the latter in *Richard
II*, and Henry seems to age quickly in the year or two
separating that play and *Henry IV, Part I*.

90 *coz*: Cousin (though often used loosely, as here).

91 *The prisoners*: Hotspur was entitled to retain all prisoners except those of the blood royal and it was, therefore, only Mordake who had to be surrendered.

97 *prune*: Preen (a term from falconry).

99 *I have sent for him to answer this*: According to
Holinshed, Hotspur and his father came of their own
accord to Windsor to outface the King. Shakespeare
makes Henry seem to have the power to command their
presence.

106 *out of anger can be utterèd*: Can be said in public in
anger.

I.2

Shakespeare does not state a location for this scene and
it has at various times since the eighteenth century been
placed in an apartment of the Prince's, in the palace,
in a room in a tavern, before a tavern, and in the street.
It has also been suggested that Hal should engage in
some silent stage business as he 'discovers' Falstaff
asleep within the inner stage – a curtained-off recess.
What is much more important than location is that Hal
and Falstaff should be seen and heard together, without
the intervention of their cronies, so that the audience
can gauge the nature of Hal's association with Falstaff

2 *fat-witted*: Thick-witted.

3 *sack*: The precise nature of Falstaff's wine is a matter
of dispute. It was probably a generic term for sweet
white wines such as sherry and canary (which are
confused in response to a cry for sack in a play by
Thomas Heywood and William Rowley called *Fortune
by Land and Sea* (1607–9)).

4–5 *thou hast forgotten . . . truly know*: Time for Falstaff is measured by sack and capons, and as time is thus meaningless to him, he has not asked about what really concerns him.

6 *What a devil hast thou . . . time of the day*: Night is Falstaff's time, not day.

9 *leaping-houses*: Brothels.

10 *flame-coloured taffeta*: Prostitutes were traditionally dressed in red taffeta.

11 *superfluous*: Needlessly concerned, with quibble on the meaning 'self-indulgent'.

14 *go by*: 'Travel by' and 'tell time by'.
   the seven stars: The Pleiades (and possibly an inn sign).

15 *'by Phoebus, he, that wandering knight so fair'*: Possibly a line from a ballad of the time.

17 *grace*: Three meanings are suggested here: refinement; the favour of God – divine grace; majesty. It is given a fourth meaning when Falstaff says, at 20–21, that Hal will not have sufficient grace (before food) as would precede so simple a meal as *an egg and butter*.

22 *roundly*: Plainly (and perhaps referring to Falstaff's girth).

23 *Marry*: This was a very mild oath derived from the name of Christ's mother, Mary; it was of such mildness that when oaths were expunged from F, *Marry* was unaffected. Its force is no more than the exclamatory use of 'why'.

24 *squires of the night's body*: Nobleman's attendants, with a quibble on *night* to give the meaning 'knight', and *body*, 'bawdy'.

25 *thieves of the day's beauty*: The general sense is clear here, but the precise sense a little awkward. Those who work, or rob, at night, waste (rather than steal) the day. Perhaps they may be said to rob the day of its beauty and what it has to offer – its 'booty'.
   Diana's foresters: Diana was goddess of chastity, the moon and hunting. Falstaff's concern is not with chastity, needles to say, but with hunting by moonlight, robbery.

26 *gentlemen of the shade*: An ironic description like that used for a pirate – a gentleman of fortune – derived perhaps from an honourable title such as Gentlemen of the Chamber or Gentlemen-at-Arms.
   minions: Favourites.

27 *of good government*: Orderly, and serving a good ruler.

29 *countenance*: With a quibble on 'face' and 'patronage'.
   steal: Both 'rob' and 'go stealthily'.

30 *it holds well*: The simile is apt.

31 *the moon's men*: It has been suggested that as Queen Elizabeth was frequently described as Diana, this reference might be to her favourites – whose fortunes certainly ebbed and flowed.

35 *Lay by*: A robber's or highwayman's command.

36 *Bring in*: A demand for food and drink.

36–7 *as low an ebb as the foot of the ladder*: For the robber, the ebb and flow of fortune is likened to the low point of his end, the foot of the ladder leading up to the gallows, and the high point of his end, the *ridge*, or crossbar, from which the hangman will launch him into eternity.

41 *Hybla*: Hybla Major, near the modern town of Melilli in Sicily, was famous for its honey in classical times.

41–2 *old lad of the castle*: This is surely a pun on Falstaff's original name, Oldcastle (see Introduction, p. xxxv), and a famous brothel of the time called The Castle.

42–3 *is not a buff jerkin . . . robe of durance*: A *buff jerkin* was a close-fitting, leather jacket worn by soldiers; *durance* means long-wearing. Durance can also mean imprisonment and it is the idea that he might end up in prison that makes Falstaff react as he does. In relating the buff jerkin and durance to the Hostess and Hyblaean honey in this way, Hal is being ironically critical of Falstaff's attitudes. Subtly, here and elsewhere, Shakespeare distinguishes the natures of the two characters one from another, making it clear that the Prince is not wholly involved in the ways of the world he has temporarily adopted.

44 *wag*: Habitual joker. The word is repeated at 58 and

this leads in to Falstaff's request regarding hanging. There is possibly a suggestion here of 'waghalter' – one destined to hang.

45 *quiddities*: Quibbles.

47 *what a pox*: The exclamation is given a particular point by its venereal association with the *Hostess of the tavern*. The prince's exclamation echoes Falstaff's *What a plague* in the preceding line.

49 *called her to a reckoning*: 'Asked for the bill', and also 'demanded that she give an account of herself' (with sexual implications).

59 *resolution*: Enterprise.
   fubbed: Fobbed off, cheated.

60 *old Father Antic the law*: An *Antic* was, in Tudor drama, a clown, and thus Falstaff makes himself ridiculous by speaking of the law in terms which describe himself.

63 *brave*: Fine.

65–6 *thou shalt have the hanging of the thieves*: Falstaff takes this to mean that he will be made hangman, but Hal presumably also implies that Falstaff shall suffer the fate of all thieves in those days, hanging.

68 *jumps*: Agrees.

69 *court*: (1) King's court (as a courtier); (2) courts of justice.

71 *suits*: Preferment at court.

72 *suits*: The condemned man's clothing, to which the executioner was entitled.

73 *no lean wardrobe*: Because there are plenty of hangings.
   'Sblood: God's blood (an oath).

74 *gib cat*: Castrated male cat.
   lugged: Baited.

76 *drone of a Lincolnshire bagpipe*: It is possible that Shakespeare is referring here to the sound of frogs or bitterns, but the word *drone* is particularly inexact for their croaking and booming. It is more likely that he is referring to an early form of bagpipe, which were played throughout England and Europe on festive occasions; certainly in Lincolnshire (there are early references to a Leicestershire bagpipe), and we have references to the

practice in Shakespeare's time (one by the man who probably played Touchstone, Feste and Lear's Fool – Robert Armin). These should not be confused with the better-known Northumbrian bagpipe, which seems to have been developed a little later. Further, it is hardly melancholy and does not have an obtrusive drone. In any case, had Shakespeare heard of this bagpipe he would surely have related it to Hotspur. Another possibility is that Shakespeare had in mind the drone of a long-winded speaker: *bagpipe* is recorded as being used with this meaning in 1603 (cf. windbag).

77 *hare*: The hare was traditionally melancholic, but *hare* here also meant 'whore'.

78 *Moorditch*: A filthy channel between Bishopsgate and Cripplegate, traditionally associated with melancholy – and with, probably, a suggestion of venereal disease.

80 *comparative*: Abusive, one who compares adversely (see also III.2.67).

82 *vanity*: Worldly things (see note to V.3.33).

82–7 *I would to God . . . and in the street too*: Shakespeare has Falstaff imitate a Puritan divine.

82–3 *commodity*: Supply (literally, a means of raising money).

84 *rated*: Scolded, rebuked.

88–9 *for wisdom cries out in the streets and no man regards it*: Proverbs 1:20: 'Wisdom crieth without, and putteth forth her voice in the streets'; and 1:24: 'Because I have called, and ye refused, I have stretched out my hand, and no man regarded.'

90 *damnable iteration*: The devil's capacity to quote the Scriptures.

94 *the wicked*: Again in imitation of the current Puritan jargon.

95 *I must give over this life*: Oldcastle (Falstaff's original name, see Introduction, p. xxxv) was a Lollard (follower of John Wycliffe) and thus a heretic. It is possible that there is an allusion here to the original Oldcastle. It might have been humour of this kind, as much as the name itself, to which Oldcastle's descendants objected.

100 *Zounds*: God's wounds (an oath).

an: If.

101 *baffle*: A knight who perjured himself was baffled, that
is, degraded by being hanged upside down. An effigy,
or the knight's shield, might be used in place of the
knight himself.

104–5 *'Tis no sin . . . vocation*: This text, much favoured by
Elizabethan divines, was one which secular writers took
much delight in perverting.

106 *Gadshill*: In *The Famous Victories of Henry V* (see
Introduction, p. xxxv) the thief is hailed by Derrick in
the second scene as 'Gads Hill': 'Whoop hollo! Now
Gads Hill, knowest thou me?' When he is tried in the
fourth scene 'for setting upon a poor Carrier upon
Gads Hill in Kent, and having beaten and wounded the
said Carrier, and taken his goods from him', he is called
Cutbert Cutter. Shakespeare takes as a proper name the
nickname used in the second scene.

106–7 *set a match*: Planned a robbery.

107 *merit*: Personal quality or good works (more frequently
the latter) which entitle one to reward from God. In
Love's Labour's Lost the Princess maintains that her
beauty 'will be saved by merit' (IV.1.21).

109 *a true*: An honest.

112 *Sack – and Sugar*: To further sweeten sack (see note to
3) was regarded as a sign of advancing years

118 *He will give the devil his due*: The devil's due will be
Falstaff himself – and in this way Falstaff will break
no proverb.

121 *cozening*: Cheating.

124 *Gad's Hill*: This was a place notorious for robberies,
two miles from Rochester in Kent. It is after this place,
where he practised his vocation, that the character
Gadshill is named.

126 *vizards*: Masks.

129 *Eastcheap*: This is the scene for II.4. A tavern in
Eastcheap is referred to in *The Famous Victories of
Henry V* but it is never named by Shakespeare. The
traditional name, the Boar's Head, is, however,
suggested in *Henry IV, Part II* when Hal asks after

Falstaff: 'Doth the old boar feed in the old frank?', and
Bardolph replies: 'At the old place, my lord, in
Eastcheap' (II.2.139–41).

132 *Yedward*: Edward.

134 *chops*: Fat cheeks.

139 *royal*: With a quibble on the meaning 'a coin worth ten
shillings'.
  stand for: (1) Be worth; (2) make a fight for.

150–54 *God give thee the spirit of persuasion . . . want countenance*: Further imitation of Puritan pulpit oratory.

153 *for recreation sake*: For amusement.

154 *the poor abuses . . . countenance*: Some *abuses of the time*
were certainly given *countenance* by Puritans at this
time but they were not those which Falstaff, or
Shakespeare, had in mind as needing attention. Philip
Stubbes's *The Anatomy of Abuses* (1583) was a violent
attack upon the stage. The players were, said Stubbes,
'painted sepulchres' and the plays they presented, did
they not 'maintain bawdry, infinite foolery, and renew
the remembrance of heathen idolatry?' and did they
not 'induce whoredom and uncleanness?'

156 *the latter spring*: Youthful old age.

156–7 *All-hallown summer*: Fine weather about All Saints'
Day (1 November).

173 *habits*: Clothing.

173–4 *appointment*: Accoutrement.

177 *sirrah*: Here *sirrah* is used as a familiar form of 'sir'. It
can be used to imply 'villain', as it is at I.3.116.
  cases of buckram: 'Rough cloth suits', or perhaps 'over-
alls'. Buckram could be stiffened with glue and *case*
suggests that this was so here.
  nonce: Occasion.

178 *immask*: Hide (a word peculiar to Shakespeare).
  noted: Well-known.

179 *hard*: Strong.

184 *incomprehensible*: Infinite, beyond comprehension.

186 *wards*: Postures of defence (a fencing term).

188 *reproof*: Disproof.

190 *tomorrow night*: The meeting at Gad's Hill is to be the

following morning; it is at the tavern in Eastcheap that
they will all meet on the next evening.

193–215 *I know you all ... men think least I will*: This speech is
considered in the Introduction, pp. xxxviii–xxxix.

194 *unyoked humour*: Unbridled inclination.

195 *the sun*: Like the eagle and the lion (see III.3.147), the
sun was a traditional symbol of royalty. When Richard
is forced to obey Henry IV when the latter is still Henry
Bolingbroke, this image, as 'glistering Phaethon', is
brilliantly combined with the physical descent of the
King from the battlements of the castle, where he
stands, to the 'base' court:

> Down, down I come like glistering Phaethon,
> Wanting the manage of unruly jades.
> In the base-court – base-court, where kings grow base
> To come at traitors' calls, and do them grace.
> In the base-court. Come down – down court, down
>   King,
> For night-owls shriek where mounting larks
>   should sing. (*Richard II*, III.3.178–83)

It is noticeable that here Hal is only *imitating* the sun:
he is not actually king yet.

201 *strangle*: Stifle.

205 *accidents*: Incidental occasions.

210 *sullen ground*: Dull background.

215 *Redeeming time*: Making amends for wasted time,
perhaps suggested by Ephesians 5:16; 'Redeeming the
time, because the days are evil.'

1.3

This scene is presumably the meeting of the Council
ordered at I.1.102–3, and in this it accords with
Shakespeare's source, Holinshed.

3 *found me*: Found me so.

5 *be myself*: The precise nature of kingship is frequently
discussed in drama of the Elizabethan and Jacobean
period. A king had two selves: one was human, one
royal (and perhaps divine). Separating these two selves

is dramatized in *Richard II* (and was enacted before an even larger audience at the execution of Charles I). Henry is now resorting to his regal self, *Mighty, and to be feared*, abandoning his humane self, *soft as young down*. The regal Richard is strikingly contrasted with the human being in the opening scenes of *Richard II*.

6   *condition*: Natural disposition.

12–13   *that same greatness . . . make so portly*: The Percys (of which the Earl of Worcester was one) had been largely instrumental in enabling Henry, as Bolingbroke, to regain his lands, and had then supported his usurpation of the throne. In all this, it is Northumberland who plays the major role in *Richard II*. Worcester does not appear (although he is mentioned) and Hotspur's part is small, though he recalls his first meeting with Henry later in this scene (239–50).

   portly: Stately.

18   *moody frontier of a servant brow*: Angry defiance of a subject's frown.

25   *delivered*: Reported.

26   *envy*: Malice.

   misprision: Misunderstanding.

28–68   *My liege . . . high majesty*: The rhythm of Hotspur's speech is particularly varied. The first line has been made a flatter denial than the punctuation of Q1 might suggest. Q1 concludes the line with a comma but the nature of Hotspur's statement demands a stop here. The division of 31–3 is almost imitative of the breathlessness of which Hotspur speaks but this gives way to lines which run on into those that follow. Then, from 48, the rhythm suggests Hotspur's short-temperedness. The three lines beginning with *And* (54, 56, 58) give vent to the force of Hotspur's feelings; there is no pausing as he hastens on from indignity to absurdity.

33   *new reaped*: Freshly barbered.

34   *stubble-land at harvest-home*: His beard was closely clipped, as is fashionable nowadays; not 'unkempt', of course.

37   *pouncet-box*: This was a word of Shakespeare's own for

a small box with a perforated lid. It held snuff, made
possibly of powdered tobacco or, more probably,
aromatic herbs.

40 *Took it in snuff*: (1) Was angry; (2) snuffed it up.

45 *holiday*: Not everyday.
   lady: Lady-like.

46 *questioned me*: Conversed with me.

49 *popinjay*: Parrot, prattler.

50 *grief*: Pain.

55 *God save the mark*: God avert evil! The meaning of *the
   mark* is uncertain; it may be the sign of the cross.

57 *parmacity*: A corruption of spermaceti – a fatty
   substance derived from the head of the sperm whale –
   by association with 'Parma city'.

59 *saltpetre*: Used in the manufacture of gunpowder.

61 *tall*: Valiant.

65 *indirectly*: Without paying him full attention.

67 *Come current*: Be accepted at its face value.

74 *wrong*: Injury.
   impeach: Discredit.

76 *yet*: Emphasized – 'despite all this'.

79 *brother-in-law*: As noted at I.1.38, there were two
   Edmund Mortimers and these Holinshed and Shakespeare confused. Glendower's daughter was married to
   Sir Edmund Mortimer (1376–1409), brother of Roger
   Mortimer, already dead at this time, and Elizabeth,
   whom Hotspur married (though Shakespeare calls
   her Kate – and Holinshed Eleanor). See also the next
   note.

83 *that Earl of March*: This is the reading of the first two
   Quartos. The later Quartos and F read *the* but *that*
   makes the relationship to Mortimer more obvious. As
   mentioned in the preceding note, Shakespeare was
   confused over the relationship of the Mortimers. The
   Earl of March, alive at the time of the play, was the
   son of Roger Mortimer (Hotspur's brother-in-law) but
   he had the same name, Edmund, as his uncle (another
   brother-in-law to Hotspur). This Earl of March was
   not married to Glendower's daughter.

86 *indent*: Bargain.
    fears: 'Things feared', and also, 'cowards'.

91 *revolted*: Rebellious.

96 *mouthèd wounds*: Cf. I.1.5: *the thirsty entrance of this soil*
    and note.

97 *sedgy*: Bordered with reeds and rushes.

99 *confound*: Spend, consume.

100 *changing hardiment*: Each displaying his valour to the
    other.

105 *crisp*: (1) Curled; (2) rippled.
    head: (1) Surface; (2) pressure of water (a head of
    water).

107 *bare*: Beggarly (and perhaps 'bare-faced').
    policy: Expediency.

112 *belie*: Slander.

116 *sirrah*: Used scornfully here; cf. the usage at I.2.177.

119 *kind*: Manner.

123 *if the devil come and roar for them*: This line has been
    likened to the 'roaring devil' of the old morality plays,
    but it is no more than the extravagant reaction we
    might expect to what Hotspur doubtless considers to
    be the King's *bald unjointed chat* (64).

124 *I will after straight*: I'll immediately chase after him.

130 *Want mercy*: Be damned.

135 *cankered*: Rotten to the core.
    Bolingbroke: Henry IV's name – as used in *Richard II*.

136 *Brother, the King hath made your nephew mad*: This is
    an ironic understatement.

140 *brother*: See the notes to 83 and 154.

141 *an eye of death*: The meaning is not quite certain. It
    could mean 'an eye threatening death' but it more prob-
    ably means 'an eye of mortal fear'.

144 *next of blood*: Heir to the throne.

147 *in us*: Done by us.

148 *Irish expedition*: Henry IV (when still Bolingbroke)
    returned to England from his banishment while Richard
    was engaged in suppressing a rebellion in Ireland.

149–50 *From whence he . . . did return . . . murderèd*: North-
    umberland's summary gives little indication of the part

he played in Richard's deposition, particularly the
treacherous interception of Richard in which he was
involved. An Elizabethan audience hearing these words
would not, however, be unmindful of the part he had
played and the way that Shakespeare had dramatized
him in *Richard II*. The audience's sympathies would
not easily be aroused for the Percys, and this must
particularly reflect upon the way in which Hotspur
would be seen, even though his part in the deposition
of Richard was so small.

151–2 *we in the world's wide mouth | Live scandalized*:
Worcester seems to imply that public opinion misjudges
the Percys. This is only true to the extent that Henry
must share the blame, but Shakespeare, in this play, is
subtly insulating Henry from his share in Richard's
deposition (see especially his description of his and
Richard's behaviour in III.2.50–73).

154 *Proclaim my brother*: The heirs proclaimed by Richard
II were the Earls of March (Roger, then Edmund). By
confusing the two Edmunds, Shakespeare took Glendower's prisoner to be Earl of March and rightful heir
to the throne. (The true Earl of March was, in fact,
loyal to Henry IV and Henry V.) See also note to 83.

161 *murderous subornation*: Aiding and abetting murder.

164 *The cords, the ladder, or the hangman rather*: The imagery
used here first suggests means of ascent (*cords, ladder*),
and from this it is an easy leap to *hangman*.

165 *I descend so low*: Carrying on the hanging image,
Hotspur 'drops' his tone.

166 *line*: Degree, and continuing the sense of *cords* at 164.
predicament:(1) Category; (2) the danger in which they
find themselves.

167 *range*: Are classified (according to *line* – degree – and
predicament – category).

171 *gage them both*: Pledge both (the *nobility and power* of
the preceding line).

174 *canker*: The wild- or dog-rose (contrasted with Richard,
the *sweet lovely* [garden] *rose*, 173); and also, both
'canker-worm' (which infects the rose) and 'ulcer'.

181 *disdained*: Disdainful.

187 *quick-conceiving discontents*: Discontented minds ready to catch the meaning.

190–91 *As to o'er-walk . . . footing of a spear*: A reference to a typical peril of medieval romances in which the knight crosses a perilous bridge.

192 *If he fall in . . . or sink, or swim*: A knight falling from such a bridge is doomed, whether he sink or swim.

194 *So*: Provided that.

196 *rouse . . . start*: From cover.

200 *bright honour*: Hotspur's attitude to honour, and how it relates to Prince Hal's, are discussed in the Introduction, pp. xlv–xlviii.

203 *locks*: Hair (but honour with flowing locks is ridiculous).

205 *corrival*: Equal.

206 *out upon . . . fellowship*: Hotspur is selfishly concerned with monopolizing honour – he has no wish to share it. Unless he has it all (both sides of the coin), it will be incomplete so far as he is concerned.

207 *apprehends*: Snatches at.
    figures: Figures of speech, and also, vain imaginings.

208 *form*: True meaning.

213 *if a scot*: If a small amount (a *scot* was a small payment).

214 *You start away*: It is small animals that start – the hare, not the royal lion (the distinction was made at 196).

223 *still*: Continually.

225 *studies*: Pursuits.
    defy: Renounce.

227 *sword-and-buckler*: A *buckler* was a small round shield. Hotspur's implication is that Hal's tastes are plebeian. In Shakespeare's day (though not in the time of Henry IV) the sword and buckler were no longer used by gentlemen, having been replaced by the rapier and dagger.

230 *pot of ale*: This is another reference to the lowliness of Hal's tastes; in theory at least, Elizabethan gentlemen drank wine as, indeed, did Falstaff; see note at I.2.3.

234 *to break into this woman's mood*: This accusation is ironic

in view of Hotspur's objection to the *certain lord* (32)
who talked *so like a waiting-gentlewoman* (54).

237 *pismires*: Ants.

239–46 *In Richard's time . . . You say true*: The colloquial urgency
of Hotspur's search for the name of the place where he
first met Bolingbroke breaks down the metre of the lines
without their completely losing their shape. Hotspur's
animation is skilfully, and attractively, conveyed.

241 *madcap Duke*: Holinshed describes the Duke of York's
love of pleasure rather than business, but this aspect is
not dramatized by Shakespeare in *Richard II*. Hal says
he will be a *madcap* at I.2.140–41 and he is called *madcap*
at IV.1.95.

241 *kept*: Lived, kept up.

244 *Ravenspurgh*: Near Spurn Head, Yorkshire, where
Bolingbroke landed; now covered by the sea.

247 *candy deal*: Sugary amount.

248 *fawning greyhound*: Sweetmeats and treacherous dogs
are frequently associated by Shakespeare – for example,
in *Antony and Cleopatra*:

> The hearts
> That spanieled me at heels, to whom I gave
> Their wishes, do discandy, melt their sweets
> On blossoming Caesar . . . (IV.12.20 23)

251 *cozeners*: Deceivers, with a quibble on 'coz', cousin.

254 *stay*: Await.

257 *the Douglas' son*: The Earl of Fife, mistakenly said to
be Douglas's son (see note to I.1.71).

259 *Which I shall send you written*: In this way Shakespeare
avoids giving details tedious to relate and unnecessary
to his major concerns.

262 *secretly into the bosom creep*: Win the confidence.

264 *True*: Hotspur's interjection, *Of York, is it not*, and the
breaking of the line into three parts, may suggest
urgency, but the effect can also be comic. Worcester's
True: can reveal pained resignation.
bears hard: Takes ill.

265 *brother's death*: The William Scrope, Earl of Wiltshire,
who was executed at Bristol by Bolingbroke in *Richard
II* was a cousin of the Archbishop. The Earl's death is
reported by his brother Sir Stephen Scroop at III.2.142
of that play. The error is Holinshed's. There is a reference to another member of the family in *Henry IV,
Part I* at IV.4.3.

266 *estimation*: Conjecture.

272 *thou still lettest slip*: Once again Northumberland
rebukes his son for his childish impetuosity.

274 *power*: Army.

278 *head*: Army.

279 *even*: Carefully.

282 *pay us home*: 'Pay us out', and perhaps also, 'send us
to eternity'.

288 *suddenly*: At once.

290 *at once*: Altogether.

294 *thrive*: Be successful.

296 *fields*: Battlefields. But if Act II runs straight on, it is
not this applause that Hotspur's plea receives, but a
mighty yawn from the First Carrier!

II.1

This scene is laid in Rochester, Kent, early in the morning.
The language of the scene depicts remarkably vividly
the uncomfortable, rough world of ordinary men and
women. It presents the other side of the merry, irresponsible world of the tavern in Eastcheap.

1 *by the day*: In the morning.

2 *Charles's Wain*: The Plough or Great Bear.

3 *horse*: Plural here.
   packed: Loaded with goods (they are packhorses).

5 *beat*: To soften.
   Cut: A work-horse.

5–6 *put a few flocks in the point*: Stuff wool into the saddle-
bow (for comfort).

6 *jade*: A worn-out horse.
   wrung in the withers: Rubbed or bruised along the ridge
between the shoulder-blades.

7 *out of all cess*: Excessively.

8 *Peas and beans*: Horse-feed.

dank: Damp, making an alliterative jingle with *dog*.

9 *next*: Quickest.

bots: Stomach worms.

10 *house*: Inn.

12–13 *since the price of oats rose*: There were too many poor harvests in the 1590s, resulting in higher prices, for this to be a specific topical allusion, although the price of oats was particularly high in 1596. It is such a passing reference as this that helps suggest another kind of low life than that shown in the tavern in Eastcheap.

15–16 *stung like a tench*: Stung, as by its markings the tench appears to have been, or because it was thought to breed parasites.

17 *By the mass*: A mild oath, but not sufficiently so to save its being expunged from F (see An Account of the Text).

17–18 *there is ne'er a king Christian could be better bit*: There is no Christian king (who might be expected to have the best of things) who could receive more bites.

19 *first cock*: By convention, the first cock-crow occurred at midnight, the second at 3 a.m. and the third an hour before dawn.

21 *jordan*: Chamber-pot.

leak: Urinate.

chimney: Fireplace.

22 *chamber-lye*: Urine. The practice described must have been common for it was specifically condemned by a Tudor physician Andrew Boorde as early as 1542.

loach: The loach, a small, freshwater fish, was thought to breed parasites. The word was also a slang term for a simpleton and this meaning may also be implied.

23 *Come away*: Come along!

26 *razes*: Roots.

Charing Cross: Charing Cross was not at this time a district of London but a village lying between the city and Westminster.

27 *God's body*: Another oath omitted from F.

28–9 *What, Ostler! . . . Canst not hear*: It was the ostler's responsibility to prepare the horses for travellers and to help them on their way. Evidently Robin the Ostler was very much better at this than his successor.

30 *as good deed as drink*: Falstaff uses this proverbial saying in the next scene (II.2.21–2). It is a little clearer as used in *Twelfth Night*:

> SIR ANDREW 'Twere as good a deed as to drink when a man's a-hungry, to challenge him the field and then to break promise with him and make a fool of him. (II.3.122–4)

30–31 *the pate on thee*: Your head.

31 *very*: True.

31–2 *Hast no faith in thee*: Can't you be relied upon?

34 *two o'clock*: That it is four o'clock was established in the very first line of the scene. But this is no oversight on Shakespeare's part. From the first the Carriers are mistrustful of Gadshill. They are not prepared to give him the time of the day, never mind trust him with a lantern. This is an effective, and very economical, juxtaposition of the workaday world of the Carriers and that of Gadshill (and Falstaff).

37 *soft*: Gently, go easy.

40 *Ay, when? Canst tell*: Oh yes, sure. But *when* do you think you'll get it? (The statement is tantamount to a refusal.)

44–5 *Time enough to go to bed with a candle*: The journey from Rochester to Charing Cross – about thirty miles – would be a long day's ride with a packhorse, but the Carrier is being evasive, again, rather than informative.

46 *along with company*: Travel in a group (for safety's sake).

47 *great charge*: Much money (or baggage).

48 *Chamberlain*: Servant in charge of guests' rooms.

49 *At hand, quoth pick-purse*: Ready, said the pickpocket (a popular catchphrase of the time).

52 *giving direction*: 'Supervising (the servants' work)', and also 'planning a robbery'.

labouring: The work of the servants, but also that of the robbers.

52–3 *Thou layest the plot how*: The double meaning here is precisely the same as for *giving direction*. Inn-servants at the time were frequently accused of providing robbers with information about those who stayed at their inns, giving details of what they had that was worth stealing, and whither they were bound and when.

54–5 *It holds current*: It's still true.

55 *that*: What.

franklin: Rich freeholder.

56 *Weald of Kent*: The land lying between the North and South Downs. The spelling of Q1 is *wilde of Kent* but the spelling of the origin of the word (Anglo-Saxon '*weald*', a forest) is the same as the modern spelling and it has been adopted here; *wilde* gives a false impression of the sense.

three hundred marks: £200; a mark was a weight of gold, not a coin.

58 *auditor*: An official of the Exchequer.

61 *presently*: Immediately.

62–3 *Saint Nicholas' clerks*: This was a slang expression meaning 'highwaymen'. St Nicholas was the patron saint of, among others, children, scholars (clerks) and travellers, and the latter came to include robbers as well as those upon whom they preyed. The saint was depicted as holding three balls or purses of gold and it has been suggested that it was these that made him appear to be a patron appropriate to robbers. Various puns explaining the association have also been suggested. Nick can refer to Old Nick (the devil) or, as a verb, to cheating and defrauding. Nicholas also sounds like 'necklace' – the halter destined for robbers who were caught.

63 *I'll give thee this neck*: You can hang me.

68 *fat*: Full-bodied.

70 *Troyans*: Roisterers, good companions, like the *Corinthian* of II.4.11.

72 *the profession*: Of highwayman.

74 *foot-landrakers*: Vagabond footpads.

74–5 *long-staff*: Quarterstaff.

75 *sixpenny strikers*: Footpads who would hold up a man
    for sixpence.

75–6 *mad mustachio purple-hued maltworms*: Roaring,
    bewhiskered, purple-faced drinkers (cf. Falstaff's
    description of Bardolph, III.3.31–47).

77 *great O-yeas*: The word given for *O-yeas* in Q0 and Q1
    is *Oneyres*; the later Quartos and F print *Oneyers*. Many
    attempts have been made to explain this word – to
    suggest either what it means as it stands or what it
    ought to be. The simplest interpretation has been 'one-
    ers' (used by Dickens and still heard colloquially); the
    most ingenious, that it comes from an obscure
    Exchequer term, 'to ony', meaning to mark the abbre-
    viation *o. ni.* (*oneratur, nisi habeat sufficientem exonera-
    tionem*) against a sheriff's name to show he was
    responsible for certain moneys. Emendations suggested
    have included 'Seigniors', 'Moneyers', 'Wan-dyers',
    'one-eyers', 'owners', 'mynheers', 'meyers' and, for the
    whole expression, 'great ones; – yes'. Though the
    simple 'one-ers' seems possible, it is a thin expression
    in such a rich flow of language.

    It is argued in An Account of the Text that the men
    who set the type of Q1 were skilled craftsmen who
    followed their copy. *Oneyres* must have seemed to them
    the word intended (which supports 'one-ers') but it does
    not guarantee that they understood the word they set.
    We can be fairly certain that *Oneyres* closely represents
    what the word looked like in the manuscript and this
    excludes words of quite different outline like
    'Moneyers'. The likely word must have been related to
    Burgomasters in the same line (cf. the preceding *nobility
    and tranquillity*), it must be capable of being used iron-
    ically, and ideally should fit the pattern of wordplay
    that follows. It ought also to be a word Shakespeare
    might have used, although he did create words for a
    single occasion (so 'ony-ers' is possible) and he was
    not always consistent in his wordplay.

    The word that fits these stringent requirements is
    O-yeas. It might well have been spelt by Shakespeare

as it was sounded – 'Owyres'; 'w', of all letters in Elizabethan handwriting, is easily misread as two letters and quite easily as 'ne'. *O-yeas* imitates the 'Oyez!' of the Town Crier (for whom it stands), an office that goes well with that of Burgomaster (the 'o' of which it incidentally echoes). Shakespeare uses *oyes* in *The Merry Wives of Windsor* (V.5.41, rhyming with 'toys') and *Troilus and Cressida* ('On whose bright crest Fame with her loud'st "Oyes" | Cries, "This is he!"', IV.5.142–3), and the expression *great O* (= capital O) is also Shakespearian (cf. *Twelfth Night*, II.5.87–8: 'and thus makes she her great P's'). The *great O* is surely Falstaff (a 'capital' crier if ever there was one). The *great O* of Falstaff (his girth – *such as can hold in*) is as a cipher, signifying nothing (cf. *King Lear*, I.4.188–9). The puns on *strike* and *speak* are given just the right comic tone and point when related to Falstaff and there is an individuality about *O-yeas* which is lacking in 'one-ers'; and it would have had a more obvious and more direct appeal than the obscure 'ony-ers'.

78 *hold in*: This is a multiple pun: (1) keep counsel; (2) stick together; (3) hold fast to the quarry (a hunting term); (4) be held within Falstaff's great girth.
     strike: Rob.
     speak: (Second time) (1) swear; (2) rob

83 *boots*: Booty.

85 *hold out water in foul way*: Remain waterproof, that is, protect you in difficulty.

86 *justice hath liquored her*: The general sense is clear and the pun on *liquored* is plain enough – 'greased' (as were boots in order to keep out water), 'bribed' and 'made drunk'. Gadshill means that he and his companions will be protected from the full rigour of the law – *the commonwealth* (84) – but *justice* ought to be equated with *commonwealth* and although, in the event, Hal intervenes, he is hardly *justice*.

87 *as in a castle*: In complete security (with, perhaps, a reference in the unrevised version to Oldcastle).
     receipt: Recipe.

88 *fern-seed*: Fern-seed was thought to be visible only on St John's Eve (Midsummer's Night). If gathered then, it was thought to confer invisibility on whoever carried it.

93 *our purchase*: What we obtain by robbery.

93, 95 *true, false*: A repetition of the fairly simple kind of wordplay used by the Chamberlain at 66.

96 *'homo' is a common name to all men*: Gadshill is prepared to give his word simply as a man (*homo*), for, whether true or false, all are men. The definition is derived from a Latin grammar by William Lily and John Colet, *Grammatices Rudimenta*, known usually as *Lily's Latin Grammar* or *The Accidence*. It was the grammar that Shakespeare learned from and it is possible that it is referred to in *The Merry Wives of Windsor*; Sir Hugh Evans, at Mistress Page's request, asks William 'some questions in his accidence' (IV.1.16).

98 *muddy*: Dull-witted.

II.2

0 *Enter Prince and Poins*: Qo has here *Enter Prince, Poines, and Peto, &c.* A separate entry is given for Falstaff (as here) after *Stand Close!* The *&c* would imply Bardolph, but if Peto and Bardolph were to enter here it would mean that these two were a party to Poins's plot for, presumably, they would hear him tell the Prince that Falstaff's horse had been removed (1, and Falstaff at 11–12) and they would have to be restrained from answering Falstaff when he called them at 20. While, doubtless, they would be willing parties to such a deception, it would rather spoil the private nature of the joke being practised on Falstaff. Furthermore, in II.4 they seem unaware of what the Prince and Poins have done and their ignorance is essential to the carrying out of the deception. It has sometimes been suggested that *Bardolph* at 49 is a speech-prefix and that the speech given him beginning at 51 ought to be Gadshill's. This is an attractive emendation from Qo, but the case for the change is not strong enough to justify alteration of the Quarto. The stage direction at the beginning of the

scene, as it is printed in Qo, ought, perhaps, to be taken
as a general call for those involved in all the to-ing and
fro-ing that this scene demands, much of which is not
indicated in the original stage directions.

2 *frets like a gummed velvet*: Just as unpiled fabric could
be treated with glue (as noted at I.2.177) so could velvet.
As a result it was more inclined to wear quickly – to
'fret' (here also meaning 'be vexed').

3 *Stand close*: Hide!

12 *square*: A measuring instrument.

13 *break my wind*: Pant breathlessly, with an obscene
quibble.

13–14 *to die a fair death for all this*: To make a good end as a
result of so much suffering.

18 *medicines*: Love potions.

20 *starve*: Die.

21–2 *as good a deed as drink*: See note to II.1.30.
true: Honest.

28 *Whew*: This may represent Falstaff's breathlessness,
but there is comic business to be derived from his
attempting vainly (because out of breath) to respond
to the whistling of the Prince and Poins.

33 *Have you any levers to lift me up again*: Although Falstaff
is unaware of the trick about to be played on him, his
capacity to make a joke of his own size here suggests
to the audience that he too is sharing in the joke. This
has the effect of stressing the playfulness of the action,
robbing it of any pain (or inhibiting sympathy), so that
an audience can enjoy the sport to the full.

34 *bear my own flesh*: Carry my own weight.
afoot: On foot.

36 *colt*: Trick.

42–3 *Hang thyself in thine own heir-apparent garters*: The heir
apparent was a Knight of the Garter and Falstaff has
adapted this honour to the popular riposte: 'He may
hang himself in his own garters.'

43 *peach*: Inform against you (thus saving himself).

44 *ballads*: The ballads to which Falstaff refers are those
which were composed to mark special occasions (a

victory, a murder, an execution) or to libel enemies. They were printed on broadsides (single sheets of paper) and sold in the street. Music was rarely printed with the ballad but an indication was given of a popular tune appropriate (in terms of its measure and rhythm if not its association) to the words of the new ballad. Such ballads were enormously popular and the practice flourished until late in the nineteenth century – until, that is, the rise of popular, cheap newspapers. Some ballads in the nineteenth century sold between two and three million copies. Figures for Shakespeare's time are not available, but from the number of references to such street ballads it is clear that they were comparably popular. A possible source of the pound of flesh story, used by Shakespeare in *The Merchant of Venice*, is 'The Ballad of the Cruelty of Gernutus', although the story appeared elsewhere. Cleopatra fears that 'scald rhymers [will] Ballad us out o'tune' (*Antony and Cleopatra*, V.2.215–16).

45 *is so forward*: Goes so far.

49 *setter*: Informant.

51 *Case ye*: Disguise yourselves.

58 *front*: Confront.

59 *lower*: Lower down.

65 *John of Gaunt*: Falstaff is, of course, very fat; Hal, according to contemporary descriptions, was tall and thin, as the descriptions of him at II.4.240–43 indicate. In *Richard II*, II.1.74, Hal's grandfather, John of Gaunt, plays on his name – 'Old Gaunt indeed, and gaunt in being old' – and this is probably recalled here.

75 *happy man be his dole*: May each man's lot be one of happiness (proverbial).

76 *Every man to his business*: This is another proverbial expression, calling to mind Falstaff's assertion *'Tis no sin for a man to labour in his vocation* (I.2.104–5).

83 *caterpillars*: These parasites are twice referred to in *Richard II*. It is the 'caterpillars of the commonwealth' (II.3.165) who, according to the Gardener, swarm on England's 'wholesome herbs' (III.4.46–7). It has been

pointed out that Falstaff's abuse is all applicable to
himself.

bacon-fed knaves: Andrew Boorde, the Tudor physician
who condemned 'pissing in chimneys' (see notes to
II.1.22), considered bacon to be good for carters and
ploughmen, 'the which be ever labouring in the earth
or dung'.

85 *undone*: Ruined.

87 *gorbellied*: Pot-bellied.

88 *chuffs*: A term of contempt for rich, and perhaps miserly,
men.

your store were here: Your property were in your bellies.

89 *bacons*: Fat men (cf. 'porkers').

90 *grandjurors*: Men of substance who served on grand
juries.

We'll jure ye: When we've finished with you, we shall
have given you reason to serve on a jury. This literary
device is still common. Another good example of its
use by Shakespeare occurs in *Coriolanus*. Referring to
the defeat of Aufidius by Coriolanus, Menenius says:
'I would not have been so fidiused for all the chests in
Corioles' (II.1.125–6).

91 *true*: Honest.

93 *argument*: Subject for discussion.

97 *An*: If.

98 *there's no equity stirring*: There's no justice in the world.

102–8 *Got with much ease . . . I should pity him*: This passage,
like a number of others in the play, is printed as prose
in Q1. Alexander Pope first arranged it as verse in the
eighteenth century and most editors have followed his
practice. It is not always possible to be sure that such
relineation is correct – the passage at V.3.42–3 is usually
regarded as prose though printed in verse in this edition
– and this is particularly true of very short passages.
The problem arises partly from the state of the original copy, where lines might be run one into another,
giving rise to uncertainty in the printing-house, and
partly because a passage of plain blank verse can read
like prose, the rhythm of such verse not being unlike

rather formal English speech. In the case of one dramatist of the period, Philip Massinger, it is not only
possible to read much of his verse as if it were prose
but it has been shown to be possible to print certain
known prose (the preliminaries to a play) as blank verse.

105 *an officer*: A constable.

106 *Away, good Ned! Falstaff sweats to death*: This line reads
awkwardly as verse (see the note to 102–8), although
one should not expect the metre to be rigidly exact. It
has been pointed out, however, that the line would read
normally if the name here were 'Oldcastle' for *Falstaff*
(see Introduction, p. xxxv).

107 *lards*: Drips fat in the form of sweat, bastes.

II.3

Shakespeare gives no location for this scene, and
Warkworth Castle in Northumberland has been
proposed. Various authors have been suggested as the
letter-writer, the likeliest being George Dunbar, third
Earl of March (the Scottish, not the Marches of Wales
with which Mortimer is associated). Dunbar, though a
Scot, fought against his own people at Holmedon, and
then informed on the Percys and fought for Henry IV
at Shrewsbury against Hotspur and Douglas (see 31–2).
He changed sides again some years later, becoming
reconciled with Douglas, and returned to Scotland.
What matters in the play, of course, is Hotspur's reaction to the letter, not its author. An eighteenth-century
critic remarked that 'did not Sir John need breathing-
space' this scene 'might well be spared'.

3 *house*: Family.

6 *barn*: Used contemptuously for the writer's residence.

13 *unsorted*: Unsuitable.

14 *for the counterpoise of*: To weigh against.

17 *hind*: Peasant.

22 *Lord of York*: The Archbishop of York.

30 *pagan*: Lacking faith.

33 *I could divide myself, and go to buffets*: I could split myself
into two parts and fall to blows with myself.

37 *Kate*: Hotspur's wife was called Elizabeth, and Hol-

inshed mistakenly called her Eleanor (the name of the loyal Edmund Mortimer's sister – see note to 1.3.83). The change of name is presumably deliberate and Kate certainly seems to have been a favourite name of Shakespeare's.

39–66 *O my good lord . . . else he loves me not*: This speech, and the discussion that follows, have often been compared with the scene between Brutus and Portia in *Julius Caesar* (II.1.233–309). The similarity of situation, and Shakespeare's capacity to handle his material differently, have been noted. What is so characteristic of this scene is the juxtaposition of playful banter and Lady Percy's deep concern. These qualities are beautifully brought together at 88–103.

43 *stomach*: Appetite.

45 *when thou sittest alone*: A sign of melancholy.

47 *given*: Given away.

48 *thick-eyed*: Dull-sighted.
    curst: Ill-tempered.

51 *manage*: Manège, horsemanship.

53 *retires*: Retreats.

54 *palisadoes*: A defensive point constructed from iron-tipped stakes.
    frontiers: Outworks (of a fortified position).

55 *basilisks*: This was the largest size of cannon, named after a fabulous snake hatched by a reptile from a cock's egg (hence its alternative name, 'cockatrice'); its breath, or a look from it, were said to be fatal. The cannon's shot weighed about 200 lb.
    cannon: Here, a cannon of medium size.
    culverin: This was the smallest size of cannon, named after the French word for an adder. A number of cannons of the Elizabethan period that have come down to us have reptiles sculptured on them and it is possible that this is the source of their names.

57 *currents*: Eddies, movements.
    heady: Impetuous, headstrong.

62 *motions*: (1) Emotions; (2) workings (of the features).

64 *hest*: Behest, command.

65 *heavy*: Weighty.

74 *Esperance*: '*Esperance*' alone, or as '*Esperance ma comforte*', was the Percy motto. It means 'Hope is my reliance'. *Esperance* is used by Hotspur as a battle-cry at V.2.96.

78 *carries you away*: (1) Takes you away; (2) excites, 'transports' you.

81 *A weasel hath not such a deal of spleen*: The *weasel* was thought to be particularly quarrelsome and the *spleen* was thought to be the organ of the body which excited sudden emotion or action and thus irritability and ill-humour.

82 *tossed*: Tossed about.

84 *my brother Mortimer*: For this relationship, see notes to I.3.79, 83 and 154.

85 *his title*: Mortimer's supposed claim to the throne (see I.3.143–4 and notes to I.3.83 and 154).

86 *line*: Strengthen (as with a lining to a garment).

88 *paraquito*: Parrot.

90 *break thy little finger*: A lovers' endearment.

91 *An if*: If.

93–4 *I love thee not . . . Kate?*: The question mark has been added in this edition. Hotspur is more troubled here, about his enterprise, and about his wife, than his childishness in I.3 suggests. Lady Percy's vivid account of his nightmares and his melancholy suggests a character rather different from that described by Hal in the next scene: *he that kills me some six or seven dozen of Scots at a breakfast, washes his hands, and says to his wife, 'Fie upon this quiet life, I want work'* (II.4.101–3). Shakespeare's depiction of this side of Hotspur, so close to Hal's comment, is for a good dramatic purpose. Thus, this is no bold statement of fact to be denied a moment later (as at 102–3). It is the kind of self-questioning that suggests that Hotspur is beginning to be aware of the implications of rebellion. The way in which Kate and Hotspur exchange banter here implies that neither can quite face what they feel will be the outcome of this revolt. This momentary sign of maturity in

Hotspur needs to be set against what often seems to be an unthinking brashness in him.

95 *mammets*: Dolls.

tilt with lips: Kiss (*tilt* has the implication of 'tourney').

97 *pass them current*: Cracked crowns (five-shilling pieces) were not legal tender (*current* coinage).

God's me: God save me! This was an oath which escaped the purging carried out when F was printed (see An Account of the Text).

107 *whereabout*: On what business.

114 *Thou wilt not utter – what thou dost not know*: An ancient witticism that goes back to the Elder Seneca and was popular in Shakespeare's time.

118 *Whither I go . . . you go too*: This echoes closely Ruth's famous promise to Naomi ('whither thou goest, I will go also', Ruth 1:16). It is indicative of a much more serious Hotspur than was revealed in I.3, and it must modify our view of him when he is described by Hal in II.4. Kate, incidentally, has the answer to her question.

120 *of force*: Of necessity.

II.4

This is the meeting planned at I.2.128–9 and traditionally the scene is set at the Boar's Head, Eastcheap (but see the note to I.2.129).

1 *fat*: 'Vat', or, 'stuffy', though a pun seems unlikely.

4 *loggerheads*: Blockheads.

4–5 *amongst three or fourscore hogsheads*: Favoured customers might be invited to drink in the cellar amid the casks.

7 *leash*: Trio.

11 *Jack*: Ill-mannered fellow.

Corinthian: Drinking companion, as *Troyans*, II.1.70.

15 *dyeing scarlet*: The obvious meaning here is that regular drinking results in a red complexion – Bardolph is *the Knight of the Burning Lamp* (III.3.26–7). There may also be a reference to the Elizabethan use of urine as lye in textile processing, to assist in washing wool, for example, and particularly to assist in fixing the colour, to prevent undue running.

15 *breathe in your watering*: This passage has been inter-
preted to mean 'pause in the middle of drinking', at
which there was a cry of *Hem!*, signifying that the
throat should be cleared, and the drink polished off
(*Play it off!*, 16). Eighteenth-century editors offered an
interpretation which Boswell castigated as 'filthy', but
which is surely nearer the truth. It is difficult to believe
that *watering* could be applied to the drinking of sack.
Although there are plenty of references to the iniquity
of those who need to take breath when they drink, none
of these uses 'water' as a synonym for beer or wine.
watering is surely 'urinating' (carrying on the implication of 'dyeing scarlet') and such breathing that evokes
the responses *Hem!* and *Play it off!* is 'breaking wind'.

18 *drink with any tinker in his own language*: Tinkers had
the reputation of being great drinkers and they had
their own slang.

20 *action*: Encounter.

21–2 *pennyworth of sugar*: Dekker, in *The Gull's Horn-book*
(1609), refers to the practice of sweetening wine 'in
two pitiful papers of sugar'. Sugar for this purpose was
sold by tapsters.

23 *underskinker*: Under wine-waiter (to 'skink' is to draw
wine).

25 *Anon, anon, sir*: Coming, sir!

26 *Score*: Chalk up.
bastard: Sweet Spanish wine.
Half-moon: A fancy name for an inn room.

29 *puny*: Inexperienced, a term applied to Oxford freshmen
and new students at the Inns of Court, at one time.

32 *a precedent*: An example (worth imitating). Q1 has
present here but this was changed in F to *President* (the
Elizabethan spelling for 'precedent'). This has been
thought by some editors to suggest that another manuscript written by Shakespeare (or copied from such a
manuscript) was available and was used in the course
of printing F. This change could, however, have been
fairly readily made without the aid of another manuscript and the word is used here because it is a sound

guess, not because it is supposed to have any special authority. (See also An Account of the Text.)

36 *Pomgarnet*: Pomegranate (another fancy name for an inn room).

40 *to serve*: That is, as an apprentice.

41 *five years*: The full term was seven years; Francis will be fourteen to sixteen years of age.

46 *indenture*: Articles of apprenticeship.

48 *books*: Bibles.

49 *I could find in my heart* – : John Dover Wilson has pointed out that the humour of this exchange lies in Francis's hopes of an appointment in the Prince's household – but the frequent interruptions dash these hopes. The interlude also delays Falstaff's entrance and builds up tension in the audience, eager to know what he will say and how he will behave.

67 *rob*: The Vintner by breaking his indenture.

67–9 *leather-jerkin . . . Spanish pouch*: This catalogue describes the Vintner's dress, presumably, but it is reeled off in such a way as to confuse poor Francis, and his wits are further muddled by Hal's next speech.

68 *not-pated*: Crop-headed. *not* is not the common adverb of negation but a word meaning 'crop-headed' even without the addition of *pated*. Although now a dialect word, *not* still can be used for a 'hornless sheep'.

agate-ring: Wearing a seal ring with a carved agate mounted thereon.

puke-stocking: Dark-coloured woollen stockings.

68–9 *caddis-garter*: Coloured tape used for garters by those who could not afford, or would not pay the price of, silk.

69 *Spanish pouch*: Spanish-leather wallet.

71–3 *Why then your brown bastard . . . it cannot come to so much*: This is nonsense uttered in order to mystify Francis even further. The wretched apprentice hardly seems game worthy of Hal.

brown bastard: A particularly sweet Spanish wine.

your white canvas doublet will sully: The implication is, perhaps, stick to your apprenticeship and, in the modern colloquial expression, 'keep your nose clean'.

73 *In Barbary . . . so much*: If Francis runs away, even to
such a far-off place as *Barbary*, it (his *white doublet*) will
not count for much. It was from Barbary (North Africa)
that sugar was imported into England.

88–90 *what cunning match . . . what's the issue*: Poins, whose
trick with Falstaff is more ingenious and more fruitful
of humour than Hal's with Francis, might well ask,
what's the issue? One result has been to put Hal in an
excellent humour. Hal's relish at his joke is not unlike
Hotspur's enjoyment of his turn of words at III.1.54–8.
One rather doubts if Poins will find it a *precedent* (32)
so much worth the repetition.

91–94 *I am now of all humours . . . at midnight*: I am now in
the mood to enjoy any jest, any fancy, that man has
enjoyed since time began.

95 *What's o'clock, Francis*: Hal has just said *this present
twelve o'clock at midnight* (the repetition being designed
to ensure that the audience is aware of the time) and
thus his request to Francis is simply a prolongation of
his *precedent* – his joke with Francis.

100 *parcel of a reckoning*: Items making up a bill.
I am not yet of Percy's mind: It has been suggested that
it is the feverish activity of Francis that calls Hotspur
to Hal's mind, or that Hal contrasts his delight in *all
humours* (91) with what he takes to be the single humour
of Percy – bloodshed – which he proceeds to satirize.
I am not yet of Percy's mind has more than one meaning.
Hal means he is not as is Hotspur (as Hal's father
wishes his son were); that he has not reached the stage
of delighting in bloodshed that Hotspur has; and also,
unwittingly, 'I am not fully aware of all that is in
Hotspur's mind' – as can be seen by comparing Hal's
satire with the perturbation dramatized in II.3. (See
note to II.3.93–4.)

101–7 *he that kills me . . . 'a trifle, a trifle'*: Although it does
not quite accord with the Hotspur we have just seen,
Hal's satire is superb. It has just the right degree of
exaggeration, just the right touches of incongruity such
as the killing of six or seven dozen Scots before break-

fast, and the excellent take-off of Hotspur's trick of delaying an answer (cf. how II.3.93 reverts to Lady Percy's words at 66; and also at IV.1.13). Although we do not have the play of Hotspur and Lady Percy which Hal suggests at 108–9, this brief satire is not at all a bad substitute.

109 *Rivo*: So far, *Rivo* has not been satisfactorily explained. It presumably means 'More wine!' A suggestion that it is derived from the Italian '*riviva*', meaning 'Another toast!', is attractive.

113 *nether-stocks*: Stockings.

116 *Titan*: The sun – Falstaff's red cheeks sunk into his cup of sack.

117 *pitiful-hearted Titan*: The repetition of *Titan* has troubled many editors and it has been suggested that the compositor should have set 'butter' for *Titan*. Although butter melts easily in the sun, *pitiful-hearted* makes a much less satisfactory epithet for 'butter' than it does for *Titan*.

120 *lime*: Added to wine to improve its sparkle.

125 *a shotten herring*: (As thin as) a herring that has shot its roe, yet another food image associated with Falstaff.

127 *God help the while*: God help these times.

128–9 *I would I were a weaver: I could sing psalms*: Weavers had a reputation for singing at their work and, as many were Puritans, they sang psalms. In *Twelfth Night* Sir Toby asks, 'Shall we rouse the night-owl in a catch that will draw three souls out of one weaver?' (II.3.55–7).

131–2 *beat thee out . . . dagger of lath*: A feature of the old morality plays was the Vice, who, equipped with a dagger of lath, or wooden sword, belaboured the devil or fought his associates. Falstaff's likening himself to the Vice is particularly interesting. It suggests the awareness of a character within a play of the part he is playing. An Elizabethan audience would be aware that the end for the Vice was to be beaten away and, occasionally, executed. It is not possible to know whether Shakespeare had this in mind for Falstaff when he wrote *Henry IV, Part I* (but see I.2.193–215); Falstaff is certainly turned away in the second part of the play, however (and in *Henry V* Bardolph will be hanged).

139 *an*: If.

145 *backing*: Supporting.

154 *a thousand pound*: At II.1.56 and II.4.505 the amount is stated to be 300 marks (£200). This is probably just Falstaff's exaggeration, but, in his defence, it could be said that at II.1.58–9 the Chamberlain says the auditor is *one that hath abundance of charge too*.

159 *half-sword*: Shortened swords (as used at close quarters).

162–3 *buckler . . . sword*: See note to I.3.227.

163–4 *ecce signum*: Latin, 'behold the evidence', a popular tag of the time.

165 *of*: On.

167 *sons of darkness*: This may have been suggested by 1 Thessalonians 5:5: 'Ye are all the children of light . . . we are not of the night, neither of darkness.'

168 *PRINCE HAL*: This speech is given to Gadshill in Q1 and the speeches at 169, 171 and 175 to *Ross*. (presumably the Russell who has been expunged from the play and replaced by Peto, as discussed in An Account of the Text). It has been suggested that when it became necessary to remove *Ross*., the speech-prefix for Gadshill was written in once, adjacent to that for the Prince, and that in this way Gadshill was given the Prince's line (and he ought to be forward in asking this question here) while the lines below remained attributed to Russell. (See An Account of the Text.)

174 *an Ebrew Jew*: A Jew of Jews, a very Jew.

187 *paid*: Settled, killed.

189 *horse*: Taken to be stupid, like the ass or donkey.

190 *ward*: Posture of defence.

192 *even*: Just.

195 *afront*: Abreast.
     mainly: With might and main.

196 *I made me*: An archaic dative construction; *me* is not now required.

197 *target*: Shield, larger than the buckler with which Falstaff was equipped.

202 *these hilts*: The hilt was in three parts, so the word could be used in the plural.

210–11 *Their points being broken – | Down fell their hose*: The joke is lost on a modern audience; *points* are not only the sharp ends of swords but were also the laces which fastened stockings (*hose*) to doublet.

212 *I followed me*: See note to 196.

213 *with a thought*: Quick as thought.

218 *Kendal green*: This was a cloth of green, associated with Kendal in Westmorland, worn by foresters, servants and country people. Robin Hood's men were said to wear Kendal green, and Robert Armin, who probably played Touchstone in the first productions of *As You Like It*, wrote in his *A Nest of Ninnies* (1608): 'Truth, in plain attire, is the easier known: let fiction mask in Kendal green', suggesting that it was also a garb worn by thieves.

223 *knotty-pated*: Block-headed (cf. note to 68).

224 *tallow-catch*: This may be a dripping-pan to catch the fat from meat being roasted, or 'keech' (rolled fat used by candle-makers) may be intended by *catch*.

225–6 *Is not the truth the truth*: A proverbial saying.

233 *strappado*: A torture or punishment in which the victim was strung up by the arms and then dropped suddenly, so jerking the arms from their sockets.
racks: An instrument of torture by which the victim was slowly stretched.

235 *reasons*: Pun on 'raisins'.

238 *sanguine coward*: Cowards were proverbially pale – lily-livered – and thus *sanguine coward* is a comic contradiction in terms. *sanguine* describes Falstaff's drink-flushed complexion.

240 *starveling*: Thin, lanky person.
elf-skin: Mere nothing. Q1 reads *elfskin*. Q3, Q4, Q5 and F have *elfskin*, with or without a hyphen, but many editors have thought the word should be 'eel-skin', a word that accords with the ensuing descriptions and was used elsewhere by Shakespeare. It has excellent support, therefore. It has also been suggested that the

word 'elshin' is intended. An 'elsin' is a northern dialect word for a shoemaker's awl – an appropriate description of Hal, but a very obscure word.

There is one curiosity about the way that this word is printed in Q1 that has led to the reading *elf-skin* being chosen here. Almost invariably when a double s was required for Q1 a ligatured long s (ſſ) was used. The difference between ſ and f was minute and mistakes sometimes occurred.

Setting the two letters, ſ and s, required the compositor to make two deliberate choices from his type case. Thus, if 'eel-skin' was intended, he has not mistaken a single letter only, but has made a rather complex sequence of errors – a mistaken letter and a reversal of letters. On the other hand, if *elf-skin* was intended, a very simple and likely error has occurred – ſ has been set instead of f. This was probably the result of faulty distribution: that is, ſ could have been put into the compartment reserved for f in the compositor's case when type previously used was being distributed.

The choice is not an easy one, but as the meaning is sound, it is felt that the implications of the setting of ſ and s should here be taken into account and *elf-skin* selected.

241 *neat's-tongue*: Ox-tongue.

bull's-pizzle: Bull's penis, which when dried was used as a whip.

stock-fish: Dried cod.

243 *standing tuck*: A small rapier standing on its end. A rapier was also said to stand when the blade was no longer resilient.

251 *with a word*: In brief.

258 *starting-hole*: Bolt-hole.

259 *apparent*: Manifest.

261–2 *By the Lord, I knew ye as well as he that made ye*: Although some critics have argued otherwise, Falstaff could not be telling the truth in any literal sense here, but there is a great dramatic truth in what he says (see Introduction, p. xl).

265 *The lion will not touch the true prince*: A belief traceable back to Pliny.

268–9 *thou for a true prince*: That Falstaff, the lion, would not touch Hal proves his legitimacy – and see I.2.138–9, 152–4.

270–71 *Watch tonight, pray tomorrow*: *Watch* means both to keep watch and to revel or carouse. Once again, Falstaff echoes a biblical text – 'Watch, and pray, that ye enter not into temptation' (Matthew 26:41) – and once again Falstaff perverts the meaning. The joke would have been more obvious, to an Elizabethan audience, if Falstaff was called after the Lollard, Oldcastle.

274 *argument*: Plot; some plays were preceded in printed editions with an outline of the plot and this was called The Argument.

276 *no more of that*: The joke is now over.

283–4 *royal man*: A noble (*nobleman*, 280) was worth 6s. 8d. (33p), and a *royal*, ten shillings (50p).

287 *What doth gravity . . . at midnight*: This is a question, in so far as *gravity* implied old age, that Falstaff might have asked of himself.

299 *swear truth out of England*: Swear so fully and so falsely that there would be no place left for truth in England.

302 *tickle our noses with spear-grass*: The nose could be made to bleed easily, and fairly painlessly, by irritating the inside of the nostril with one of a variety of grasses. It was done by beggars at one time; it is still done by children. Derrick, in *The Famous Victories of Henry V*, tells how he did this when a soldier:

> Every day when I went into the field,
> I would take a straw and thrust it into my nose
> And make my nose bleed.

305 *that*: Something.

308 *taken with the manner*: Caught in the act (a legal expression).

309 *fire*: Referring to Bardolph's complexion – as does Falstaff, III.3.26–7.

313 *exhalations*: Fiery meteors.

316 *Hot livers, and cold purses*: Liverishness and an empty purse (the results of drinking).

317 *Choler*: Bardolph maintains he is not to be trifled with.

318 *rightly taken*: (1) Properly understood; (2) justly arrested.

halter: Destined for hanging.

320 *bombast*: (1) Cotton or wool used for padding; (2) high-flown language.

324 *thumb-ring*: Used in sealing documents.

329 *Amamon*: A devil.

bastinado: Beating on the soles of the feet.

330 *made Lucifer cuckold*: Was the reason why horns grew on Lucifer's head.

331 *liegeman*: Subject.

Welsh hook: Pike or bill – having no hilt, forming a cross, it could not be sworn on. See note to II.4.202.

341 *So did he never the sparrow*: Hal's wit is, at times, very like Hotspur's – cf. the latter's response to Glendower's claim that he *can call spirits from the vasty deep. But will they come*, says Hotspur, *when you do call for them?* (III.1.50, 52).

342 *good mettle*: (1) A good spirit (and so no coward); (2) good metal (which does not run).

346 *cuckoo*: To *cuckoo* is to repeat incessantly.

350 *blue-caps*: Scots (in blue bonnets).

361 *spirit*: 'Spirited', and perhaps, 'devil'.

368 *practise an answer*: This is the *play extempore* suggested by Falstaff at 273, but the subject is of Falstaff's choosing. A play is also given in *The Famous Victories of Henry V* in which John Cobbler plays the Lord Chief Justice and Derrick the young Prince.

371 *state*: Chair of state.

374 *leaden*: And therefore useless.

376–7 *an the fire of grace be not quite out of thee*: At I.2.17–18 Falstaff maintains the Prince has none.

379 *in passion*: With deep emotion.

379–80 *in King Cambyses' vein*: After the style of *Cambyses*, Thomas Preston's extravagant but primitive tragedy

(1569). Dr Johnson thought Shakespeare may not have
known the play at first hand (though he seems to parody
its title in *A Midsummer Night's Dream*). Certainly
Shakespeare does not imitate its rhymed fourteeners.
Falstaff begins in an exaggerated style (384 and 386–7),
but with his *Peace, good pint-pot* he quickly relapses
into a form of humour more suitable for him. It is
doubtful if an extended parody of Preston's play was
ever intended. Lyly is a more likely object of parody
and Kyd has been suggested for 386–7.

381 *my leg*: My bow (to introduce myself).

384 *Weep not*: Preston's *Cambyses* has a stage direction
instructing the queen to weep. The Hostess's tears are
of laughter, of course.

385 *holds his countenance*: Keeps a straight face.

386 *tristful*: The reading of all the Quartos and F is *trustful*.
This emendation comes from the Dering Manuscript
(see An Account of the Text) but that does not mean
the reading has special authority: it is simply an excellent conjecture which later editors have been glad to
accept.

388 *harlotry*: Used affectionately, not abusively.

390–91 *tickle-brain*: A cant name at the time for a strong drink.

393–4 *camomile*: The camomile proverbially grew faster the
more it was trodden on. The style parodies Lyly's *Euphues*.

397 *trick*: Characteristic.
foolish: Wanton, roguish.

398 *nether*: Lower.
warrant: Indicate.

400 *pointed at*: Spoken contemptuously.

400–401 *prove a micher, and eat blackberries*: To mitch or
mooch was to play truant, especially to gather blackberries. This passage has also been said to be imitative of Lyly.

402 *son*: A quibble on 'sun', the symbol of royalty; see note
to I.2.195.

405 *ancient writers*: One ancient writer who stated that 'Who
so toucheth pitch, shall be defiled withal' was the author
of Ecclesiasticus (13:1) and another, less ancient, was

Lyly. The joke lies in giving ancient authority for the most common expression.

408   *in passion*: With emotion.

412   *portly*: Stately.
      corpulent: Well-made.

416   *lewdly*: Wickedly.

417–18   *If then the tree may be known . . . as the fruit by the tree*: This was a popular saying. It occurs in Matthew 12:33 and Luke 6:44.

418   *peremptorily*: Decisively.

426   *for a rabbit-sucker, or a poulter's hare*: For (something as slight as) a baby rabbit or a hare hanging in a poulterer's shop.

427   *set*: Seated.

434   *ungracious*: Graceless.

436   *tun*: 'Large barrel', with a quibble on 'ton weight'.

438   *humours*: Secretions, with the implication of 'diseases'.
      bolting-hutch: Sifting-bin for separating bran.

439   *bombard*: Large leather wine-vessel.

440   *cloak-bag*: Portmanteau.
      Manningtree ox: East Anglia was well known for its cattle but not Manningtree specifically. Thomas Heywood, however, in his *An Apology for Actors* (1612), states that 'to this day, in divers places in England, there be towns that hold the privilege of their fairs, and other charters by yearly stage-plays, as at Manningtree in Suffolk, and Kendal in the North, and others'. The reference to fairs suggests that such festivities included the roasting of a whole ox – something that might well have had pleasant associations for actors concerned with the plays – and a sequence of morality terms occurs in the next two lines.

441   *pudding*: Stuffing.

441–2   *Vice . . . Iniquity . . . Ruffian . . . Vanity*: These are all names of characters in morality plays. A *Ruffian* (or ruffin) was a devil. For the *Vice*, see note to 131–2.

444   *cleanly*: Deft.
      cunning: Skilful.

447   *take me with you*: Let me know your meaning.

455–6 *saving your reverence*: A formula excusing possible offence.

459 *Pharaoh's lean kine*: See Genesis 41.

466 *I do, I will*: This key line can be spoken in as many ways as there are actors to play Prince Hal. It marks a major shift in his relationship with Falstaff (see Introduction, p. xli).

468 *watch*: Watchmen, officers to maintain order.

472–3 *the devil rides upon a fiddle-stick*: What the devil's all the fuss (proverbial).

476 *Dost thou hear, Hal*: This first sentence of a puzzling speech can refer to two things: Falstaff's wish to say what he has to say *in the behalf of that Falstaff* (470; his situation being very like that of Francis at the beginning of the scene when Poins kept interrupting – see note to 49); and Falstaff's attempt to get Hal to take the arrival of this *most monstrous watch* (467–8) seriously. As Falstaff tries to get rid of Bardolph and his unwelcome news, it is more likely that he is trying, with some desperation, to hold Hal's attention for just a moment longer. If this is so, it suggests the meaning underlying the obscure lines that follow.

476–8 *Never call a true piece of gold . . . without seeming so*: Many interpretations have been offered of these lines. One possibility, quite different from that suggested here, is that Falstaff is begging not to be given away. Some editors have suggested amending *made* to 'mad'.

The first sentence clearly means do not mistake the genuine for the false. The key word in the second sentence (addressed to Hal) is *essentially*. This occurs in *Hamlet*, III.4.188–9, being opposed to 'craft' (a word associated with *counterfeit*): 'I essentially am not in madness, | But mad in craft.' The opposition in this second line is, again, between the genuine and the false. The whole passage may be explained, however, from within *Henry IV, Part I*, as a whole, and from this scene in particular. Frequently in the play the word *true* occurs. In this scene it is used by Falstaff of Hal and of himself. At 263–9 we have the business of the lion recognizing a *true prince* – and this Hal is, with some emphasis, recognized as being. At 460–65 Falstaff makes his appeal – not comic, but deeply felt – that *true Jack Falstaff* (with many other qualities besides) should not be banished.

It is in these lines that we have the essence of Falstaff's plea. He begs that he will not be regarded as anything but true: and as Hal is a true prince (which, however he behaves, essentially he is), he will not neglect (*banish*, 420) a comrade, for to do so would be the reverse of being true.

This interpretation is in accord with the play as a whole. Hal is seeking his true self and his awareness of this, and ours, is made clear in I.2.193–215, where he compares himself, among other things, to *bright metal on a sullen ground* (210). As *bright metal* he is *essentially made* even if, because his (the sun's) beauty has been smothered from the world, he is *essentially made without seeming so*. (And if the metaphors appear to be mixed in this explication, it might be claimed that gold was thought to be a product of the sun.) See also Hal's answer at III.2.92–3.

481–2 *I deny your major . . . let him enter*: Falstaff has failed to get his message through to Hal – he has been dismissed as *a natural coward without instinct*. He resorts to an involved pun (on *major* and 'mayor' – the *sheriff* being his officer) and attempts to use syllogistic logic to answer Hal – he denies his major premiss. But more important than this involved quibbling is the anticipation this moment has of Falstaff's rejection in *Henry IV, Part II*. Faced with the possibility of arrest, Falstaff retains a certain dignity (which he will soon lose): *If you will deny the sheriff, so; if not, let him enter.*

483 *bringing up*: (1) Upbringing; (2) being summonsed.

485 *arras*: Here, the curtain closing off the inner stage from the main playing area.

492 *hue and cry*: General pursuit.

497 *not here*: This is not strictly 'true'. Falstaff is not in the room because he has hidden behind the arras.

500 *dinner-time*: Dinner was served some time before noon and could last two or three hours.

502 *withal*: In addition.

511 *Paul's*: St Paul's Cathedral.

524 *ob*: Obolus, halfpenny (sometimes modernized in performance).

526 *intolerable*: Exceedingly great.

527 *close*: Safely, secretly.

at more advantage: At a more convenient time.

530 *a charge of foot*: An infantry company.

531 *twelve score*: 240 paces.

532 *advantage*: Interest.

III.1

Shakespeare gives no location but an eighteenth-century editor suggested the Archdeacon's house in Bangor, North Wales, where, according to Holinshed, such a meeting took place.

2 *induction*: Opening scene (of a play).

prosperous hope: Hopes of success.

11 *my nativity . . .* : These portents may have been suggested by those that are reported by Holinshed to have occurred at Mortimer's birth. Holinshed also mentions a blazing star which was seen in 1402 and was said to foretell Glendower's success in battle against Lord Grey; this may have suggested to Shakespeare the idea of associating portents with Glendower's birth.

13 *cressets*: Metal baskets, suspended or carried on poles, into which were put combustible materials, the result, when set alight, being like blazing torches. The word here suggests 'blazing stars', perhaps from the star observed in 1402 (see note to 11).

25 *eruptions*: Outbreaks (as in the eruption of spots in the course of a disease).

25–30 *oft the teeming earth . . . and moss-grown towers*: This explanation of earthquakes goes back to classical times. It is mentioned by Aristotle and Pliny.

teeming: Pregnant, over-full.

beldam: Grandmother (with a suggestion of witchcraft

from the second meaning of *beldam*: hag or witch).

31   *distemperature*: Disorder.

32   *passion*: Agony.
     of: From.

33   *crossings*: Contradictions.

35   *front of heaven*: Sky.

41   *clipped*: Bound.

42   *chides*: Contends with, beats against.

43   *read to*: Lectured.

45   *trace*: Follow.

46   *hold me pace*: Keep up with me.
     deep experiments: Investigations into the depths – the occult.

47   *speaks better Welsh*: The surface meaning is obvious but beneath the compliment is a double insult. To 'speak Welsh' was to speak double-Dutch – nonsense; it was also to brag.

55   *Tell truth, and shame the devil*: Hotspur's delight in his use of this proverbial saying is very clear and rather childlike. His humour in these exchanges is not unlike Hal's in his little game with Francis (II.4).

60   *Three times*: 1400, 1402 and, antedated here, 1405.
     made head: Raised an army.

63   *Bootless*: Unsuccessful.
     weather-beaten: According to Holinshed, 'by mists and tempests sent'.

65   *scapes*: Escapes.

66   *right*: Rights, what we claim.

67   *threefold order taken*: Triple entente.

70   *hitherto*: To this point.

76   *indentures tripartite*: Triple agreement.
     drawn: Drawn up.

77   *sealed interchangeably*: So that each party to the agreement has a copy signed by the other two.

78   *this night may execute*: May be done this evening.

83   *father*: Father-in-law.

88   *in my conduct*: Escorted by me, in my care.

92   *Methinks my moiety*: When Hal imitated Hotspur, he parodied this habit his rival had of delaying his

response (II.4.106–7).

moiety: Share (not necessarily a half).

Burton: On the river Trent.

94 *cranking*: Winding.

96 *cantle*: All the Quartos print *scantle*, which means a small portion. F has *cantle*, a segment. F's emendation has generally been accepted. *scantle* may have been the result of the final letter of *monstrous* being attracted to *cantle* as the compositor said the line to himself as he set it in type.

98 *smug*: Smooth.

101 *bottom*: Valley.

106 *Gelding*: Cutting.

continent: Bank (that which contains).

111 *charge*: Expenditure.

120 *gave the tongue a helpful ornament*: Glendower quibbles. When he sang *an English ditty*, he graced it with a delightful accent (a defence of his Welsh), set it to music (*framèd to the harp*), and gave to the English language (*tongue*) something of literary worth (*a helpful ornament*) – achievements Hotspur could not claim.

124 *metre*: Metrical, doggerel.

125 *canstick*: Candlestick.

128 *mincing*: Affected (poetic) feet.

131 *I do not care*: Hotspur may seem capricious, but his attitudes, though they change rapidly, are not unbecoming to him by Elizabethan standards. He is at one and the same time quixotically generous and determined to maintain his rights (as he understands them).

138 *Break with*: Break the news to.

142–3 *Sometime he angers me | With telling me*: It is a trifle ironic that Hotspur, so free with his views, should complain of Glendower's capacity for talking. As events prove, however, Hotspur's talking is supported by his actions whereas Glendower is *o'er-ruled by prophecies* (IV.4.18). It is noteworthy that Hotspur, on hearing the news that Glendower has failed them, wastes no breath in bemoaning his absence (IV.1.130–34).

143 *moldwarp*: Mole.

144 *Merlin*: Wizard or prophet at King Arthur's court.

147 *couching, ramping*: Parodic forms of heraldic terms: couchant – lying; rampant – rearing.

148 *skimble-skamble*: Nonsense (a word coined by Shakespeare).

149 *faith*: Faith in Christ.

152 *'Hum', and 'Well, go to'*: Simulating interest when bored.

156 *windmill*: Because noisy and unsteady.

157 *cates*: Delicacies.

160–61 *profited | In strange concealments*: Proficient in secret arts (cf. 46).

171 *wilful-blame*: Wilfully blameworthy.

175 *blood*: Spirit.

176 *dearest*: Noblest.
    grace: Credit.

177 *present*: Show.

178 *want of government*: Lack of self-control.

179 *opinion*: Conceit.

183 *Beguiling*: Cheating, defrauding.

184 *good manners be your speed*: May it be good manners that gives you success (in battle). In view of the way in which Worcester beguiles Hotspur by not revealing *The liberal and kind offer of the King* (V.2.2), this is rather an ironic exchange.

185 *and*: In Elizabethan English *and* could connect an affirmation and a command. Another instance occurs at V.4.33.

190 *my aunt Percy*: The Mortimer who was Glendower's son-in-law was Lady Percy's brother; the Mortimer who was proclaimed heir to the throne was Lady Percy's nephew – but he did not marry Glendower's daughter. The family relationship is described in notes to I.3.79 and 83.

191 *Glendower speaks to her in Welsh*: It has been suggested that when the play was first performed, a Welsh singing boy was available to Shakespeare's company.

193 *harlotry*: As at II.4.388, *harlotry* is not used here to imply prostitution. It is intended affectionately, if

slightly deprecatingly, as if to say Glendower's daughter is a silly little wretch, a misery.

195 *swelling heavens*: Eyes filled with tears.

196 *I am too perfect in*: I understand only too well.

197 *should I answer thee*: Answer by weeping also – were
it not shameful.

199 *feeling disputation*: Dialogue of feelings (not speech).

202 *highly penned*: High-flown.

204 *division*: A rapid passage of short notes based on a
simple theme.

207 *wanton rushes*: Rushes covered the floor (and also the
stage in all probability), and these have been spread
wantonly – without restraint.

210 *crown*: Give absolute power to.

214 *heavenly-harnessed team*: The sun (from the team of
horses driven by Helios, the sun god).

217 *book*: Indentures tripartite (mentioned at 76).

218–19 *those musicians . . . thousand leagues from hence*: The
musicians who are to provide the music are spirits, like
those which Prospero requires to give 'Some heavenly
music' (*The Tempest*, V.1.52).

221 *thou art perfect in lying down*: With sexual innuendo.

225 *he is so humorous*: The punctuation of Q1 at the end of
224 and 225 (given in this text) does not make it clear
whether the devil (*he*) is humorous because he speaks
Welsh (a comical language to learn, in Hotspur's
opinion), or because of the association of humour and
music with the devil (cf. II.4.472–3: *the devil rides upon
a fiddle-stick*). Q6 (1622) made the matter clear by punc-
tuating with a full stop after *Welsh* (224). This is attractive (though that Quarto has no special authority) as
an emendation, but it has not been used here because,
whether intended or not, the punctuation given us in
Q1 suggests the way Hotspur's mind moves from one
association to another. Lady Percy, it will be noted,
takes up the association of *humorous* and *musician*,
punning on the first word to give *humours* – whims (see
note to IV.1.31).

229 *Lie still . . . sing in Welsh*: This banter delightfully

expresses Lady Percy's love for her husband (see also
the note to II.3.93–4).

230 *brach*: Properly, this is a hound that hunts by scent;
loosely it means a 'bitch', and is used as a term of
abuse. Hotspur is surely using a word that has all the
appearance of being Welsh (though it is not) as a kind
of joke – a rather more subtle one than he usually
makes. The phrase 'the Lady Brach' occurs in *King
Lear* (I.4.111), and 'brach' within a list of dogs at III.6.68
in that same play.

233 *still*: Silent.

234 *'tis a woman's fault*: To be unable to remain quiet or
still.

241–2 *you swear like a comfit-maker's wife*: Just as Hal parodied Hotspur in II.4, so now Hotspur mimics his wife.
comfits were sugar-plums – crystallized fruits.

243 *mend*: Amend.

245 *sarcenet*: (Light as) silk.

246 *Finsbury*: In Shakespeare's day, a favourite walk and
place of recreation was Finsbury Fields. It was the sort
of entertainment enjoyed by sober citizens – or so it is
implied. The joke is not so much at Lady Percy's
expense (though it fits the context well enough if one
allows for the anachronism), as an allusion for the
enjoyment of the audience for whom it would be local
and topical. This is an example of a character stepping
out of his role, though not to the same extent as Falstaff
does in recounting the events at Gad's Hill.

247 *a lady*: An aristocrat (a plebeian concept, surely, and
hardly appropriate to Hotspur).

249 *protest*: Protestation.
pepper-gingerbread: The precise meaning is not clear –
perhaps 'mealy-mouthed' with a touch of pepper, a
touch of 'acid', is the nearest equivalent. Whatever the
exact meaning, Hotspur's protest comes across vividly.

250 *velvet-guards*: Velvet trimmings, that is, those who wear
them – citizens in their finery.

253–4 *'Tis the next way to turn tailor ... teacher*: Hotspur offers
mock encouragement, realizing Lady Percy will not

sing: 'It's the best way to fit yourself to be a tailor, or to become a teacher of robins.' Tailors, like weavers (see II.4.128–9) and robins, were held to be good singers.

258 *By this*: By this time.
book: Agreement.
but: Just.

III.2

1 *give us leave*: Leave to be alone.
6 *doom*: Judgement.
8 *passages*: Events, incidents.
9–11 *thou art only marked . . . my mistreadings*: The meaning here is ambiguous. The passage can mean that Hal will suffer for Henry's sins (Richard's deposition) or that Henry is already being punished for his sins by the manner of Hal's behaviour. The second meaning is probably intended. There seems no justification on this occasion for arguing that both meanings are meant.
12 *inordinate*: (1) Immoderate; (2) out of order (unworthy of your high rank).
13 *bare*: Wretched.
lewd: Base.
attempts: Exploits.
14 *rude*: Uncivilized.
15 *withal*: With (also at 21).
17 *hold their level with*: Put themselves on a level with.
19 *Quit*: Acquit myself of.
20 *doubtless*: Certain.
22 *extenuation*: Mitigation.
23 *many tales devised*: Much malicious gossip.
25 *pickthanks*: Talebearers (the word is derived from Holinshed).
28 *Find pardon on my true submission*: Hal asks forgiveness for what he has truly done especially as he is guiltless of many things said against him.
30 *affections*: Inclinations.
hold a wing: Take a course (a term from falconry).
31 *from*: Away from.
32 *rudely lost*: Shakespeare omits the reason here, although

it is mentioned in all the sources, including *The Famous Victories of Henry V*, and by Falstaff in *Henry IV, Part II* when he says to the Lord Chief Justice, 'For the box of the ear that the Prince gave you, he gave it like a rude prince, and you took it like a sensible lord' (I.2.195–7). It is noticeable that 'rude' (uncivilized) is used on each occasion.

39 *Had I so lavish of my presence been*: It was not thought proper for a king to show himself over-frequently to his people.

40 *common-hackneyed*: One part of this word duplicates the other; in combination the result is forceful and individual. Henry's account of his behaviour does not tally with that given by Richard in *Richard II* where, with a variety of detail, he is said to court the common people, seeming 'to dive into their hearts | With humble and familiar courtesy' (I.4.25–6).

43 *possession*: The possessor (King Richard).

45 *likelihood*: Likelihood of having a future.

50 *I stole all courtesy from heaven*: I assumed a divine graciousness. The word *stole* is not without significance. Although Henry is being shown in a favourable light here, he did steal Richard's throne.

54 *Even in the presence of the crownèd King*: The allusion is probably to the entry of Bolingbroke (Henry) and Richard into London, described in *Richard II*, V.2, by York.

56 *pontifical*: As worn by a Pope or bishop.

60 *skipping*: Frivolous. Richard's faults are, not surprisingly, exaggerated by Henry.

61 *rash*: Quickly lighted.
   bavin: Faggot used for kindling (and soon burnt out).

62 *carded his state*: To 'card' wool is to tease out impurities and to straighten the fibres by means of a comb-like device. It is not, as has sometimes been suggested, a process in which various qualities of fibre are mixed (hence implying that the King debased himself by associating with inferiors), but essentially a cleansing and straightening process. Carding of the mixing kind was

used for shuffling cards, but as this fault is described in the line that follows (*Mingled his royalty with capering fools*), there is no need to repeat it. The word *carded* here means, surely, 'tortured' – tore at, or scratched, his state – a form of torture practised in the period. The textile association of *carded* presumably led Shakespeare to think of mingling. (Another textile processing term is used at III.2.137 – *scour*.)

65 *countenance*: Authority.
   against his name: That is, to the detriment of his reputation.
66 *push*: Pushing and shoving.
67 *comparative*: Dealer in insults (see also I.2.80).
69 *Enfeoffed*: Surrendered.
   popularity: The common people.
77 *community*: Familiarity.
79 *sun-like majesty*: The sun is a traditional symbol of royalty (see note to I.2.195). Its association here with *cloudy men* (83), hostile to the sun, is similar to the association of the sun with *the base contagious clouds* at I.2.196.
87 *vile participation*: Low companions.
91 *foolish tenderness*: Tears.
94 *As thou art to this hour was Richard*: The King's likening of Prince Hal to Richard II, and Hotspur to himself, are the most telling lines in his long rebuke to his son (see Introduction, p. xliv–xlv).
97 *to boot*: As well.
98 *worthy interest*: Right by worth.
100 *colour*: Semblance.
101 *harness*: Armed men.
102 *Turns head*: (1) Turns his eyes; (2) turns the army he has raised.
103 *And being no more in debt to years than thou*: Hotspur was actually older than Henry IV, Hal's father (see note to I.1.86–7).
109 *chief majority*: Pre-eminence.
112 *Thrice*: The battles were Otterburn (at which the English were defeated and Hotspur was captured; Hal was then

aged one), Nesbit and Holmedon (see note to I.1.55).
Douglas's father was killed by Hotspur at Otterburn.

116 *To fill . . . up*: To increase, to enlarge.

120 *Capitulate*: Sign agreements.

are up: Up in arms.

123 *dearest*: The first meaning is 'most precious' but there
is also a pun on *dearest* \ 'direst'.

124 *vassal*: Base, abject.

125 *start of spleen*: Fit of pique.

126 *To fight against me under Percy's pay*: This very serious
charge had no foundation at the time but it is possible
that Shakespeare had in mind a reported usurpation of
the crown by Hal in 1412, a decade later. There is a
dramatic moment in *Henry IV, Part II* when Hal,
believing his father to be dead, puts the crown on his
head, only to be bitterly rebuked by Henry:

> I stay too long by thee, I weary thee.
> Dost thou so hunger for mine empty chair
> That thou wilt needs invest thee with my honours
> Before thy hour be ripe? (IV.5.94–7)

See also V.4.50–56 of this play.

136 *favours*: Features.

141 *unthought-of*: Poorly thought of, despised.

147 *factor*: Agent.

151 *worship of his time*: Honour of his lifetime.

156 *intemperance*: Wild behaviour. F substitutes *intemperature*, which is an attractive reading (for it means
both 'licentiousness' and 'distempered condition') but,
as is argued in An Account of the Text, has no
authority.

159 *parcel*: Portion.

161 *charge*: A command.

sovereign trust: (1) A most important command; (2) the
King's wholehearted trust.

164 *Lord Mortimer of Scotland*: This is yet another, but a
different, confusion concerning the Mortimers, who
were Lords of the Welsh Marches (or Borders). George

Dunbar was Earl of the Scottish Marches (see note
introducing II.3).

167 *head*: Army.

172 *advertisement*: News.

175–6 *Harry . . . through Gloucestershire*: This would require
a journey by a secondary route. Shakespeare, or Hal,
forgets this plan, for Hal meets Falstaff in IV.2 near
Coventry on the main Shrewsbury road.

177 *Our business valued*: Our affairs put in order.

180 *him*: Himself.

III.3

As the Hostess enters after line 50, we are evidently in
the tavern in Eastcheap.

2 *last action*: At Gad's Hill, or possibly the engagement
with Hal in II.4.

bate: Lose weight.

4 *old apple-john*: A kind of apple noted for its long-
keeping qualities. Although the flesh remained sound,
the skin shrivelled.

5 *suddenly*: At once.

am in some liking: (1) Feel like doing so; (2) still have
some flesh on me.

5–6 *out of heart*: (1) Dispirited; (2) in poor condition.

6 *no strength*: Of body, and, of purpose.

7 *An*: If.

8 *peppercorn*: Mere nothing (as in 'a peppercorn rent').

brewer's horse: notoriously worn out.

11 *fretful*: (1) Anxious; (2) fretted (worn).

13 *there is it*: There it is.

18–19 *in good compass*: Within bounds.

19–20 *out of all compass*: With a glance at his girth.

25 *admiral*: Flagship.

27 *Knight of the Burning Lamp*: A parody of Amadis,
Knight of the Burning Sword, a chivalric figure.
Beaumont parodies him in his *The Knight of the Burning
Pestle* (1607–8).

29–30 *as good use of it . . . death's-head*: This seems to be
ambiguous, perhaps deliberately so. Rings were
engraved with a skull and these served as a reminder

of death (memento mori). But they were regularly worn
by prostitutes, of which many a man makes use.

31 *Dives*: The rich man who feasted while Lazarus starved
(Luke 16); see also IV.2.24.

35 *God's angel*: The allusion is probably to the story of
Moses and the Burning Bush in which, it is said, 'the
angel of the Lord appeared unto him in a flame of fire'
(Exodus 3:2).

given over: Given over to Satan.

39 *ignis fatuus*: Latin, fool's fire, will-o'-the-wisp.

ball of wildfire: Firework (and possibly, erysipelas – a
skin disease).

40 *purchase*: Value.

triumph: Illumination for a festival.

42 *links*: Small flaming torches.

44 *drunk me*: An archaic construction; modern English
does not require *me*.

44–5 *good cheap*: Cheaply.

46 *salamander*: Fabulous lizard that lives in and on fire.

48 *I would my face were in your belly*: Proverbial retort.

51 *dame Partlet*: A traditional name for a hen, and so a
fussy woman. 'Pertelote' is the name of the hen in
Chaucer's *Nun's Priest's Tale*.

58 *shaved*: In addition to its usual meaning, *shaved* could
mean 'cheated' and 'to have caught syphilis' (which
was believed to lead to baldness).

60 *you are a woman*: And thus unreliable if not untrust-
worthy.

68 *Dowlas*: Cheap linen from Doulas in Brittany.

69 *bolters*: Cloths used for sieving.

70 *holland*: Fine linen, and rather over-priced at eight
shillings an ell.

71 *ell*: In England, 45 inches.

72 *by-drinkings*: Drinks between meals.

78 *denier*: One-tenth of a penny.

79 *younker*: An alternative name for the prodigal in the
parable of the prodigal son was 'the younger'.

81 *forty mark*: About £27, approximately eighteen months'
pay for a skilled craftsman in London, if fully employed.

84 *Jack*: Knave.

86 *playing upon his truncheon like a fife*: Presumably when Falstaff says at 85 that he would *cudgel* Hal, he imitates the action. When Hal enters, Falstaff rapidly and comically changes his stage business to meet the new situation.

87 *door*: Quarter.

89 *Newgate fashion*: Two by two (as prisoners).

111–12 *stewed prune*: Prostitute.

112 *drawn fox*: The meaning is not clear; perhaps the joke has been lost to us. It has been explained as a fox drawn from cover and so relying upon cunning for its life; a disembowelled fox; a dead fox used to give a false trail; and a drawn sword (so named because of the figure of a wolf engraved on the blade which was mistaken for a fox).

113–14 *Maid Marian . . . ward to thee*: The *deputy* of a *ward* was a highly respectable citizen, and his *wife* was expected to be so also. *Maid Marian*'s reputation was very low, however, and thus Falstaff says that compared to the Hostess, Maid Marian was a highly respectable woman.

116 *What thing*: A sexual quibble.

117 *no thing*: Another sexual quibble.

126 *where to have her*: With a sexual quibble.

147 *The King himself is to be feared as the lion*: The *lion*, like the sun, was a symbol of royalty (see note to I.2.195).

149 *I pray God my girdle break*: Proverbial.

155 *embossed rascal*: There are probably puns on both words; *embossed* can mean (1) swollen; (2) slavering like a hunted deer; *rascal* is (1) a knave; (2) a lean, inferior deer.

157–8 *sugar-candy to make thee long-winded*: Even in Shakespeare's day sugar was prescribed to aid stamina – particularly that of fighting cocks!

159 *injuries*: Things whose loss you complain of as injuries. The use of *injuries* with this meaning makes possible a pun on *wrong* at 160.

167 *by*: According to.

168 *Hostess, I forgive thee*: Doubtless Dame Partlet will be

so flustered by now that she will feel gratified at being forgiven for what is Falstaff's fault.

171 *still*: Now.

177–8 *double labour*: Taking it and returning it.

182 *with unwashed hands*: Without wasting any time.

184 *charge of foot*: Company of infantry (see II.4.530).

196 *the Temple hall*: Inner Temple Hall, a popular meeting-place.

199 *furniture*: Furnishing, equipment.

203 *I could wish this tavern were my drum*: This has not been wholly satisfactorily explained. It has been suggested that there is a pun on *tavern* and 'taborn', a kind of drum; or that Falstaff wishes the *tavern* were the only *drum* he must follow, which, as it stands, is not very close although the sense is reasonable.

There seem to be two other possibilities. A *drum* was at this time a small party of soldiers sent, with a drummer, to discuss terms with an enemy. Falstaff might feel that any military party discussing terms might for preference meet at a tavern. Secondly, Falstaff says *my drum* – Jack's Drum. Jack Drum's Entertainment was a rowdy reception – a fair description of a battle, and of the behaviour of Falstaff and company in the tavern (as, for example, when the Sheriff arrives in II.4). Shakespeare uses the expression 'John Drum's entertainment' in *All's Well That Ends Well* (III.6.35) and Marston wrote a play called *Jack Drum's Entertainment*, published in 1600.

IV.1

The scene is set in the camp of the rebels at Shrewsbury.

2 *fine*: Refined.

3 *attribution*: Attribution of praise.

4 *stamp*: Stamping, coinage.

5 *general current*: Widely accepted (and see note on the use of *current* at II.3.97).

6 *defy*: Distrust.

7 *soothers*: Flatterers.
  braver: Finer.

9 *task*: Test.

approve me: Put me to the proof.

11 *ground*: Earth.

12 *beard*: Come face to face (literally, 'pull by the beard', and particularly 'beard the lion').

13 *I can but thank you*: Hotspur's reply is delayed – a trick imitated by Hal (see note to II.4.101–7) – but here with some reason as he responds naturally to the Messenger's entry.

16 *he is grievous sick:* Northumberland's illness occurred earlier. It is mentioned by Holinshed immediately after his account of how Worcester, 'that had the government of the Prince of Wales', conveyed himself 'in secret manner' out of the Prince's house. Shakespeare brings news of Northumberland's illness to light just before the battle of Shrewsbury, so bringing out his son's impetuosity and courage, and perhaps suggesting that the father was as devious as the son was outspoken. His reasons for not sending a force to support his son (32–8) are not very convincing. Whereas Shakespeare refashions history for dramatic effect in this instance, he makes no use of the fact, available in the same section of the same source, that Worcester 'had the government' of Hal – except possibly to pick up the word *government* (command) at 19.

20 *His letters . . . my lord*: This reply, what Touchstone might have called 'the Retort Courteous' (*As You Like It*, V.4.70), is not as deferential in tone as one would expect from a mere messenger – especially the carrier of bad tidings. The Messenger ought, perhaps, to be a member of the Percy household, a squire. In the Quartos and F *bear* is given as *bears*. Though a plural subject sometimes did have a verb in the singular in Elizabethan English, this has been emended here.

24 *feared*: Feared for.

30 *'Tis catching hither*: It will infect us here.

31 *inward sickness* – : The Quartos merely have a comma after *sickness*. Clearly the sense cannot run on to the next line. It is conceivable that a line has been lost, but the text as we have it is more likely a representation of

the way in which Hotspur's thoughts run ahead of what he says (see also note to III.1.225).

32 *deputation*: Others acting as his deputy.

33 *drawn*: Drawn in, involved.

   meet: Appropriate.

35 *removed*: Not closely connected.

36 *bold advertisement*: 'Confident advice' or 'instruction to be resolute'.

37 *conjunction*: Forces so far joined together.

   on: Go on.

44 *present want*: Absence now.

45 *more*: Greater.

   find it: Find it to be.

47 *main*: Quibbling on 'stake' in a game of chance, and 'army'.

48 *nice*: Delicate.

50 *very bottom*: Whole extent.

   soul: Essence; possibly with quibble on 'sole', the 'bottom' of the shoe, and the 'singleness' of such hope – but such is Shakespeare's potentiality for quibbling that we are inclined to see puns where none were intended and where they may be inappropriate.

51 *very list*: Extreme limit.

54 *reversion*: Inheritance (prospect) to look forward to.

56 *of retirement*: Into which to retreat.

58–9 *look big | Upon*: Threaten.

59 *maidenhead*: First trial.

61 *hair*: Appearance.

62 *Brooks*: Permits.

64 *mere*: Downright.

66 *apprehension*: Idea, belief.

67 *fearful*: Timorous.

69 *offering side*: Side offering a challenge; *offering* is spelt *offring* in Q1 to make it, strictly, a two-syllable word. It has been spelt in full here, the speaker being expected to adjust the stress to suit his own style of speech (see also the note to I.1.8).

70 *strict arbitrement*: Impartial adjudication. Worcester's behaviour at the opening of V.2 accords with the

opinion expressed here.

71 *loop*: Loop-hole.

73 *draws*: Draws aside.

74 *a kind of fear*: That is, fear in us.

75 *strain too far*: Exaggerate.

77 *opinion*: Repute.

78 *dare*: Risk.

80 *make a head*: Raise (such) a force.

83 *joints*: Limbs.

92 *intended*: On the point of setting out.

95 *nimble-footed*: Hal was reported in the histories to be
    particularly fleet of foot.

    madcap: See I.2.140–41.

96 *daffed*: Tossed aside (cf. 'doffed').

98–9 *All plumed like estridges . . . lately bathed*: These lines
    introduce a passage rich in images. Vernon's speech
    is no more representative of character than the
    Queen's speech in *Hamlet* that begins 'There is a
    willow grows askant a brook' (IV.7.166). Vernon's
    words evoke that spirit of pride, honour, royalty and
    ceremony, which is appropriate to this occasion. The
    moment here is one of chivalric challenge. It will be
    contrasted by Shakespeare with its opposite, Falstaff's
    consideration of honour, his 'killing' of the dead
    Hotspur, and his comment on the *grinning honour as
    Sir Walter hath* (V.3.59) (see also Introduction, pp.
    lv–lxi). These two lines of Vernon's speech have been
    called the 'chief crux of the text' by John Dover
    Wilson and a number of emendations have been
    proposed. Two of the most interesting are the substi-
    tution of 'wing' for *with* and a much more radical
    rearrangement involving the omission of *estridges*,
    which, it is suggested, Shakespeare had failed to cancel
    clearly during revision. This would give the single
    line, 'All plumed like eagles having lately bathed',
    instead of the two lines printed in this edition (and
    Q1). The first proposal is helpful, but not essential;
    the second, though attractive, requires the omission
    of a particularly appropriate and colourful image, the

Prince of Wales's plumes (ostrich feathers) ruffled
(*Bated*) in the breeze. *Bated* can mean refreshed
(exactly as in the dialect noun, 'bait', for food between
main meals), but it is applied to food, not the refresh-
ment that comes from bathing; *estridges* could be
goshawks, though this seems unlikely here. The
passage may have been inspired by descriptions in
Thomas Nashe's *The Unfortunate Traveller* (1594),
Spenser's *Faerie Queene* (I.xi.33–4), and most inter-
estingly George Chapman's *De Guiana Carmen
Epicum* (1596), where the following lines occur as
Raleigh is about to leave on his second expedition to
Guiana:

> where round about
> His bating colours English valour swarms . . .
> And now a wind as forward as their spirits,
> Sets their glad feet on smooth *Guiana's* breast . . .
> And there doth plenty crown their wealthy fields,
> There *Learning* eats no more his thriftless books,
> Nor *Valour* estridge-like his iron arms.

100 *coats*: Surcoats (worn over the armour and usually
having the knight's arms depicted thereon).
images: Effigies (of saints or warriors).

104 *beaver*: Part of a helmet protecting the lower jaw.

105 *cuishes*: Cuisses, thigh-armour.

107 *vaulted with such ease*: To jump, fully armoured, into
the saddle was a feat requiring great strength and agility.

109 *turn and wind*: Turn and wheel-about, terms in horsemanship.

110 *witch*: Bewitch.

111–12 *Worse than the sun in March . . . nourish agues*: The sun
in March was thought to be strong enough to assist in
the breeding of fevers without dispelling them. Some
contemporary references relate to this action of the sun
on the bodily humours, but the expression may also be
related to the effect of the sun on marshland, for there,
sun of this strength would encourage the marsh vapours

to rise and propagate but would not be strong enough
to dry up the marsh. (Cf. *King Lear*: 'You fen-sucked
fogs drawn by the powerful sun', II.4.162.)

113 *like sacrifices in their trim*: Decked like this, they are as
beasts for sacrifice.

114 *fire-eyed maid of smoky war*: Bellona, Roman goddess
of war. Macbeth was described by Shakespeare as
'Bellona's bridegroom' (*Macbeth*, I.2.56).

116 *Mars*: Roman god of war.

118 *this rich reprisal*: The phrase is appropriate to describe
the style of Hotspur's rhetoric in reply to Vernon's
description of Hal's chivalric company; *reprisal* means
'prize'. The language in this speech is of blood, mail,
smoke and sacrifice. The images in Vernon's speech are
altogether different; indeed, they are *full of spirit as the
month of May* (101) as opposed to Hotspur's *Worse than
the sun in March* (111).

123 *corpse*: In Q1 the spelling *coarse* is used (for 'corse'),
indicative of the Elizabethan pronunciation of this word.

126 *He cannot draw his power this fourteen days*: He cannot
collect his army together for a fortnight. Hotspur is
now let down again, yet there is no outburst from him
as there is when he describes the tedium of Glendower's
conversation (III.1.142–58). In Holinshed's chronicle,
the Welsh are said to be present at the battle, but in
Daniel's poem on the civil war, it is said that 'The swift
approach and unexpected speed' of Henry's advance
did not give time for the Welsh forces to reach
Shrewsbury. Shakespeare evidently follows Daniel's
account at this point and the reason is plain – Hotspur
is further isolated.

129 *battle*: Battle array.

130 *thirty thousand*: It is not possible to take too certainly
estimates of numbers involved in medieval battles.
Hotspur was said by Holinshed to have had 14,000
men, but his chronicle does not give a number for the
King's army; another chronicle does give a figure of
30,000, and Hall gives a figure of 40,000 for those
engaged on both sides.

132 *powers of us*: Forces we have.
    serve: Suffice.

134 *Die all, die merrily*: If die we must, let it be cheerfully.

135 *out of*: Free from.

IV.2

3 *Sutton Coldfield*: To the north-east of Birmingham, well off the Coventry–Shrewsbury route.

5 *Lay out*: Use your own money.

6 *an angel*: A coin with the Archangel Michael stamped on it and worth between 33 and 50p – 15 to 35p being a journeyman's weekly wage at the time.

8 *answer the coinage*: Be answerable for making money that way ('coining' money on bottles).

9 *Peto*: At III.3.195 Hal tells Peto they have thirty miles to ride together. It may seem (as it did to Dr Johnson) that as Peto is with Falstaff here, some other name (such as Poins's) should be substituted at III.3.195. As, however, Hal was to travel through Gloucestershire (III.2.175–6) but appears in this scene, it is clear that the plans have been changed, wittingly or not, by Shakespeare.

12 *soused gurnet*: Preserved gurnet, a small fish with a big head.

12–13 *I have misused the King's press damnably*: Falstaff provided the original audience with a living example of the rapaciously corrupt captains of Elizabeth's army (see Introduction, pp. xlix–li).

15 *good*: Substantial (with money to buy themselves out).

17 *commodity*: Falstaff speaks of his men as merchandise which he can trade in order to make a profit.
    warm: Well-to-do.
    slaves: Contemptuous for 'subjects'.

19 *caliver*: Light musket.

20 *toasts-and-butter*: Milksops.

23 *ancients*: Ensigns (of which the word is a corruption).

24 *gentlemen of companies*: Gentlemen volunteers who held no formal rank (see also note to I.2.26).

24–5 *Lazarus in the painted cloth*: Falstaff has already referred to the parable of Dives and Lazarus (III.3.31) and it is, once again, an instance of Falstaff's store of biblical knowledge; *painted cloth* was a very inferior form of tapestry. (See also note to 33.)

27 *unjust*: Dishonest.

27–8 *younger sons to younger brothers*: That is, having no prospect of inheritance.

28 *revolted*: Runaway (see II.4.45–7).
   trade-fallen: Out of work.

29 *cankers*: Parasites.
   long peace: Considered to be unhealthy – as if the state needed its blood let in accordance with the current medical practice.

30 *fazed*: Frayed.

33 *prodigals*: Another biblical reference from Falstaff, this time to the best-known of all parables. The prodigal son, when he had spent all his money, was reduced to eating the food he had to serve the pigs. Shakespeare uses the word *husks*. (This is found in the Geneva Bible, not the Bishops' Bible, where 'ceddes' is used.) Falstaff also refers to the parable of the prodigal son in *Henry IV, Part II*, II.1.143–4.

34 *draff*: Pig-swill.

40 *out of prison*: Often as corrupt as the army officers, Justices of the Peace, such as Justice Shallow of *Henry IV, Part II*, would often use military conscription to empty out the jails (see Introduction, pp. xlix–li).

46 *find linen . . . on every hedge*: Linen was put out to dry by draping it over hedges.

47 *blown*: (1) Short-winded; (2) swollen.
   Jack: Besides Falstaff's name, a contemptuous word for 'fellow' and also the name for a soldier's quilted jacket.

48–9 *What a devil dost thou in Warwickshire*: Falstaff quickly asks Hal (perhaps bearing in mind the original arrangement – III.2.175–6 – though Falstaff was not present on the occasion that this was revealed to the audience), before Hal can ask him what he's up to.

58 *steal cream*: A pun on 'stale cream' has been suggested here.

61 *Mine, Hal, mine*: The absence of any shame here

(despite his earlier assertion that he will not march through Coventry with such a rabble), indeed, the positive pride, is quite outrageous.

63 *to toss*: On pikes, as in *Henry VI, Part III*, I.1.244: 'The soldiers should have tossed me on their pikes.'

63–4 *food for powder*: English officers were known to send their men to their deaths on purpose, in order to pocket their pay (see Introduction, pp. xlix–li).

71–2 *three fingers in the ribs*: A finger measured three-quarters of an inch and thus Falstaff's ribs are well covered with flesh. In *The Merchant of Venice* there is a contrary use of the relationship of ribs and fingers. Launcelot refers to his being badly fed by saying, 'you may tell every finger I have with my ribs' (II.2.99), and traditionally he makes his blind father feel his fingers spread over his chest.

IV.3

The scene is set in Hotspur's camp at Shrewsbury.

3 *supply*: Reinforcements.

10 *well-respected*: Well-considered.

17 *of such great leading*: Who are such experienced generals.

22 *pride and mettle*: Spirit.

26 *journey-bated*: Weakened by travel.

29 *stay*: Wait.

30 *I come with gracious offers from the King*: The King's ambassador was the Abbot of Shrewsbury, but, as in the first scene of the play, Blunt's role is enlarged (see note to I.1.63). From Hotspur's response, Blunt is clearly regarded highly by the rebels as well as by Henry. Thus his death, and Falstaff's reaction to it (see V.3.58–9), are built up to be more than incidental.

31 *respect*: Attention.

36 *quality*: Party, with no reference to 'worth'.

38 *defend*: Forbid.
   still: Always.

39 *limit*: Bounds of allegiance.

41 *charge*: Official duty.

42 *griefs*: Injuries.
   whereupon: Wherefore.

43 *conjure*: Call up.

51 *suggestion*: Temptation (*suggestion* being a more sinister
   word than it now is).

52–3 *The King is kind . . . when to pay*: These lines are neatly
   phrased by Hotspur to give just the right satiric impression. Whether the injuries Hotspur feels he has suffered
   are sufficient to justify rebellion or not, he here makes,
   very coolly and satirically, an exposé of Henry's
   usurpation of Richard's throne. Blunt's response, *Tut,
   I came not to hear this* (89), could be as much embar-
   rassment as awareness that this was not the reason for
   Hotspur's present feelings of injury.

62 *sue his livery*: Beg for his inheritance following his
   father's death. ('As I was banished, I was banished
   Hereford; | But as I come, I come for Lancaster',
   Richard II, II.3.112–13.)
   beg his peace: From Richard.

64 *in kind heart and pity moved*: Northumberland's heart
   was moved solely by self-interest.

68 *more and less*: High and low.
   with cap and knee: Cap in hand and on bended knee.

70 *Attended*: Waited for.

73 *golden*: Richly dressed

75 *Steps me*: An archaic construction; *me* is no longer
   required.
   his vow: That is, to seek no more than the inheritance
   to which he was entitled.

79 *strait*: Overstrict.

82 *face*: Appearance assumed for the occasion.

83 *seeming brow*: Front, semblance.

85–6 *cut me off the heads . . . favourites*: This refers to the
   execution of Bushy, Green and Wiltshire in *Richard II*
   (the two first-named in III.1). Bolingbroke had no right
   to order these executions; he was already assuming
   Richard's prerogative. The word *me* would be omitted
   in modern English; it does not imply that the heads
   were cut off to please Hotspur.

87 *In deputation*: As his deputies.

88 *personal*: Personally engaged.

92 *in the neck of*: Immediately after.

   tasked: Taxed, a technical term for a tax of one-fifteenth.

93 *his kinsman March*: See note to I.3.83.

95 *engaged*: Held hostage.

98 *intelligence*: Use of spies.

99 *Rated*: Berated, dismissed with abuse. This refers to the dismissal of Worcester, I.3.14–20. Hal, of course, had also been *rated* (III.2.32–3).

100 *In rage dismissed my father from the court*: The King's words at I.3.120–22 are hardly in rage.

103 *head of safety*: Army with which to protect ourselves.

    withal: In addition.

105 *indirect*: 'Not of the true line of descent', and also 'morally crooked'.

108 *impawned*: Pledged (by exchange of hostages).

111 *purposes*: Proposals.

113 *And may be so we shall*: Hotspur's conciliatory tone is surprising. Although it accords with Holinshed, that is not the reason for Shakespeare's use of it. Henry is not without fault (as he himself knows, III.2.4–11). His deception in the course of usurping Richard's throne is recounted not only here but also in *Henry IV, Part II* –

        God knows, my son,
        By what by-paths and indirect crooked ways
        I met this crown (IV.5.184–6)

    – and even by Hal himself in *Henry V*:

        Not today, O Lord,
        O not today, think not upon the fault
        My father made in compassing the crown! (IV.1.285–7)

    This is not just the opposition of right and wrong. Henry's faults were very serious and the implications of his usurpation of Richard's throne were well known

in Shakespeare's day. It still left the problem unre-
solved as to whether it was permissible to rebel against
a sovereign, as Hotspur is doing. Shakespeare, however,
in addition to making clear Henry's guilt, also brings
out two elements from the chronicles that favour the
character of Hotspur. First, his willingness to reflect
(here), and secondly, Worcester's deception of Hotspur
(V.2).

IV.4

The scene is presumably set in York. *Sir Michael*
(*Mighell* in Q1) is not known to history. 'Sir' was a
courtesy title for priests, and a priest might well be the
Archbishop's messenger, or Sir Michael might be a
knight. The scene serves to heighten the desperate state
in which Hotspur finds himself. There would not, of
course, have been any point in Shakespeare keeping
secret the outcome of the battle: an Elizabethan audience would know only too well who had won.

1 *brief*: Letter.

2 *Lord Marshal*: Thomas Mowbray, Duke of Norfolk.

3 *my cousin Scroop*: It is uncertain to which of several
Scroops this refers. The Sir Stephen Scrope (members
of the family spelt their name differently) who tells
Richard II of his younger brother's execution by
Bolingbroke at Bristol (referred to at I.3.265) seems
likely. It could, however, be Sir Henry Scroop, executed
as a traitor in *Henry V*, II.2.

7 *tenor*: Purport.

10 *bide the touch*: Be put to the test.

15 *first proportion*: Greatest magnitude.

17 *rated sinew*: Valued source of strength.

18 *o'er-ruled by prophecies*: Shakespeare here maligns
Glendower. According to Holinshed, the Welsh were
at Shrewsbury, but Daniel states (see note to IV.1.126)
they did not reach Shrewsbury in time, owing to the
King's rapid advance.

20 *instant*: Immediate.

31 *corrivals*: Associates.
   dear: Noble (as at I.1.62).

35 *prevent*: Forestall.

38 *our confederacy*: Our united opposition.

V.1

The scene is the King's camp at Shrewsbury.

3 *distemperature*: Cosmic disorder.

4 *his*: The sun's.

6 *Foretells a tempest and a blustering day*: The relation of cosmic to human affairs was frequently observed by the Elizabethans and occurs often in Shakespeare.

13 *our old limbs*: Henry was younger than Hotspur (see note to I.1.86–7).

17 *obedient orb*: Sphere of loyal obedience (the idea being that the planet circles the earth, which most people in Shakespeare's day believed to be fixed).

19 *exhaled*: Dragged from rightful course.

20 *prodigy of fear*: Fearful omen.

26 *dislike*: Discord.

28 *Rebellion lay in his way, and he found it*: Falstaff's witticism puts Worcester's *protest* (25) perfectly in its place, as Hal's affectionate *chewet* indicates.

29 *chewet*: (1) Jackdaw (a chatterer); (2) minced meat dressed with butter (both applicable to Falstaff).

32 *remember*: Remind.

34–5 *For you my staff of office did I break | In Richard's time*: This event is recorded by Holinshed and, though Worcester does not himself appear, it is mentioned twice in *Richard II* (II.2.58–9 and II.3.26–7). The Percys' case has already been presented in detail by Hotspur in IV.3 and described in I.3.146–74. That it is now described a third time suggests the importance attached by Shakespeare to Henry's mode of accession. Lines 41–5 are particularly noteworthy, repeating what Hotspur said at IV.3.60–63. Worcester's interest was no more selfless than was Northumberland's, needless to say.

44 *new-fallen*: Newly fallen due to you.

50 *injuries*: Abuses.

wanton time: Period of misgovernment.

57 *gripe*: Seize.

sway: Rule (of the whole country).

60 *gull, bird*: Nestling.

69 *dangerous countenance*: Threatening looks.

71 *younger enterprise*: Earlier undertaking (his claim to his inheritance).

72 *articulate*: Formulated item by item.

74 *face*: The meaning here seems to be to cover (as with one fabric by another) – to put a different *face* on things, rather than simply to adorn.

75 *colour*: The colour of the facing, with also the metaphorical implication of misrepresentation.

77 *rub the elbow*: Hug themselves with pleasure, arms crossed. Joy was believed to make the elbows itch.

78 *innovation*: Revolution.

80 *water-colours*: Painting in *water-colours* was not considered permanent – they might easily be washed off; *impaint* here is the first recorded use of this word. The effect of the line must have been striking.
    his: Its.

81 *moody*: Sullen.

88 *set off his head*: Removed from his account, not counted against him.

89 *braver*: Finer.

100 *in a single fight*: Hal's challenge is an important element in his pursuit of honour (see Introduction, pp. li–liii).

105 *cousin's*: 'Cousin' did not in Shakespeare's time necessarily imply the precise family relationship which the word denotes to us (and see note to I.1.90).

106 *grace*: Pardon.

111 *wait on us*: Are at hand.

114 *We offer fair*: As Holinshed says: 'the King had condescended unto all that was reasonable at his hands to be required, and seemed to humble himself more than was meet for his estate.'

122 *bestride me*: Stand over Falstaff to protect him.

123 *a Colossus*: A statue considerably larger than life size, of which there were a number in the ancient world. *The* Colossus, however, was that of Helios at Rhodes, which was over 100 feet high. It was destroyed by an

earthquake after standing for fifty-six years, about 224 BC, but many Elizabethans believed that its legs still stood over the entrance to the harbour.

124 *Say thy prayers, and farewell*: Hal's abruptness is understandable in the circumstances, but its degree is, perhaps, a little surprising.

125 *I would 'twere bed-time, Hal, and all well*: One of the most human touches in all Shakespeare. The Prince in his reply takes the sense of *bed-time* to be debt-time (a similar quibble occurs at I.3.183–4).

129 *pricks*: Spurs.

130 *prick me off*: Select me for death (cf. select by picking with a pin).

131 *set to a leg*: Almost certainly a reference to the famous courtier-soldier Sir Philip Sidney, who died at the siege of Zutphen after a bullet shattered his thigh bone (see Introduction, pp. xlvi–xlvii).

132 *grief*: Pain.

137 *insensible*: Not perceptible to the senses.

138–9 *Detraction*: Slander.

139 *suffer*: Allow.

140 *scutcheon*: Funeral hatchment (a square or lozenge-shaped tablet).

catechism: This describes the question and answer technique which Falstaff has just used.

V.2

The scene is the rebels' camp at Shrewsbury.

1 *my nephew must not know*: Worcester's deception of Hotspur is recounted by Holinshed.

6 *still*: Always.

11 *trick*: Trait.

12 *or . . . or*: Either . . . or.

18 *an adopted name of privilege*: A nickname licensing him (to be rash).

19 *a spleen*: An impulse.

20 *live*: Are active.

22 *taken*: Caught, as in 'take cold'.

28 *Deliver up my Lord of Westmorland*: Westmorland was evidently the *surety for a safe return* of Worcester and

Vernon (IV.3.109); he is now to be released. It has been
suggested, as we are not told that Westmorland is to
be held hostage, that a passage has been omitted, by
accident or through revision. It is at least as possible
that Shakespeare is using a shortcut to avoid cluttering
the action with unimportant details. (See note to
I.3.259.)

32 *Douglas*: Strictly speaking, this line has only nine syllables, but, if it were desired that the iambic metre be
preserved exactly, *Douglas* could be pronounced as
three syllables. The situation is the reverse of that
discussed at I.1.8. Rhythm in Shakespeare, and indeed
in much English verse, is more subtle than counting
syllables will allow.

34 *seeming*: Semblance of.

38 *forswearing*: Denying by a false oath.

43 *engaged*: Held as a hostage (as Mortimer at IV.3.96).

48 *draw short breath*: Become short-winded (by exertion in
battle). Short of breath to the point of death is also
implied.

50 *showed his tasking*: Offered he the challenge.

52 *urged*: Proposed.

54 *proof*: Trial.

55 *duties of a man*: Praises due a man.

59 *dispraising praise valued with you*: Disparaging praise
itself as compared to you yourself, the object of praise.

61 *blushing cital of himself*: Either, he gave a modest recital
of his own merits, or, in his recital of his own merits
he blushingly called himself to account.

64 *instantly*: Simultaneously.

66 *envy*: Ill-will.

67 *owe*: Own.

71 *liberty*: Reckless freedom.

74 *That*: So that.

76–8 *Better consider what you have to do . . . with persuasion*:
You are better able to consider for yourselves what you
have to do than I am able, by gifts of oratory, to inspire
you. The tortuous expression of Hotspur's meaning
here might suggest he did lack *the gift of tongue* were

it not that elsewhere he hardly strikes one as being tongue-tied. The highly compressed style may occur by chance, or it might, perhaps, be intended as a humorous touch. He does, nevertheless, make a modest address to his followers at 90–100. This has a half-comic beginning which supports the suggestion of humour in these three lines.

82–4 *To spend that shortness basely . . . arrival of an hour*: If life lasted but an hour, it would be too long if it were spent basely.

83 *dial's point*: Hand of a clock.

90 *cuts me from my tale*: Stops me talking.

91 *I profess not talking*: Talking is not my profession.

91–2 *Only this – | Let each man do his best*: The effect of bathos here is at once comic and touching.

94 *withal*: With.

96 *Esperance*: This was the Percy battle-cry (see also the note to II.3.74).

99 *heaven to earth*: Odds of infinity to nothing.

V.3

Although the rest of the play is divided into three scenes, the place and time are not differentiated. What is said in the opening comment to I.1 applies here with particular force.

21 *Semblably furnished*: Seemingly armed.

22 *A fool go with thy soul*: Q1 has *Ah foole, goe with thy soule*, but the emended form, proposed in the eighteenth century, seems to give what was intended, as this makes a popular colloquial formula – 'the name of fool go with you'.

25 *coats*: Surcoats (see note to IV.1.100).

29 *stand full fairly for the day*: Are a fair way to victory.

30 *shot-free*: (1) Unwounded; (2) without paying the bill.

31 *scoring*: (1) Charging to an account; (2) cutting (wounding).

33 *Here's no vanity*: All (in life) is vanity, but here in death there is no vanity. Another biblical reference by Falstaff (to Ecclesiastes 12:8).

35 *led*: But not necessarily from the front – 'I have led

them to a place where they might be peppered'.

37–8 *the town's end*: Near the town gates.

39 *What*: Why (exclamation).

43 *Lend me thy sword*: In Q1, *thy sword* is printed as prose
in the same line as *Whose deaths are yet unrevenged. I
prethee*. The sudden shift to a line of prose is awkward,
though most editors accept it – it is not, of course,
exceptional. The arrangement in this edition makes a
slightly smoother transition to Falstaff's prose, but the
result cannot be called remarkable poetry. (See also the
note to II.2.102–8.)

45 *Turk Gregory*: The Turks had a reputation for ferocity.
Two popes have been suggested as the Gregory referred
to: Gregory VII, who reigned in the eleventh century,
and, much more convincingly, Gregory XIII (1572–85),
who not only was credited with encouraging the
Massacre of St Bartholomew and plots to murder
Elizabeth I, but, with Nero and the Grand Turk,
appeared in a coloured print called *The Three Tyrants
of the World*, being sold in the streets of London in
Shakespeare's time.

46 *paid*: Killed.

53 *'tis hot*: Hot with great use.

56 *pierce*: Pronounced 'perce'.

58 *carbonado*: Rasher for grilling.

59 *such grinning honour*: See note to IV.3.30.

61 *there's an end*: Of life or of the subject.

V.4

4 *make up*: Go to the front.

5 *retirement*: Retreat.
amaze: Dismay.

12 *stained*: (1) Blood-stained; (2) disgraced (by defeat).

23 *mettle*: Spirit.

24 *Hydra's heads*: The Hydra was a many-headed monster,
eventually killed by Hercules, which grew two heads
for each one cut off.

26 *those colours*: The King's.

29 *shadows*: Imitations.

30 *very*: True.

33 *assay*: Try.

42 *Who never promiseth but he means to pay*: This is surely
an echo of I.2.206–8, especially the second line: *And
pay the debt I never promisèd.*

47 *opinion*: Reputation.

48 *makest some tender of*: Have some regard for.

50–51 *they did me too much injury . . . death*: There was no
ground for such accusations at this time, but see note
to III.2.126.

hearkened for: Desired.

53 *insulting*: Contemptuous, exultant.

57 *Make up*: Advance.

64 *Two stars . . . in one sphere*: According to Ptolemaic
astronomy, each star had its own course.

65 *brook*: Endure.

68–9 *would to God . . . as great as mine*: It was a principle of
chivalric combat that a knight only fought another of
equal rank. Hal's rank is above Percy's, but not the
honour he has won. Hotspur's statement is not as self-
regarding as it sounds to us. In *Richard II* Aumerle
makes much the same point when insulted by Bagot:

> Shall I so much dishonour my fair stars
> On equal terms to give him chastisement? (IV.1.21–2)

74 *Well said*: Well done!

75 *boy's*: Child's.

80–82 *But thoughts . . . a stop*: Thoughts, life and, eventually,
time itself must all end.

82 *I could prophesy*: Prophecy was associated with dying
men. Gaunt, in *Richard II*, thought himself 'a prophet
new-inspired' (II.1.31).

87 *Ill-weaved ambition*: Poorly woven cloth shrank easily.

89 *bound*: Boundary.

92 *stout*: Valiant.

93 *sensible of*: Able to respond to.

94 *dear a show*: Warm a display.

95 *favours*: In Hal's case these would seem to be the plumes
from his helmet, which were mentioned by Vernon at

IV.1.98 (see note). In a tournament, a 'favour' was
usually a scarf or glove worn by a knight as a sign of
a lady's favour. It has been argued that such a favour
is intended here, on the grounds that Hal's badge, the
three ostrich feathers, was not well known in
Shakespeare's time.

104 *heavy*: A pun – Falstaff's flesh is compared with
Hotspur's *stout* spirit (92).

107 *dearer*: The pun here is obvious – 'more loved' and
'more noble' – and it is clear that there are many who
have fallen (Sir Walter Blunt, for example) who are
more noble than Falstaff. But do we expect any of
them, even Sir Walter, to be more loved by Hal? The
ironical banter of the opening of the speech (so similar
in tone to that exchanged by Hotspur and Lady Percy)
is certainly affectionate, and the implication of *I could
have better spared a better man* perfectly sums up Hal's
affection for Falstaff and his realization of Falstaff's
shortcomings. Possibly, as Dr Johnson complained, a
pun was irresistible to Shakespeare and we ought not
to attach too great significance to this apparent lowering
of Falstaff in Hal's affections.

108 *Embowelled*: Disembowelled (for embalming). A
sequence of puns involving hunting terms begins here.
Falstaff has just been called *a deer* (106), and deer, on
being killed, were disembowelled. When Hal leaves
Falstaff to lie *in blood*, he metaphorically refers to
Falstaff's own blood (Falstaff has suffered no wound),
Hotspur's blood, and also uses a hunting term which
meant 'in full vigour'. Some critics argue that this shows
that Hal knows Falstaff is faking, but that is most
unlikely (see Introduction, pp. lix–lx).

109 *Falstaff riseth up*: Hal's speech over Falstaff is sufficiently
serious and deeply felt to suggest that Falstaff might
have seemed to be truly dead to an audience as well as
to Hal. The stage direction after 75 is ambiguous: *he
fighteth with Falstaff, who falls down as if he were dead.*
Falstaff's rising up here should not follow immediately
on Hal's exit. There ought to be a pause because,

whether a modern audience believes him to be dead or not (and many members of a modern audience will know he is feigning), his coming to life is a moment of comedy of which an actor can make much. It is comparable to the situation in II.4.261 when, even if we know what Falstaff's answer is to be, we await it with anxiety and receive it with delight.

112–13 *that hot termagant Scot*: Douglas.

113 *scot and lot*: In full, with a pun on 'Scot'.

119 *part*: Quality (not 'portion').

124–5 *Nothing confutes me but eyes*: No one can prove me wrong but an eye-witness (and there is none here, except the audience, who Falstaff assumes will take his part).

126 *thigh*: Falstaff's wounding Hotspur in the thigh, like *Can honour set to a leg* (V.1.131), is probably a reference to Sir Philip Sidney (see Introduction, pp. xlvi–xlvii).

128 *fleshed*: Used (your sword) for the first time. John of Lancaster was then only thirteen. The attention given him at the end of *Henry IV, Part I* has been thought by some critics to be a preparation for his part, as Bedford, in *Henry IV, Part II*. If that is so, it is one piece of evidence to indicate that Shakespeare had a second part of *Henry IV* in mind when writing this part (but see Introduction, pp. xxiv–xxv).

137 *Jack*: Knave.

149–50 *I'll take it upon my death*: An oath of particular solemnity.

156 *a lie*: A lie of yours.

157 *happiest terms*: Most favourable expressions of support.

159 *highest*: Highest part of the ground.

161 *I'll follow . . . for reward*: This is another quibble based on hunting. The hounds are said to *follow* and they are given as *reward* portions of the deer that has been brought down.

163 *purge*: (1) Repent; (2) take laxatives.

V.5

1 *rebuke*: Violent check.

2 *Ill-spirited*: Evil-minded.

did not we send grace: Cf. *will they take the offer of our grace* (pardon) at V.1.106.

6 *Three knights*: Ten in Holinshed.

15 *pause upon*: Postpone taking a decision.

20 *Upon the foot of fear*: With the speed of panic.

36 *bend you*: You direct your course.

dearest: Best.

41 *his*: Its.

43-4 *And since this business . . . be won*: This does not read like the end of *Henry IV* as Shakespeare conceived it: it almost invites our attention to a second part.

fair: Successfully.

Read more in Penguin

PENGUIN SHAKESPEARE